LIVING WITH UNCLE

Canada-US Relations in an Age of Empire

**Edited by
Bruce Campbell
and Ed Finn**

James Lorimer & Company Ltd., Publishers
Toronto

James Lorimer & Company Ltd. acknowledges the support of the Ontario Arts Council. We acknowledge the support of the Government of Canada through the Book Publishing Industry Development Program (BPIDP) for our publishing activities. We acknowledge the support of the Canada Council for the Arts for our publishing program. We acknowledge the support of the Government of Ontario through the Ontario Media Development Corporation's Ontario Book Initiative.

Cover design: Meghan Collins

The Canada Council | Le Conseil des Arts
for the Arts | du Canada

ONTARIO ARTS COUNCIL
CONSEIL DES ARTS DE L'ONTARIO

National Library of Canada Cataloguing in Publication

Living with Uncle: Canada-US relations in an age of empire / edited by Bruce Campbell and Ed Finn.

Includes bibliographic references and index.
ISBN 978-1-55028-960-2. ISBN 1-55028-960-8

1. Canada--Foreign relations--United States. 2. United States--Foreign relations--Canada. I. Campbell, Bruce, 1948- II. Finn, Ed, 1926- III. Title.

FC249.L58 2006   327.7'1073   C2006-903634-9

James Lorimer & Company Ltd.,
Publishers
317 Adelaide Street West, Suite #1002
Toronto, Ontario
M5V 1P9
www.lorimer.ca

Printed and bound in Canada.

CONTENTS

ACKNOWLEDGEMENTS

This book grew out of a conference of the same name that was part of the Canadian Centre for Policy Alternatives' Twenty-fifth Anniversary in 2005. Some of the contributions to this book were adapted from conference presentations. Others were written following the conference. We are grateful for the authors' willingness to come together with us, and for their presentations, which were so integral to the success of our event.

Our thanks to the CCPA National Office staff who organized this event, to the staff in Ottawa and across the country whose talent and dedication sustain the Centre's prolific body of work, to our volunteer board for their guidance and direction, to the research associates for the depth they add to the Centre's reputation. We also thank the hundreds of people who helped us celebrate our first quarter-century, the thousands of people who support the work of the CCPA through their membership contributions and donations, and to the scores of enlightened individuals and organizations who saw the need for a progressive counterweight to the business-sponsored think tanks and stuck with us through the hard times. Our thanks as well to the people who make up the labour, social, and environment organizations with whom we work day in and day out to advance the ideals of social and economic justice, democracy, and peace.

Finally, we thank James Lorimer for his support of and collaboration with the Centre over the years, and for encouraging us to complete this book.

PART I

INTRODUCTION

Perhaps it is best to begin this book by taking the long view of Canada's relationship with the United States. For the last two-and-a-half centuries, the relationship has been relatively civilized—with some notable rough patches—at least by international standards. Our view of the United States has fluctuated from good neighbour to neighbourhood bully, from bastion of democracy to be emulated to rogue state to be shunned. Our sense of the American view of Canada has also fluctuated with long periods of benign neglect punctuated by episodes of callous disregard. The huge power imbalance is the central defining reality of the relationship explaining the obvious fact that, while Canadians' self-image is deeply influenced by our relation to our American neighbours, Canada barely registers on the American consciousness.

Within Canada, there is the ancient and enduring tension between two political currents. One camp focused on the north-south axis, today referred to as continentalist/globalist/neoliberal. The other camp, oriented east-west, is variously described as nationalist/internationalist/progressive.

For Canadian policy makers of either camp, though they may define it differently, the challenge is to preserve sufficient policy space to maintain a requisite level of independence on the American periphery. Developments of the last two decades have made this challenge especially difficult: the "free trade" agreement, neoliberal globalization, the end of the cold war, September 11, and the war on terror. The term *crisis* is frequently used to describe the current state of relations. On the other hand, considering this term has been used repeatedly in the past, perhaps crisis also describes an enduring characteristic of the bilateral relationship, at least from a Canadian perspective.

The contributors to this volume may differ somewhat in their assessment of the state of Canada-US relations and where that relationship is going. But they share a common vision of an independent Canada open to the world and able to chart its own course: a Canada that is on friendly terms with the United States, but at a distance; a Canada able and willing to resist the powerful forces that would draw it deeper into Fortress America. They share a vision of a Canada that is able to advance, democratically, an agenda that builds on a social democratic–just society vision that emerged after World War II from the struggles of the 1930s and 1940s, but with a much longer history rooted in the concept of sharing for survival.

They understand that a powerful competing political force in the world and within Canada—often referred to as neoliberal globalization—has made the ability to pursue just society goals more difficult. This force reflects a very different vision and one that also has a long history.

The north-south pull has been strong in the post-war era, driven by business interests and by the realities of the cold war. The Canadian economy has become vastly more integrated with the United States over the last six decades. Scores of policies, agreements, and protocols have managed, redirected, or slowed down this integration process: the Auto Pact, NORAD, "Third Option," GATT, FIRA, the NEP—to name some of the most prominent. Their purpose was generally to manage or develop counterweights to integration forces in order to preserve our independence.

The great 1988 free trade debate and election—in which many of the contributors to this book were prominent players—resulted in the passage of the Canada-US Free Trade Agreement (FTA). It was a watershed event that set the country on a course more closely aligned with Fortress America. It enhanced the power of capital relative to workers and communities, and limited the power of government to regulate and shape the market. It thus ensured that integration would not only accelerate, but do so within a neoliberal policy mold. This has made it more difficult for progressive-minded governments to advance their policy agendas, and more difficult to advance just society goals, let alone hold onto existing social achievements. Five years later, the FTA—deepened and extended to Mexico—was converted and expanded to the North American Free Trade Agreement (NAFTA).

September 11, 2001, jolted the Canada-US integration process again. Security trumped trade, security and trade became indivisible, and Canada—more dependent than ever on the US market—had even less bargaining room to resist or moderate US demands. Security became the new engine of integration. Amid the threat of border disruptions the Smart Border Declaration and Action Plan was signed in December 2001. The flow of goods, services, and people normalized, although with the border considerably thicker than it used to be. And Canada paid the price in major security concessions with significant harmonization of intelligence policies and procedures affecting everything from refugee, immigration, visa, and transportation policies to the criminal justice system, civil liberties, and privacy protections.

The big business push for deeper integration policies has been driven by fear, in the 1980s by the fear of increased US protectionism, and since 9/11 by the fear of security-related border disruptions. But it has also been driven by the goal of harmonizing Canadian policies, regulations, and institutions with those of a more "business friendly" America, reducing the significance of the border, and foreclosing the ability of any future Canadian government to return to the interventionist policies of the 1960s and 1970s. It is a way to smuggle a corporate agenda, unpopular with most Canadians, through the back door.

NAFTA was an important step—but only a step—toward the goal of economic union with the United States. September 11 was a threat, but also an opportunity to inject new life into a flagging deep integration initiative. Business think tanks cranked up their policy mills producing, notably, the "Big Idea," which proposed a deep integration mega-deal with everything on the table. The big business lobby, the Canadian Council of Chief Executives, still headed by Tom d'Aquino, launched its Security and Prosperity Initiative, which contained a host of ambitious deep integration measures: a continental security perimeter, an energy and resources (likely including water) security pact, a regulatory harmonization action plan, a customs union, and the introduction of common institutions. D'Aquino parlayed this project into a tri-national business task force on North American integration, co-chaired by John Manley and with members including himself and Michael Wilson.

While business is driving the agenda, at the political level the executive branch and elements of bureaucracy are moving deep integration forward by stealth. There is little public debate or consultation. Information is scarce. Parliamentary oversight is minimal. There is the sense that the less Canadians know about what is going on, the better. Although elite attitudes and values have converged with their US counterparts—on Iraq and other foreign policy matters, on lower taxes and minimalist government, for example—they have diverged greatly from those of the Canadian public. This divergence also extends to attitudes about deeper integration and whether Canada should be more like the United States. Most Canadians don't want to be more like Americans. They are confused about the term *integration,* but wary of such initiatives, particularly when they are thought to affect Canadian policy autonomy. Thus, it is not surprising that the issue, a hard sell at the best of times, is being kept low-key.

The Chrétien and Martin governments, convinced of its desirability (or at least inevitability), advanced elements of the deep integration project, but were not enthusiastic about the Big Idea approach. The Canadian public's hostility to the Bush administration, US indifference, and division within their own parliamentary ranks made them incrementalists. They moved more visibly on the security front, where the pressure from the United States was greatest, and less so on the economic front.

The Martin government played a lead role in creating the North

American Security and Prosperity Partnership agreement signed by the three NAFTA leaders in March 2005. The SPP became the umbrella—absorbing NAFTA and the Smart Border Action Plan—under which deep integration is moving forward. The handprints of Tom d'Aquino and his big business colleagues are all over the SPP (the name is almost identical), which is in sync with the business blueprint for North American integration. At the second Leaders' meeting in March 2006, to which business representatives were invited, a new body, the North American Competitiveness Council of CEOs, was announced, to give direction and guidance to the political leaders on the SPP.

Though it is early days in the life of the Harper Conservative government, there is every indication that not only will it continue the deep integration initiatives started by the Liberals, but will push them more aggressively and more openly. Its ideology is more overtly integrationist. It identifies more closely with American military and intelligence priorities. The Conservatives might even risk going for another ambitious deal with the United States if it gets a majority in the next election.

Several Mulroney-era free trade warriors have prominent positions in the new government, including Michael Wilson, recently appointed ambassador to the United States. It has acted quickly on the security front by bolstering the intelligence budget, expanding the scope of NORAD to include maritime approaches to North America, and announcing a huge spending spree on military hardware to facilitate the integration of Canadian forces with US global military actions. It renounced Canada's Kyoto treaty commitment to reduce greenhouse gas emissions, and aligned itself with George Bush's made-in-North America approach as urged by d'Aquino and company. It buckled under US intransigence on softwood lumber and, in a singular act of appeasement, negotiated a controversial settlement to the dispute—this despite the fact that Canada had won all the NAFTA dispute panel decisions.

How has Canada fared in the free trade era? The promised closing of the long-standing productivity gap between the two countries and diversification of the economy beyond our traditional resource base has been disappointing, to say the least. We are more than ever a "hewer of wood and drawer of water" in the international division of labour—albeit (so far) a wealthy one. The unparalleled domination of our economy by foreign-owned (mainly US) transnational corporations, for a time reversed, is on the rise again. The political centre of the country has weakened as powers have been handed over to the market and devolved to provincial governments. As north-south economic flows have grown relative to east-west flows, provincial governments have come to exercise more power in the federation. At the same time, lowest common denominator tax competition within Canada, and from south of the border, has weakened fiscal capacity at all levels of government. Thus, as North American integration has deepened, so too have the pressures of national dis-integration intensified.

Economic and media elites paint a glowing picture of a strong Canadian economy with a bright outlook. Scratch the surface, however, and all is not well. Canada is a more unequal society—more so than at any time since the 1920s. Profits now take a record share of the income pie from labour. Gross domestic product (GDP) growth is strong, but average wages and personal incomes are stagnant. Some groups, some sectors, and some regions have done well. Those in the top 10 percent of the income scale have prospered—those in the top 1 percent have gained spectacularly. Those at the bottom have lost ground, and those in the vast middle are just treading water trying to hang onto a standard of living under threat of erosion. Our system of social programs, safety nets, and public services has shrunk. Canadians have less protection against the vagaries of the market. The market has made big inroads into the public space. Unemployment at the moment is relatively low, but "good jobs" have declined, and employment is more precarious.

The contributors to this book generally agree that the impact of

NAFTA—interacting with other neoliberal policies—on the lives of most Canadians has been negative, that the loss of policy space has been serious, and that the further deep integration initiatives under-way or contemplated would make what has already been given up seem modest by comparison. While they would welcome Canada withdrawing from NAFTA, most would also question its political fea-sibility at this time. Most would also caution that the loss of policy space should not be overstated, that considerable room to manoeu-vre remains for a government willing to exercise it aggressively and creatively. They hold our political leaders—not outside forces—pri-marily responsible for the direction the country has taken. They believe that the political destiny of the country is still largely in the hands of Canadians and the politicians they elect.

While there has been considerable social and fiscal harmonization downward (to US levels), notably in the areas of taxation, income inequality, and social spending, Canada-US social and fiscal differ-ences remain substantial—and they can be reversed, given the political will. While north-south flows have grown proportionately to east-west flows, the border still remains a powerful insulation against continental integration. We urge caution, however, against nostalgia for a time that is passed, pragmatism about what can be reclaimed and what cannot, and optimism about a future in which the vision of Canada outlined at the beginning of this introduction remains as valid as ever.

Deep integration is a slippery slope. As we move further down it, how much more difficult is it becoming to restore the pre-existing balance? Is there a tipping point beyond which it is irreversible? At what point does deepening economic integration spill over into the political realm? Is it already happening? How can we contain, reshape, or reverse the deep integration juggernaut? How can we chart a sensible alternative course? These are some of the key ques-tions and challenges of living with Uncle in this age of empire.

CHAPTER 1

The North American Deep Integration Agenda: A Critical Overview

BRUCE CAMPBELL

I will address the concept of *deep integration*—still largely unknown in the Canadian public arena—by addressing six questions: What is it? Where did it come from and where is it now? Where is it going? Why is it a bad idea? And what are the alternatives?

What Is It?
Corporate continental integration—driven by goals of efficiency, competitiveness, and profits—has been underway for five decades or more. What is being referred to here is a policy agenda designed to support and reinforce corporate goals. Embraced to varying degrees by both the current Conservative government and its Liberal predecessor, it is an ambitious, interventionist agenda to forge ever deeper levels of policy and regulatory harmonization, and structural and institutional integration. This to create a unified continental free market in which goods and serv-

ices, capital and labour, can move throughout the continent with minimal government interference, and where the border is of negligible significance.

Aimed in the first instance at economic and security policies, it requires the harmonization of an ever-widening swath of policies—social, environmental, immigration, cultural, and so forth. Policy uniformity, even without common decision-making institutions, is in fact a key measure of *political* integration.[1]

In the European Union, political integration is being achieved through supranational institutions and formal agreements, a pooling of sovereignty with the explicit goal of political union. In North America—where governance structures are weak or non-existent—this is occurring through Canada (and Mexico) aligning to the dominant power. The ultimate goal, though rarely stated explicitly, is economic union with the United States. While no overtly political end-game is ever mentioned, the consequence of this deep integration project, whether intended or not, is a kind of de facto political association or union (but with no political representation).

Use of terms such as *interoperability, common, compatibility,* and *mutual recognition* mask the reality that harmonization in most cases means Canada bending its policies and regulations, or simply adopting US policies and regulations. The term *integration,* as defined by the Oxford dictionary, implies the creation of a new entity that combines roughly equal elements of the pre-existing entities. A process of coming together where one entity is dominant and the resulting combination resembles the dominant entity implies *assimilation.* What is being referred to here as deep integration is a series of incremental or big measures that together are more akin to assimilation than integration.

Where Did It Come From? Where Is It Now?
How to discipline integration forces in order to maintain essen-

tial policy autonomy in our relations with the United States and avoid slipping into a satellite status is an age-old Canadian public policy challenge. Given the complexity of managing the Canadian federation, and the dominant social, cultural, economic, political, and ideological influence of the United States, sufficient policy "room to manoeuvre" is required to give expression to Canadian identity (our imagined community) and democracy.

Two deep integration policy initiatives underway for the last seventeen years have rendered this public policy challenge more difficult.

The first, the 1989 Free Trade Agreement (FTA)—later folded into the North American Free Trade Agreement (NAFTA)—provided the constitutional framework for locking in neoliberal policies and accelerating continental economic integration.[2] NAFTA locked in property and mobility rights for capital, constrained government policy choice, and weakened the bargaining power of workers. It represented a shift (structural adjustment, in the language of the World Bank) to a more market-centred or Americanized state-market relationship.

The second, the post-September 11 US military/security agenda, has replaced NAFTA as the dominant driver of North American policy integration. Beginning with the Smart Border Declaration, and Action Plan, security-driven integration has manifested itself in the restructuring and harmonization of a wide range of Canadian intelligence, surveillance, and anti-terrorist policies and practices—information sharing, no-fly and terrorist-watch lists, security certificates, preventative detention, for example. Security integration also extends to military integration, which is proceeding under the guise of common defence. These actions have affected related policies such as immigration, visas, and refugees. They are—as we have learned from the Arar Commission—having a major effect on basic civil rights, privacy, and respect for international law.

Since 2005, the North American Security and Prosperity Partnership (SPP) agreement has absorbed NAFTA and the Smart Border Action Plan, providing the new overarching framework within which the deep integration agenda is moving forward.

These economic and security-led integration initiatives have narrowed the scope of choices available to policy makers over the last fifteen years and compromised this fundamental tenet of Canadian policy making. The deep integration proposals and initiatives now on the table, or underway, would shrink policy space much further.

There are two sets of forces and competing visions of the country at play here. At the risk of oversimplification, they are: (1) the struggle between neoliberal or market fundamentalist forces and the social democratic or progressive forces; and (2) the struggle between the nationalist/internationalist forces on the one hand and continentalist/globalist forces on the other. These fault lines are deep and long-standing. They are overlapping, but not identical. (For example, John Turner and Mitchell Sharp's opposition to the FTA was more about their concern for the loss of Canadian independence, per se, than it was about the constraints it put on social democratic policies.)

Finally, the attitudes and priorities of the Canadian economic elites driving this process are converging with their US counterparts and diverging from those of the Canadian public. Economic elites are closer to US policy makers in their attitudes on a range of issues, from the war in Iraq to missile defence to Kyoto. EKOS polling research over the last decade has shown that, unlike the general public—which is in large measure committed to public institutions, universal social programs, and equality—business elites tend to favour minimalist government, low taxes, US-style social programs, and self-reliance.[3] They believe we must fall in lockstep with US policies or risk our economic security.

A majority of Canadians has come to accept NAFTA. However, most think NAFTA covers only border issues such as tariffs. Elites count on public misunderstanding of what NAFTA really is, coupled with deference on foreign policy issues generally, in advancing their agenda. Public support drops sharply the more NAFTA and deep integration initiatives are seen to impair domestic policy choice on foreign investment and on social and environmental polices, among others.[4]

Where Is It Going?

There are a number of ambitious deep integration initiatives and proposals underway or on the table.[5] Proponents say that the deep integration process is indivisible, inevitable, and irreversible. They argue that we can go on deepening our economic and security ties to the United States without compromising fundamental policy autonomy. There are differences between those who favour a new mega-deal, or "big bang" approach, and those who favour an incremental approach—many small deals away from the public spotlight. These are not mutually exclusive. The latter may help prepare the ground for, or facilitate, the former. Both contend that, with deepening integration an inevitable force, the only real debate is over the speed and scope that integration will take.

Some proposals are moving forward and some are stalled. Some are on the back burner and some are on the front burner. It is likely that the Conservative government—especially if it eventually gets a majority—will move more aggressively than its predecessor. The major proposals are:

- A common security perimeter with fully harmonized immigration, refugee, intelligence, and defence policies, including the expansion of NORAD to land and sea command.

- A North American energy and resources pact, possibly including water.
- A customs union and common trade policy.
- A monetary union.
- A North American regulatory harmonization agreement.
- Full incorporation of NAFTA disciplines in the agriculture, finance, telecom, and culture sectors.

Initiatives now underway in several of these areas are moving incrementally toward the realization of these proposals.

Several authors in this volume examine these deep integration initiatives. Maureen Webb and Kent Roach each cover aspects of the emerging security perimeter and its implications for civil liberties. Michael Byers looks at its military dimensions. Diana Gibson and Dave Thompson analyze oil and gas; Marjorie Cohen looks at electricity integration; and Tony Clarke examines water—all cornerstones of a potential resources deal. Marc Lee and I give a glimpse into the underworld of regulatory harmonization. Elsewhere, Lee critically examines the customs union proposal,[6] and Mario Seccareccia[7] and I[8] evaluate monetary union proposals.

The latest tri-national big business consensus around a deep integration agenda was reached in a May 2005 report, *Building a North American Community*.[9] The NAFTA leaders' North American Security and Prosperity Partnership agreement, reached several months earlier, provides a framework that, though vague, is sufficiently broad to accommodate advancement of this agenda.

There are a number of actual or potential flashpoints that may provoke a public and/or political reaction that could either slow down, disrupt, or speed up this deep integration initiative. Flashpoints include: the softwood lumber dispute, cross-border water conflicts such as the Devils Lake diversion, a new wave of civil rights violations, another major terrorist incident, or an energy crisis.

Why Is Continuing Down This Road a Bad Idea?

These deep integration initiatives and proposals will further shrink policy space—the range of choices open to Canadian policy makers. My fundamental concern is about the potential adverse effect this could have on governments' ability to manage the federation—on social cohesion, regional balance, economic prosperity—and ultimately about its effect on Canadian identity and democracy.[10]

There are a number of reasons the case for deep integration is on particularly shaky ground these days.

Failed Promises.

The first set of reasons relates to the fact that the first deep integration agreements—the FTA and NAFTA—did not fulfill their proponents' promises. To put it charitably, NAFTA in particular was oversold. The government has never undertaken an honest examination of the costs and benefits of NAFTA. The proponents just gloss over the inconvenient facts: NAFTA, they say, has greatly increased exports and investment; Canada's trade surplus is up, unemployment is down, inflation is low, wages are flat, business is experiencing record profits, growth is steady. Therefore NAFTA has been a success. What is there to re-examine? Let's just move forward and build on what we have achieved.

The question is this: *Did NAFTA deliver the goods in terms of bettering the lives of Canadian citizens?* Surely this is a fundamental test of a good public policy decision, and a reasonable question to ask before we go further down this road. I recognize the difficulty of isolating the impacts of such a complex and far-reaching agreement from those of other policies and from the interplay of external and domestic forces. My view is that it has to be seen as part of a mutually reinforcing policy package whose effects are cumulative over time. These difficulties do not absolve those pushing a NAFTA-plus agenda from having to submit to an independent review of NAFTA itself.

Did NAFTA contribute to increasing exports? Yes—although a 2001 Industry Canada study by Ram and others found that by far the largest factor—accounting for 90 percent of the export surge in the 1990s—was the depreciated Canadian dollar.[11] Did increased exports lead to an increase in jobs? Yes—but an earlier Industry Canada study by Dungan and Murphy found that hidden in the trade figures was an increase in the import content of Canadian exports to the point where, by 1997, more jobs were being destroyed by imports than created by exports.[12]

Let's look briefly at some of the promises:

- NAFTA-led integration was supposed to increase productivity and close the productivity gap with the United States. The NAFTA gains predicted by computer (CGE) models were premised on this assumption.[13] It has not. The gap has in fact widened.
- NAFTA was supposed to help us escape the resource export trap that has been our history— hewers of wood and drawers of water—and move us toward a more diversified high valued-added economy. If anything, we are now even more dependent on resource-based exports. Our key capital goods sectors (machinery, equipment, electrical, and electronic goods) remain very weak, account for most of the productivity lag, and have persistent trade deficits. And we have given up policy tools that could help to overcome this weakness.

- NAFTA was supposed to attract investment and establish Canada as a preferred platform for export into the US market. Canada has lost out to both the United States and Mexico in attracting greenfield investment. Canada's share of inward North American foreign direct investment (FDI) has dropped. The attractiveness of Canada as a launching pad for the North American market has diminished further since the September 11 attacks.
- NAFTA was supposed to give us privileged access to the US market, but our share of US imports has not increased. And in many sectors it has fallen. Other countries—without the "NAFTA advantage"—have been more successful in penetrating the US market than Canada.

We were promised that the income benefits of NAFTA would be widely shared among Canadians. However, average wages have stagnated while profit income as a share of the income pie has (at the expense of labour) increased to record levels. After four decades of declining inequality, after-tax-and-transfer family income inequality widened during the free trade era. According to Statistics Canada, the bottom 20 percent of families saw their incomes fall by 7.6 percent during 1989–2004, while the incomes of the top 20 percent of families rose 16.8 percent. After declining during the 1980s, the incomes of the top 20 percent of families grabbed an unprecedented extra share of the income pie during 1989–2004—41 percent to 44 percent—at the expense of the other 80 percent of Canadian families.

A study by Saez and Veall highlights how concentrated at the very top inequality growth has been.[14] The top 1 percent of Canadian taxpayers increased their share of total taxable income from

9.3 percent to 13.6 percent during the first free trade decade, 1990–2000. The top 0.1 percent increased their share even more sharply—from 3 percent to 5.2 percent. The authors attribute this in large part to pressure from deepening integration with the United States where income inequality is much greater and where Canadian senior executives can move more freely across the border. Subsequent US tax cuts under the Bush administration for the highest income earners have likely aggravated this situation.

Contrary to prior assurances, there has been a deliberate shrinking of the Canadian social state—a structural adjustment of the public sector and of fiscal capacity. The convergence to the US model, although far from complete, has been significant. While Canadian governments still spend significantly more on social programs and public services than their American counterparts, the difference has been shrinking rapidly, as shown by a 2003 federal Finance Department study. Canadian governments (non-military) program spending fell from 42.9 percent of GDP in 1992 to 33.6 percent of GDP in 2001. This compares with US (non-military) program spending, which increased marginally from 27.7 percent to 27.9 percent of GDP. The gap in non-military spending between the two countries—5.7 percentage points of GDP in 2001—is down dramatically from a gap of 15.2 points of GDP in 1992.

On the environment, NAFTA has entrenched environmentally unsustainable practices. Most dramatically, the rise in CO_2 emissions from Alberta tar sands development to fuel the voracious US appetite for oil is the biggest single reason Canada is failing so miserably in meeting its Kyoto commitments. Moreover, one result of the fact that Canada lags behind US environmental standards in many areas is the 400 percent increase in hazardous waste imports from the United States.[15] And governments wanting to raise standards may face corporate legal challenges under the Chapter 11 investor-state dispute system.

Finally, there is the troubling issue of our increased dependence on the US market for our exports and our heightened vulnerability to border disruption or other forms of US trade retaliation. For example, the BSE (Bovine Spongiform Encephalopathy) ban on live cattle exports to the United States is a cautionary tale of the vulnerability of an industry that integrated continentally under free trade—closing many of its Canadian processing plants—only to find itself suddenly cut off from its main market, and with a surplus of product and a lack of domestic slaughter capacity (of which over 80 percent is now owned by two US multinationals).

It would be simplistic and wrong-headed to lay all the blame for these negative developments and unfulfilled promises at NAFTA's door, just as it would be equally simplistic and wrongheaded to credit NAFTA with all that is positive about our economy. Nevertheless, the prima-facie evidence does not support the case that NAFTA has been a success. Deep integration proponents may well respond by saying that NAFTA was not responsible for these adverse developments and that without it things would have been worse. But this would be a weak defence and one that has not been very well substantiated. It is certainly not a credible basis on which to argue that we should be proceeding further down this deep integration road.

To return to the question—has this deep integration project delivered the goods?—one can surely point to gains: elites have benefited; certain groups and sectors have benefited. But, overall, the answer is No. Benefits have not been widely shared. Canadians were persuaded once to take a leap of faith into the future. We have now seen the future. Why should we be contemplating a further leap?

A fundamentally flawed dispute mechanism:
The softwood case.
The softwood lumber dispute has exposed the weakness at the

heart of NAFTA. A binding dispute-settlement mechanism, designed to mitigate power politics and reduce trade harassment, was the Canadian negotiators' central goal in the original FTA negotiation. Twenty years ago, the softwood dispute was the trigger for entering into bilateral negotiations. Today, the softwood dispute is still here to remind us of their failure to achieve this goal.

The negotiators did not get the exemption from US trade laws that the Mulroney government had sought, but they did get a dispute mechanism that they thought would ensure that US trade agencies applied their own laws properly, and therewith greatly reduce the harassment that Canadian exporters faced. Misapplication of US trade laws, not the laws themselves, was seen to be the nub of the problem.

The key feature of the dispute mechanism negotiated at the eleventh hour was the ad hoc bi-national panel system, which replaced the US Court of International Trade's (CIT) judicial review of the US trade agency decisions. The panels, composed of nationals of both countries, did not judge the legality of US trade law, per se, but only whether it was being properly applied. It did little to prevent the US Congress from changing its own law. A panel's final decision was binding in the limited sense that it obliged the US trade agency to go back and review the case again. The process contained an *extraordinary challenge appeal* procedure that was only supposed to be used in extreme cases such as where a panellist had a conflict of interest, or a panel had overstepped its authority. This three-person panel, drawn from a roster of American and Canadian judges, was supposed to insulate against a constitutional challenge in the United States. Finally, the FTA process was supposed to be much faster than the CIT review.

Hailing it as the jewel-in-the-crown of the original Free Trade Agreement, the Canadian team would never have signed off on a

deal without it. This is confirmed in the memoirs of two principal negotiators, Gordon Ritchie[16] and Derek Burney.[17] Burney
said it was the *sine qua non* of the negotiation. Ritchie said recently that they would never have signed the Agreement if they had
thought that the US government would treat its commitment
with such disregard. In his memoirs, Burney wrote that the US
legal team assured the Canadians that this mechanism—which
they referred to as the "dead judges" panel—would never be
invoked.

The United States invoked the Extraordinary Challenge Committee (ECC) procedure in Lumber Round III, and invoked it
again in the current round (Lumber IV). Both times the panel
has ruled in Canada's favour. The United States has used the ECC
six times in all, making it a routine, not an unusual, part of the
process. Congress has changed US law several times to avoid
future defeats. NAFTA panel disputes now take, on average,
seven-hundred days to resolve (Lumber IV is in its fourth year).
This is more than twice as long as they were supposed to, and
longer than those settled at the US Court of International Trade,
the very process the NAFTA panels replaced.

Canadian companies have taken their fight back to the US
Court of International Trade, recognizing, as a report by the US
law firm Baker and Hostetler concluded: "It is now arguable that
Canadian private interests ensnared by anti-dumping and subsidies disputes with the United States would be better off in U.S.
courts than before bi-national panels." The final irony is that the
Canadian government is also back in the US domestic trade
court, the very process it sought to replace under the FTA.

The Bush administration simply refused to accept the final
ruling of the Extraordinary Challenge panel, and refused to stop
collecting or return the more than five billion dollars–plus in
duties it had thus far collected from Canadian exporters. The
US lumber lobby has launched a constitutional challenge to

Chapter 19—its second.

In a singular act of appeasement, the Harper government negotiated a controversial settlement to the softwood dispute, signalling that it will not seriously challenge the US government's refusal to live up to its NAFTA commitments. It sends a message that Washington can ignore the rules because Canada is so deeply dependent on the United States that it would not walk away, no matter what.

The government had another option. It could have invoked a little-known, but powerful and as yet unused, NAFTA provision—Article 1905. Article 1905 can be invoked where a party does not implement a Chapter 19 ruling. It would allow Canada to convene a special bilateral panel drawn from the ECC roster of judges. It would have given Canada the right to withdraw *any* benefits it extended the United States under NAFTA over and above those it has conferred at the World Trade Organization (WTO). It is not restricted to tariffs. It would have given Canada considerable latitude in withdrawing benefits as long as they were not "manifestly excessive."

The key trade-off in the original FTA negotiation was Chapter 19 (the Canadian demand) for investment guarantees (the American demand). Thus, it would be reasonable for Canada to suspend WTO–plus investment benefits to the United States. These could include foreign investment review provisions, or investor-state privileges for US companies; or it could suspend NAFTA's energy-sharing obligations (the proportionality clause), restoring much-needed policy flexibility to address our looming domestic energy problems.[18]

What Are the Alternatives?

To restate: I am not talking about rolling back the market integration that has occurred under NAFTA—or over the last five decades, for that matter. To think otherwise seriously overestimates the power of government in modern capitalist society. The current debate is around a specific policy agenda that is designed to support and encourage the creation of a single continental free market and the sweeping policy harmonization that this implies. My argument is that this agenda is neither inevitable nor irreversible at this point. There are viable alternatives for managing the vast and complex Canada-US relationship that would preserve independent policy space and reinforce national identity. There are alternatives that would reshape the terms of integration so as to curb corporate power and enhance the power of citizens.

The key questions are: As we move further down this deep integration road, how much more difficult is it to slow down, halt, and restore the pre-existing balance? Is there a tipping point beyond which it is irreversible? What strategies can or should be employed to discipline, reshape, or reverse further continental integration? How to counterbalance corporate power in the integrated market? How can policy makers restore a more sustainable balance between national policy capacity and the strategic pooling of sovereignty that is the reality of modern international cooperation?

My approach might be termed the deliberate pursuit of small steps (and where appropriate, big ones) to maintain and reclaim national policy flexibility. My view is that the correct and still valid role of policy is to lean against the forces of continental integration, not to reinforce them; to reshape them where appropriate; to negotiate multilateral counterweights where possible; and, where necessary, to reach bilateral arrangements in areas where the power differential is mitigated and the loss of autonomy is minimized.

As a policy outsider, the exercise of putting forward alternatives has, for me, an element of unreality. I recall attending a lecture at Carleton University in the 1970s by the great British economist Joan Robinson. In the question period, an audience member repeatedly asked her what she would do about the intractable problem of the day—stagflation. Professor Robinson repeatedly responded in turn with her own question: What power do you give me? I will assume a measure of power and conclude with a few broad policy suggestions—mainly economic—that I have elaborated elsewhere.[19]

First, government should re-assert its capacity to actively manage the domestic economy. It should focus on strengthening the *national* economy through a variety of policy tools. There is still substantial policy space remaining, despite the constraints imposed by NAFTA or the Smart Border accord. Many policy tools are not affected, but simply not acknowledged or properly used. The government should identify and maximize existing policy space, and test its limits where appropriate.

On social policy, NAFTA, by increasing the weight of the business demands for a *level playing field*, has intensified pressures for social harmonization downward to US levels. However, it is Canadian governments sympathetic to business demands that is the main culprit here. And the (far from complete) social convergence that I have described can be reversed.

On security, policy space does exist to take bold steps that reflect our own assessment and response to terrorist and other security threats. Foreign policy does not have to be whatever pleases the Bush administration. Cooperation in the defence of North America is essential, but it does not preclude our own assessment of US initiatives that we think are legitimate and those that are excessive, especially those that violate our commitments under international law. Creating a Canadian military niche within a US command-and-control structure would seriously compromise independent decision making about when, where, and for what purpose to engage Canadian troops. Worse, it would foster a perception of Canada as an appendage of the US global military strategy.

Second, the government should deal with Canada-US issues and irritants as they arise and, where possible, develop ways of dealing with them before they reach crisis proportions. It should deal in areas where the impact of the size differential is minimized. In general, government should avoid linking issues when negotiating bilateral agreements. Most agreements are, as they should be, compartmentalized and of limited scope. As military analyst Stephane Roussel argues, "the principle of compartmentalization means that progress or benefits in one area should never be linked to obtaining concessions or results in another."[20]

It is also important for the Canadian government to acknowledge that secure market access is unattainable. There is no permanent solution short of political union. The US Congress will never surrender power over its trade protection laws.

Third, given the current high degree of market integration, there is a case to be made for bilateral cooperation in reshaping policy measures to discipline and counterbalance corporate power and globalization pressures. The Auto Pact is an example of how continental market forces were reshaped by deliberate policy measures to ensure minimum levels of production in Canada. Governments could resist pressures on fiscal capacity by implementing common or complementary measures that would limit the ability of corporations to use transfer pricing and other accounting tricks to shift profits to the lowest tax jurisdiction. They could develop common or complementary strategies to combat global warming. They could develop common or complementary measures to prevent social dumping—the corporate practice of playing one jurisdiction off against another in the search for the most generous subsidies, tax breaks, and labour and environmental regulatory exemptions.[21]

These measures are not part of the deep integration agenda that Canadian elites are pushing. Nor are they realistic options under the current US administration and Congress. But they could be feasible in the future under more progressive American and Canadian governments.

Fourth, international economic diversification should be a priority. That past efforts have had very limited success should not be an excuse for giving up, but rather a spur to learning from past mistakes. Among positive incentives for diversification is the emergence of economic giants—China, India, and Brazil—that could provide opportunities for lessening our dependence on the US market. Among the negative incentives for diversification is the fragility of the US economy—its huge fiscal and trade deficits and foreign debt—which reinforces the need for Canada to reduce its vulnerability in the event of a major US economic "correction."

However, the limits of such diversification policies should be acknowledged and expectations adjusted accordingly. Canadian business is risk-averse and, for the most part, comfortable staying in its North American backyard. There is little evidence that NAFTA has served as a testing ground and springboard to the world for Canadian business, as proponents had thought. Moreover, the business landscape is dominated by foreign multinationals whose goals and plans for their Canadian affiliates do not often coincide with national priorities.

Fifth, where bilateral agreements are not necessary or feasible, Canada should favour multilateral forums. Canada should work to maintain and strengthen the United Nations system, to establish counterweights, however imperfect, to mitigate US unilateralism.

Sixth, Canada should work in multilateral forums to forge agreements in the areas of human rights, the environment, health, culture, and taxation, that are enforceable and that circumscribe and discipline the commercial imperatives of the international trade agreements. Examples of treaties that seek to move in this direction include the Framework on Tobacco Control and the recently signed UNESCO cultural diversity treaty in which the Canadian government played a lead role.

Finally, the discussion among policy insiders is all about NAFTA-plus, about new agreements—big and small—that would move us farther down this deep integration road. But I want us to reconsider what for the economic establishment is the ultimate heresy: that it is time to re-examine our future under the FTA/NAFTA. We should undertake a comprehensive assessment of its costs and benefits and take a hard-headed look at the advantages and disadvantages of pulling out of NAFTA. It is time to stand back and ask: Is NAFTA working for us? Do the costs outweigh the benefits? Is it serving our needs? I suggest it is time to reconsider whether NAFTA, in its current form, is outdated and contrary to the national interest as the overarching frame-work for managing Canada-US economic relations.[22]

Chapter 19 clearly has not provided the security of market access that was anticipated. The panel review process is deeply flawed. United States trade laws continue to apply to Canadian exports, and the United States can amend its laws without Cana-dian consent. The Chapter 19 process is lengthier, costlier, without finality, and less likely to bring satisfactory compensa-tion than the United States Trade Court. Would we not be better off managing our trade disputes through the US courts, through the WTO dispute system, and more generally through the myri-ad bilateral channels—formal and informal and at all government levels—that are flexible and able to evolve and adapt to the changing realities of the relationship?

Nor have many of the FTA/NAFTA's anticipated benefits been fulfilled: not the expected productivity gains, nor the preferred access gains, nor the investment and income gains. And it has produced adverse social consequences. Has the "NAFTA advan-tage" really been that significant? The NAFTA tariff advantage is admittedly significant in some sectors, but the snap-back to most favoured nation (MFN) levels would be manageable. Many exporters already pay the MFN rate.

NAFTA is institutionally dysfunctional, with an inactive commission and a miniscule secretariat. The trilateral labour and environment institutions set up as a result of the side-agreements negotiated by the Clinton administration are more substantial. The Environment Commission (NAAEC) has been modestly effective in monitoring environmental conditions, but has done nothing to moderate the negative effect of NAFTA on the environment. The Labour Commission (NAALC) has failed on both counts. In any case, they are both independent of NAFTA.

NAFTA has been superseded in many areas by the WTO agreements in areas such as intellectual property, standards setting, agriculture, and services rules. Differences between the two agreements in these areas are now minor.

Finally, withdrawing from NAFTA would allow us to reclaim important policy space to address potential national energy shortages. We would be free of corporate challenges to government policies under the investor-state mechanism, and would no longer be subject to the very broad concepts of expropriation and compensation to which we are bound under NAFTA. Provincial governments would be free again to bring in public auto insurance without fear of prohibitive costs, and Crown corporations would be free again to pursue non-commercial mandates where appropriate. It would help protect against the encroachment by for-profit health care investors. We would also regain some important industrial policy tools, such as performance requirements.

In his 1981 book *Life with Uncle,* respected foreign policy expert John Holmes wrote:

> The effort of governments in agreements reached with
> the United States was to control and discipline that

force [continentalism], not to encourage it ... The rules, commitments, or even institutions established between Canada and the United States, while designed to reduce conflict, are not necessarily designed to bring us closer together ... Their purpose, rather, is to regulate forces which, unless a Canadian place is staked out, would inevitably erode our sovereignty and identity.[23]

Holmes articulated a fundamental principle of Canada-US relations, which stands the test of time as a guidepost for Canadian policy makers, now and into the future.

CHAPTER 2

The Security Agenda: Driving Deep Integration

MAUREEN WEBB [24]

At the time the Free Trade Agreement and later the North American Free Trade Agreement were negotiated, Canadians were told they could enjoy the benefits of free trade with the United States without losing the benefits of sovereignty.

It is now fairly apparent that neither part of this promise is true. NAFTA has not been very beneficial for Canadians. The effects of the agreement on workers, the environment, and public health have been pernicious, and the softwood lumber case proves that any benefits the agreement does offer certain industries cannot be counted on since the United States—and particularly the Bush administration—will act unilaterally and refuse to be bound by the contract and arbitration decisions made pursuant to it.

At the same time, the agreement has severely undermined Canadian sovereignty. NAFTA's Chapter 11 allows investors to

hold governments at all levels hostage when it comes to legislat-
ing in the public interest, and potentially allows important policy
areas like health care, agriculture, and resource management to
be taken out of government control. In fact, NAFTA was never a
trade agreement in the traditional sense, but rather the first of a
new generation of agreements that give investors unprecedented
rights against national governments and subject important areas
of public policy to rules that privilege the interests of capital over
those of citizens.

The business lobby in Canada has been pushing the government to expand NAFTA and to replicate its provisions in the
World Trade Organization regime and the proposed (but indefinitely stalled) Free Trade Agreement of the Americas (FTAA). It
is apparent from reading the Canadian Council of Chief Executives' *North American Security and Prosperity Initiative* document
of January 2003 and the report of the tri-national Independent
Task Force on the Future of North America of May 2005 (co-
chaired by former industry minister John Manley) that this lobby
would be content to have Canadian social and regulatory policy
brought into line with that of the United States, as it would have
to be in the kind of economic union the lobby is proposing.
Indeed, the Canadian business lobby appears to be willing to
achieve economic union whatever the cost to Canadian sovereignty or the public good. As a result, it has become a formidable
advocate for deep integration in all realms of policy with the
United States.

Some pundits have speculated, however, that the Canadian
business lobby might not get what it wants. The United States
might calculate that, in the economic sphere as in other spheres,
it is more advantageous not to be bound by international regimes
like NAFTA that have binding dispute resolution mechanisms.
This may be particularly so, in the United States' current unilateralist mood, if it continues to lose cases under NAFTA and the

WTO and fails to get the concessions it wants under the FTAA and new WTO rounds.

But even if the United States—or Canada, reacting against US failures to honour its contractual obligations—were to withdraw from NAFTA or the other new generation "trade" agreements, deep integration between Canada and the United States would continue to be a live project. Since September 11, 2001, the United States is demanding it—calling for unprecedented integration among Canada's customs, immigration, transportation, security intelligence, policing, and military functions and those of the United States, and threatening economic sanctions in the form of border delays and closures if its demands are not met.

Security is overtaking trade as a driver of deep integration.

A Global Agenda
The security agenda that the United States is pushing is aimed not just at Canada but at countries around the world.

There are a number of factors engendering the myriad of new security initiatives being introduced by the United States. At a superficial level, the Bush administration is responding to real feelings of vulnerability on the part of a deeply shaken population. At the same time, however, the administration is taking advantage of the politics of fear to consolidate its power. It is using security to divert attention away from social policies it wants to implement in the interests of the corporate and upper classes. It is using security to project the neoconservative foreign policy expressed in think tank documents like *Rebuilding America's Defenses: Strategy Forces and Resources for a New Century*[25] onto the international stage— and to sell it at home. It is positioning the United States in strategic regions such as the Middle East, the Caspian Sea, and the Philippines in ways that allow it to better enforce its hegemonic interests. It is using the security agenda to concentrate unprecedented power in the hands of the executive branch of government.

And it is using security measures to increase control over domestic dissent and the population in general.

US demands have been backed by UN Security Council Resolution 1373, under which member states failing to comply risk Security Council sanctions, and by the economic, political, and military power of the United States. Under this pressure and for their own reasons, many governments have followed the United States, enacting a web of anti-terrorism laws and measures that have led to a growing harmonization and integration of security functions globally.

Canada—An Incremental Approach
Canada is one of the nations that have advanced furthest down this road, but a lot of what has been done has taken place under the public radar. The federal government has avoided being seen to toe the line on the more hot-button security integration issues: Iraq and missile defence. And, apart from the fairly high-profile promulgation of the Canadian *Anti-Terrorism Act*, which is modelled on the *USA Patriot Act*, the government has taken a low-key, incremental approach to implementing security initiatives. Most have been put in place through administrative agreements, international joint working groups, regulations, and the use of international forums such as the International Civil Aviation Organization and the G-8. In this way, the government has avoided having to table initiatives before Parliament, and the public debate and democratic accountability that go along with that process. The Canada-US Smart Border Agreement and Action Plan, an administrative agreement negotiated in December 2001 by John Manley when he was deputy prime minister, is the blueprint for security integration between the two countries. The Canadian National Security Policy unveiled in April 2004, the Security and Prosperity Partnership of North America announced in March 2005, and the three-hundred proposals out-

lined in the report to ministers in June 2005 more or less reflect the content of the Smart Border Action Plan.

The Smart Border Action Plan calls for common biometric standards for identity cards that can be used across different modes of travel, coordinated visa and refugee policy, coordinated risk assessment of travellers, integrated border and marine enforcement teams, integrated national security intelligence teams, coordinated terrorist lists, new counter-terrorism legislation, increased intelligence sharing, and joint efforts to promote the Canada-US model internationally.

Complying with the Smart Border Action Plan, Canada has harmonized its visa requirements with those of the United States and coordinated its refugee policy by entering into a Safe Third Country Agreement with the Bush administration. As mentioned earlier, Canada has also put into place new anti-terrorism legislation, the *Canadian Anti-Terrorism Act*, which follows the template of the *USA Patriot Act*.

The "Plan": Registration, Linkage, Risk Management

The best way to make sense of the remaining Smart Border initiatives is to see that what the United States is aiming to set up, with the help of Canada and other G-8 countries, amounts to a global infrastructure for the registration and surveillance of populations. The premise of the infrastructure is that states can register populations using biometric identifiers, link information to individuals' identifiers from as many sources as possible, and use the resulting dossiers of personal information to assess the risk individuals pose to the state.

A major paradigm shift is occurring. The United States and its allies are no longer focused on ordinary police and intelligence work, where state agents concern themselves with specific risks, starting with specific leads on specific suspects and work outwards. Rather, they are pursuing a project of mass surveillance, in which everyone is viewed as a suspect, and the aim is to eliminate risk. States are not just trying to identify known terrorists or those suspected of terrorism on reasonable grounds from out of the crowd as they cross borders or conduct transactions. They are trying to *predict* who might be a terrorist—a little like the film *Minority Report* in which officials use technology to read people's minds to stop criminal acts before they happen (although the reality falls far short of the Hollywood fantasy).

In effect, states that have thrown away or allowed the precautionary principle to be severely undermined in policy areas like public health and the environment over the past two decades, through new-generation trade agreements like NAFTA and the loosening of environmental protections, are now embracing it unquestioningly in the area of security.

The precautionary principle is an extremely beneficial principle when applied to many areas of public policy, but when it is applied to security matters, the effects are adverse. The rights and interests of individuals carry very little weight in a security regime premised on the precautionary principle. Ordinary legal protections that are fundamental to democratic societies, like the presumption of innocence, rights against unreasonable search and seizure, and rights against arbitrary detention and punishment, are viewed as intolerable risks in a precautionary regime. Guilt and innocence and the real identity of individuals are beside the point in such a regime. What matters to the risk screeners is the management and avoidance of risk from the point of view of the state.

There are historical antecedents of this kind of system: the witch hunts of the McCarthy period, the secret files of the Stasi. But the system that is currently being constructed is unlike systems that we have seen before in that its technological capacity far outstrips earlier systems, and its global reach ensures that one has to worry, not just about what one's own state might do with one's personal information, but about what any other state might do with it.

In the current period, as in earlier periods, the stakes are very high. Already, we have seen states acting aggressively on the information they are gathering and sharing through global registration and surveillance to stop dissidents from flying, stop activists and intellectuals at borders, detain people without reasonable grounds, and, at the far end of the continuum, render people to third countries and extraterritorial camps run by the United States, where they face indefinite detention without charge, and torture, even death.

Registration
One of the first actions of the United States after 9/11 was to systematically register all males between the ages of sixteen and forty-five with links to Muslim and Arab countries visiting or travelling through the United States under the National Security Entry-Exit Registration System, or NSEERS. Under the program, all registrants were required to provide fingerprints as a biometric identifier.

Biometric registration was then expanded to most visa-carrying visitors to the United States under the US Visitor and Immigrant Status Indicator Technology (US-VISIT) program. Under US-VISIT, visa applicants are fingerprinted at the US consulate in the country in which they apply for their visa, and their fingerprints and other personal information are stored in a US database for 100 years.[26]

The next challenge for the United States was to expand registration to citizens. In common-law democracies like the United States, however, the idea of a national identity card has historically been anathema. The American people and Congress have, in the past, always rejected the idea of a national identity card. In Canada, a proposal for a new national identity card was floated by the Liberal government in the fall of 2002, and was soundly shot down by public opinion and the parliamentary committee reviewing the matter. A similar hot debate occurred in the UK where the government was forced to shelve plans for a national identity card for a period of time.

The US solution for registering citizens in all countries with biometric identifiers was the imposition of a global requirement for biometric passports. The United States ensured the realization of this goal with its *Enhanced Border Security and Visa Entry Reform Act* of 2002. The Act requires all countries wishing to retain their visa waiver status with the United States to adopt a passport with biometric identifiers by October 2004, and designated the International Civil Aviation Organization (ICAO) as the standard-setter. This legislation, along with a May 2003 agreement among the G8 member countries to adopt a biometric passport system, provided the momentum that resulted in a global standard being set. In its spring 2004 meeting in Cairo, ICAO set a face-recognition standard with optional fingerprint and iris scan standards. In fall 2004, Canada announced the introduction of a mandatory biometric passport using face recognition, starting in 2005. The EU announced the introduction of mandatory biometric passports with facial scans required from 2006 and fingerprints from 2007; and the United States introduced a mandatory biometric passport with facial recognition starting in 2005.

Once the British and American publics were "softened up" to the idea of biometric travel identification documents, proposals for biometric national ID cards were resurrected in each country. The UK government has introduced a scheme proposing a new national identity card with mandatory biometric requirements. In the United States, where most people do not carry passports, the government managed to pass the *Intelligence Reform and Terrorism Prevention Act* and the *REAL ID Act*, which contain plans for creation of a de facto national ID card, using drivers' licences. In light of these developments, the prospect of a mandatory biometric national ID card being introduced in Canada is not out of the question.

Until very recently, Canadian citizens were exempt from providing a biometric identifier at the US border. Canada was not part of the US Visa Waiver Program and had its own special exemption from US requirements that visitors carry either a biometric visa or a biometric passport. However, the *Intelligence Reform and Terrorism Prevention Act* of 2004 closes that exemption. The Act requires Canadians to present a biometric passport or some other approved biometric identity document at the US border. Negotiations over what those other approved documents should be might be the opener to a resurrection of the idea of a national ID card for Canadians. And if the US and Canadian governments follow through with the Smart Border Action Plan item requiring biometric identity cards with common standards designed to be "used across different modes of travel," one wonders how Canadians will avoid having a new biometric national identity card imposed on them.

Whatever document is used, US—and Canadian—agencies will henceforth have a biometric identifier with which to build information dossiers on Canadians.

Linkage, Acquisition, and Convergence of Databases Nationally and Internationally

Since 9/11, the United States has made enormous efforts to collect data on individuals from as many sources as possible and to link this data. The government buys commercial information from data-aggregating companies;[27] it asks companies and institutions in the United States to give it vast amounts of data voluntarily, and they have;[28] it gives the FBI broad authority to access the records of businesses under the *USA Patriot Act* (access which extends to the personal information of citizens in other countries wherever it is held by US companies and their subsidiaries);[29] it buys entire voter registers and other government records of foreign countries;[30] it institutes new requirements on banks and businesses to report financial transactions;[31] and it enters into international agreements that provide for the sharing of information on financial transactions,[32] electronic communications,[33] and law enforcement records.[34]

Information is shared among US agencies,[35] and the government has also linked public and commercial databases under programs like US-VISIT,[36] the Computer Assisted Passenger Pre-screening System or CAPPS II,[37] and its successor program, Secure Flight,[38] and the Multi-State Anti-Terrorism Information Exchange or MATRIX program.[39] Unlike in Canada, the federal *Privacy Act* in the United States "regulates records the government stores, but does not regulate how [government] agencies access records from the private sector."[40] Insiders have spoken of a "black box" of information the United States is amassing for security purposes: no one knows exactly what it will eventually contain, only that it will be as comprehensive as possible.[41]

Under the Smart Border Action Plan, there have been arrangements for increased sharing and interoperability of databases between Canadian and US customs and law enforcement, and for increased sharing among diplomatic missions.

Canada and the United States have also set up integrated border, marine, and security intelligence units. Recently, the Arar Inquiry heard shocking testimony about the RCMP's investigation into alleged terrorist cells in Toronto and Ottawa, which swept Canadian citizen Maher Arar into its net. Code-named AO Canada, it was an international effort in which the FBI and another US agency, left unnamed for security reasons (likely the CIA), participated as partners, having access to all information gathered by the RCMP, without caveats. In fact, there were regular joint information meetings in Canada, and the US agencies were provided with CDs containing the entire investigation file, which included twenty-six hard-disk drives that the RCMP had seized from seven raids, but did not have the manpower to analyze themselves.[42]

In addition to the linkage and convergence just described, the United States has been demanding that the air carriers of other countries hand over advanced passenger information (API) and passenger-name record information (PNR) in order to allow US agencies to track and control movement of people across borders. API is the list of passengers on the airline manifest. PNR is the information kept in air travel reservation systems. It can include over sixty fields of information, including the name and address of the traveller, the address of the person with whom the traveller will stay, the trip itinerary, the date the ticket was purchased, credit card information, seat number, meal choices (which can reveal religious or ethnic affiliation), medical information, behavioural information, and linked frequent-flyer information.

The Smart Border Action Plan provides for the sharing of API and PNR information between the United States and Canada. Canada has facilitated this by passing three pieces of legislation. Bill C-44 amendments[43] to the *Aeronautics Act* exempt Canadian air carriers from the *Personal Information Protection and Electronic Documents Act* to allow them to give the personal information of passengers to foreign agencies requesting it. Bill S-23 amendments[44] to the *Customs Act*, and regulations made pursuant to it,[45] give Canada Customs and Revenue Agency (CCRA) access to all information relating to passengers in airline or travel agent reservation systems in respect of incoming flights to Canada. CCRA is storing and tracking the information for up to six years and sharing it with domestic and foreign law enforcement agencies. The *Public Safety Act* provides for the collection and sharing of API, PNR, and other information by Canadian agencies in respect of domestic and incoming and outgoing international flights, and for any flights by Canadian carriers departing from anywhere in the world. According to a White House progress report on the Canada-US Smart Border Action Plan, Canada started collecting API at Canadian airports on October 8, 2002, under a program called PAXIS, and an automated US-Canada API/PNR data-sharing program was to have been in place by spring 2003.[46]

The United States has forced the EU into a PNR-sharing agreement even though it violates the EU Data Protection Directive. Canada also signed a PNR-sharing agreement with the EU in October 2005, and ICAO has been asked to develop global standards for PNR sharing.

Risk Assessment

Having collected and linked all of the information just described, the United States and other countries are faced with the challenge of sorting through it to assess the risk that different individuals pose to security. There are "low-" and "high-tech" approaches to this.

The high-tech approach.

The high-tech version of risk assessment involves data mining and risk scoring: using computer programs to scrutinize masses of data for selected criteria or patterns which are supposedly indicative of the level of risk individuals pose.

The United States is pursuing high-tech solutions with fervour. Its most ambitious project was the Total Information Awareness (TIA) program, run by John Poindexter (a key figure in the Iran-Contragate scandal) out of the Defense Advanced Research Projects Agency (DARPA). The goal of the program, as described by Poindexter, was to mine "the transaction space" to find "signatures" of terrorist activity.[47] According to the project's website, the transactions mined would include individuals' financial, medical, travel, "place/event entry," transportation, education, housing, and communications transactions. Poindexter planned to develop software that could analyze "multiple petabytes" of data.

In fall 2003, Congress pulled the funding for the TIA program, but many of its component parts live on in hidden research and other programs. Steve Aftergood, of the American Federation of Scientists, has written that "the whole Congressional action looks like a shell game. There may be enough of a difference for them to claim TIA was terminated while for all practical purposes the identical work is continuing."[48]

The MATRIX program mentioned earlier is also a data mining program, as was the CAPPS II program. According to a notice published in the US Federal Register in January 2003, the intent of CAPPS II was to create a passenger screening database that would be linked to virtually unlimited amounts of data from private and public sources, including "financial and transactional data." The program was also supposed to "risk-score" passengers as red, amber, or green (high, medium, low) risks based on undisclosed criteria. CAPPS II was withdrawn over privacy and operational concerns, and replaced with a new program called "Secure Flight." Secure Flight was to forgo the use of private sector data and risk scoring that its predecessor had employed, and the Transportation Security Administration (TSA) made assurances to this effect. However, reports have recently revealed that the TSA did in fact link passenger information to commercial databases under the program[49] and had plans to test whether the program could be adapted to predict which passengers might be involved in terrorist activity.[50]

The Smart Border Action Plan called on Canada and the United States "to explore means to identify risks posed by passengers on international flights arriving in each other's country," and the

Canadian National Security Policy unveiled in April 2004 confirmed that Canada would spend resources "to study emerging technologies that could ... improve our ability to screen passengers."[51] Pursuant to these commitments, Canada and the United States have agreed to implement an interoperable "risk-scoring mechanism"—presumably what is being tested is the Secure Flight program. According to a *Smart Border Action Plan Status Report*, dated December 17, 2004, on the Department of Foreign Affairs' website, the first phase of this exchange was implemented on August 10, 2004. The project is currently located in the Canadian Risk Assessment Centre, under the auspices of the Department of Public Safety and Emergency Preparedness. It is not known what criteria are being used or tested, only that the program, like the American CAPPS II program, is a data mining one: it uses computer algorithms to sort through personal information and identify the risk posed by travellers.[52] A news report of January 2004[53] established that the program was going to score passengers as red, amber, or green risks, as did the CAPPS II program, but whether this aspect has been retained or not since the revamping of the CAPPS II program in the United States is not known.

Finally, it would seem that in Canada the risk-scoring project has been recently recast as the second phase of a new program called Passenger Protect. Announced in August 2005, Passenger Protect is composed of a terrorist watch list administered by the Department of Transport and an "advanced automated air passenger assessment system" (presumably a risk-scoring system) that is to be tested and administered by the Department of Public Safety.[54]

Data-mining programs like the ones described above are alarming because the technology they use and the assumptions upon which they are based are dangerously flawed. First, the facts they rely on are often inaccurate, incomplete, and lacking context, and the programs contain inadequate mechanisms to allow individuals to correct, contextualize, or even know the information that is being used against them. Second, the criteria used are necessarily overbroad and mechanically employed so that ethnic and religious profiling is endemic.

The CAPPS II program provides a good example of the unacceptable margins of error associated with these kinds of systems. The TSA estimated that 5 percent of the travelling public would be rated as amber or red under the CAPPS II program. The Association of Corporate Travel Executives has observed that, if only 2 percent were rated red, there would be up to eight million passengers detained or denied boarding every year in the United States.

The low-tech approach.
In the low-tech approach to risk assessment, human beings make judgments about other human beings. However, in the current political climate there are strong bureaucratic incentives for risk assessors to err on the side of caution. No one wants to be the one who fails to flag, detain, or identify someone who later turns out to be a terrorist. This environment leads to indiscriminate interpretations of information and indiscriminate actions on the part of authorities. In the low-tech approach to risk assessment, as in the high-tech approach, ethnic and religious profiling is endemic.

In the United States, some fifteen-hundred to two-thousand innocent people, mostly with origins in Muslim countries, were swept off the street immediately after 9/11 and imprisoned, in violation of their constitutional rights, on immigration charges or material witness warrants.

Under the US no-fly list, peace activists and civil libertarians have been detained and denied boarding. Many other people have been stopped merely for having a name similar to one on the list. Senator Edward Kennedy was stopped from flying on several occasions and had to call the head of the Department of Homeland Security three times before his name was removed from the list.

The United States had at least a dozen terrorist watch lists administered by nine different agencies until most of them were consolidated in fall 2003 under the new FBI-CIA Terrorist Threat Integration Center (TTIC). News reports have put the number of names on the US lists in the millions.[55]

The United States has also been engaged in seizing and rendering individuals, often on the slimmest evidence, to extraterritorial camps and prisons, where they have been detained indefinitely without charges and tortured. Pentagon figures and estimates of intelligence experts put the number of people being held by the United States directly or at its request at nine thousand, as of May 2004.[56]

The Smart Border Action Plan calls for the coordination of Canadian and U.S. terrorist lists. Canadian airlines are already enforcing the US no-fly list even in respect of flights within Canada.[57] Former defence minister Bill Graham and NDP MP Pat Martin can be counted among the innocent Canadian casualties of the list.[58] Canadian authorities are enforcing the UN list for freezing assets, which is made up largely of names from the American list for freezing assets. As mentioned earlier, Canada is also developing its own no-fly list, which will likely be largely congruent with the US list.

More ominously, testimony at the Arar Commission has been revealing possible Canadian complicity in the US practice of extraordinary rendition. The testimony has suggested that Canada may also have had its own practice of allowing persons suspected of terrorist activities (often on the flimsiest grounds) to travel to third countries where local authorities were tipped off by Canadian officials and the individuals were detained arbitrarily, interrogated without legal rights, and even tortured.

Conclusion

The report of the tri-national big business Task Force on the Future of North America, co-chaired by John Manley, calls for a high-tech biometric security system to manage the US-Canada and US-Mexico borders, tied to integrated multinational databases, integrated visa regulations, integrated refugee laws, increased sharing of information on travellers, the creation of joint border authorities, and integrated watch lists.

Much of this, and more, has already been accomplished. Deep integration in the security realm is upon us, and its touted benefits are likely to be as illusory as the benefits of the free trade regime it is meant to guarantee.

CHAPTER 3

Security and Civil Liberties After September 11: The Canadian Response

KENT ROACH

In the context of dealing with the problems facing Canada from both the deep integration agenda and the aftermath of 9/11, the challenges of preserving Canadian civil liberties and democracy, Canadian sovereignty, and finally Canadian security are paramount.

First, let's ask ourselves, where are we on civil liberties and democracy in Canada since September 11? Let's begin by recalling the vibrant and controversial debate over Bill C-36, the *Anti-Terrorism Act*, our own version of the *USA Patriot Act*—massive legislation that was enacted in the few months after 9/11.

There is a huge difference, however, between our *Anti-Terrorism Act* and the Patriot Act. The Patriot Act was passed quickly, with some of the legislators not even bothering to read the text. In contrast, in Canada, it was rushed, it was tough, but we had a lively civil society debate. We had unions, we had charities, Muslim and Arab communities, Aboriginal groups, lawyers and civil libertarians all criticizing Bill C-36 as it was originally introduced on October 15, 2001.

I played some role in that debate, and one of the things that makes me proud to be Canadian is, as I opposed that law, I was never made to feel that I was being unpatriotic or that it was somehow un-Canadian to be objecting to that law. The experience, I'm sure, would have been quite different if I had lived south of the border and were opposing the Patriot Act.

The civil society engagement in Canada was the most effective campaign mounted against the expansion of a criminal law that we have seen for the last two decades—and it had some effect. The government was forced to go back and make some amendments. Maybe those amendments were not enough—they certainly were not enough to satisfy me—but they did make the bill somewhat less harmful. For example, one amendment took out the word *lawful* for an exemption for advocacy protest and strikes. The definition of *terrorism*, admittedly, still remains too broad, but even so, that was a substantial achievement. We also got a five-year "sunset clause" with respect to investigative hearings and preventive arrest. Perhaps most importantly, there was a three-year review added, providing the opportunity to look at the entire Act and challenge its necessity.

An EKOS public opinion poll found that about 50 percent of Canadians think the government got it right with the *Anti-Terrorism Act*, 43 percent think that we are not doing enough about terrorism, and only 7 percent think that the Act goes too far to curtail our rights and freedoms. That would seem to leave me with the dissenting 7 percent minority. I think that there are some changes that still need to be made to the *Anti-Terrorism Act*. The definition of *terrorism* remains in my view overbroad. It is much broader than a universal definition of *terrorism* that the United Nations has recently proposed, and it is much broader than a definition of *terrorism* that the Supreme Court of Canada has read into the *Immigration Act*, which has no definition of *terrorism*.

There is still too much secrecy in the new *Official Secrets Act* and amendments to the *Canada Evidence Act*. Our security agencies, for example, have been authorized to conduct electronic surveillance on Canadians without judicial warrant. The *Anti-Terrorism Act* lacks an anti-discrimination—or, better still, an anti-profiling—clause. Such a clause would certainly complement the cross-cultural round table on security issues that was introduced by the former Liberal government, in recognition of the fear and resentment aroused among minority communities in Canada, particularly the Arab and Muslim communities.

The upshot is that, yes, we have overreacted at times, but I think in general we have taken a more balanced approach to the threat of terrorism than has the United States. For example, let's update the Sunera Thobani case. You may recall that in 2001 the RCMP said that they were investigating her with a view to laying a charge under the hate propaganda provisions because she made a speech highly critical of American foreign policy. That certainly suggests that there was a bit of hysteria and fear in Ottawa after September 11.

What happened next? The University of British Columbia supported Ms. Thobani from the beginning by upholding her academic freedom, for which the UBC deserves credit. Then she made a complaint to the police complaints commission that oversees the RCMP, and that complaint was upheld. The commission ruled that the RCMP had acted inappropriately, both in terms of publicizing the investigation (which is something the police are not supposed to do), and in making reference to her race.

So, yes, there was overreaction in Canada, but I think that there was also some countervailing balance. But the greatest use of anti-terrorism measures has been with the immigration law, not the *Anti-Terrorism Act*. So far, only one person has been charged under the *Anti-Terrorism Act*, but we have to remember things like Project Thread, where twenty-one men from Southeast Asia were picked up, again with inappropriate publicity, under powers of investigative detention that we would not tolerate if they were used against Canadian citizens.

Similarly, we have security certificates, which have been used to hold five men in long-term detention, again, in violation of their right to a fair trial—a denial that we would not tolerate for Canadian citizens.

The British House of Lords, in the case of the Bellmarsh detainees in that country, has raised quite fundamental questions about this post-9/11 tendency to use immigration law as anti-terrorism law—a tendency of which Canada, as well as many other countries, is also guilty. The House of Lords' decision asks two questions: (1) Is it really an effective and rational response to the threat of terrorism to use immigration law, which has the ultimate club of simply removing a person from a country? And (2) Is it fair to impose procedures that would not be tolerated with respect to citizens and nationals of the country? In its decision responding to these questions, the House of Lords, by an eight-to-one ruling, overturned a British law enacted after 9/11 that denied the right to a fair trial to non-citizens.

Canada needs to take the same corrective action. Unfortunately, the Federal Court of Appeal, in a ruling on the Charkaoui case released about a week before the House of Lords' decision, declared that our new security certificate process was Charter-proof. And this decision—which pales in comparison with that of the British House of Lords—was handed down despite the fact that our security certificate process allows you to be removed from Canada or subjected to long-term detention on evidence that you never see, and that your lawyer never sees, and that is never even seen by a special advocate who can be appointed to intercede for you with the government.

Security certificates are largely about hearings that take place with a judge and the government's lawyer, and nobody else. I don't think that is something we would tolerate for Canadian citizens. So why are we tolerating it for non-Canadian citizens?

The US influence on our political decision makers cannot be discounted. Nor can the influence of those among the Canadian elite who are pushing for an even closer relationship with the United States. I see these influences in the US proposal for a joint security perimeter. It seems to me that we don't yet have a joint security perimeter despite the Smart Border agreement (with its objectionable features like integrated intelligence and the "safe third country" agreement), and I don't think Canada is willing to go so far as to cede power over visa policy and refugee policy to the United States.

Still, there is no room for complacency. I think it is shameful that in Canada there was not more concern—even outrage—expressed at our Canadian forces in Afghanistan handing over prisoners to the Americans, who are now detaining them in Guantanamo Bay.

When it comes to threats to sovereignty, I think we also have to remember it is not just the United States we have to be concerned about. Since 9/11, there is also the UN getting into the security business with Resolution 1373. It was under the regulations of Canada's *United Nations Act* that an Ottawa man, Liban Hussein, was wrongfully listed as a terrorist. Just because the words "United Nations" accompany something does not necessarily mean that it is benign. This idea of listing people as terrorists without trial is a fundamental challenge to the rights that an independent judiciary should have in determining who is a terrorist and who is not.

As for the overall challenge of preserving Canadian security, I think there is some reason for optimism. After 9/11, we relied on the criminal law, which I argued was inadequate. But in April

2004, the federal government produced a national security policy called *Securing an Open Society: Canada's National Security Policy*. It strikes me as a good and sensible document—and I can say that with some objectivity since no one consulted me about the wording of the document.

A significant point to keep in mind is that our national security policy, unlike that of the Americans, is not based on the notion of pre-emptive self-defence (which would be a joke given the state of our military) but rather on the multiple risk that Canadians face to their human security. Yes, anti-terrorism is part of our national security policy, but so are responses to things like SARS, blackouts, and floods. It is a much more balanced national security policy than the American policy, with its obsession with terrorism.

I think our post-9/11 experience suggests that Canada can survive, and perhaps even thrive. George Grant was wrong when he said that Canada self-destructed when we accepted "nukes" after the trauma of the Cuban missile crisis. And the deep integration people are also wrong when they argue that Canadian sovereignty is a luxury we can no longer afford after September 11.

This is not to say that there is room for complacency. We still need to focus on the dangers of discrimination against minority communities, including non-citizens. We need to ensure that we get the review and accountability of national security activities right. And we can't be smug about Guantanamo. We put people there. We have people there. We have to make sure that our spending on security is broad and rational, and that it responds to all the threats that Canadians face to their human security, and not simply the threat of terrorism.

CHAPTER 4

A Made-in-Canada Defence Policy

MICHAEL BYERS

When I left Canada fourteen years ago, I was what has been called a Red Tory, or an organic conservative, in a long and honourable tradition of organic conservatism. I left Canada for post-Thatcherite Britain and, in my seven years there, began a thought process that perhaps my views were not quite right (or perhaps too "right"). After seven years in post-Thatcherite New Labour Britain, I moved to another place that was considerably more extreme—North Carolina, the state in the United States with the lowest rate of unionization of any member of the Union.

My five years in North Carolina at Duke University radicalized me politically. There was something about hearing gunshots at night and realizing that one in four children in Durham, North Carolina, did not have access to health care that made me realize that being a Canadian social democrat was actually something quite special, something to be very proud of, something to be fought for, and something that was worth coming back to Canada to be.

In my first nine months back in Canada, I have to say that it feels like a huge burden has been lifted from my shoulders and I can say what I think and be with people who think like me. In 2004, I wrote a discussion paper for Bill Blaikie, then defence critic for the NDP. It was entitled "An Alternative Defence Policy." I wrote it to try to shake the federal NDP a little bit into thinking whether its defence policy was really attuned to some of the challenges of the early twenty-first century, and whether there might be room for movement in ways that could be politically advantageous—in terms of positioning itself on the Canadian landscape at this very important time.

The paper begins with a positive assessment of the professionals who work in our Canadian Forces. We can be very proud of the nearly sixty-thousand men and women who serve in Canadian uniform. We used to have the best small army in the world. We still have one of the best small armies in the world. They are a remarkable group of people, many of them. And also, it needs to be said, they have some pretty good equipment, too. We often tend to denigrate them without appreciating that.

Yet the Canadian Forces, in my assessment, fall short in a number of different areas. First of all, we don't treat our military personnel very well. We have a serious recruitment and retention problem. Some of our new recruits sit in barracks for a year and a half before being trained, because we don't have enough people to train them. The starting salary for a private in the Canadian army is derisory, by Western developed-country standards. We don't have as many of the high-tech capable soldiers and pilots that are necessary to operate some of our equipment. In fact, we have a destroyer that is more-or-less mothballed in Victoria because we don't have enough professional sailors in our navy to operate four destroyers.

We don't have very much in the way of light infantry for peace-keeping. We had to take a break from overseas missions a couple of years ago because the few that we had were tired and over-stretched. We lack heavy-lift aircraft to the point that, when we were planning to lead a peacekeeping mission to the Congo nine years ago, we had to abort that plan because we couldn't move our troops there and the Americans weren't going to do it for us. We have almost nothing in terms of a capability to assert sover-eignty and engage in police functions over our vast territory, and, most notably, our Canadian North and our coastline, which we need to remember is the longest coastline of any country in the world. In fact, we are operating, on average, only one Aurora sov-ereignty-assertion flight over the Arctic per year, which is quite remarkable when you think about it. The defence budget, rough-ly 1.2 percent of GDP, is a bit low by comparable standards. For example, the middle-power, non-nuclear NATO countries like the Netherlands or Norway are around 1.6 percent. But, of course, we are a lot bigger than they are in terms of geographic space, so I am not convinced that that number is quite where it should be. Mind you, we do live in a safe neighbourhood. We have a large and very powerful friend next door, and, as long as the United States doesn't invade us, well, what do we have to worry about? Or so goes the argument.

The 2005 defence budget increase, seen against the backdrop of very significant budget cutbacks from 1989 onwards (the so-called peace dividend), essentially repairs some of the damage that was done by a decade and a half of neglect.

I want to take this situation apart, in terms of how the Canadi-an Forces and military planners have responded to what they, at least, regard as a budget crisis. Their response has been to seek to maintain some war-fighting capabilities and some overseas mili-tary projection capability by linking themselves ever more closely with the American war-fighting machine. This happens most significantly in a push to achieve and maintain technological inter-operability with the world's largest and best-funded military force. We see this in terms of the current upgrades to the Hali-fax-class frigates, to the CF-18s, to serious consideration about cooperative engagement capability (CEC) for our maritime force, and the discussion—now put on hold—with regard to Canadian participation in missile defence.

Technological interoperability has been the mantra of the Canadian Forces for the last decade or so. If you are a military planner in this country, it is a good way of ensuring that military budgets don't decline any further—because this equipment is expensive, so budgets need to be kept where they are. The down-side of this, of course, is that expensive machines—expensive high-tech machines—draw money away from what might be considered other comparable or perhaps more important priori-ties. There are now less than three hundred Canadian soldiers engaged in UN peacekeeping. We are way down the list in terms of contributions to UN peacekeeping. We do have a force in the coalition operation in Afghanistan, but that is not a UN opera-tion. We have no heavy-lift aircraft, which is fine if it is available for rent or the Americans are prepared to lend it, but it is a little bit embarrassing and perhaps inconvenient if you want to move Canadian Forces personnel to a flooded Manitoba and you need the American air force to get you there.

In 2002, Jean Chrétien axed a plan to buy six Boeing C-17 heavy-lift aircraft. I was struck by the fact that, shortly after the tsunami struck Southeast Asia in late December 2004, one of the first things that Kofi Annan did was plead for more C-17s. It would have been nice to have been able to offer him six of them.

Interoperability, however, is the overriding policy. We are not going to see the kind of investment we need in Arctic ice break-ing capability and sovereignty assertion in the North, or serious peacekeeping, under current projections. Instead, we are going to buy F-35 strike fighters and probably move towards a generation of Aegis-class naval vessels that can operate seamlessly in US carrier task forces and provide theatre missile defence.

That, at least, is the sort of direction that some defence planners seem eager to go. We won't be investing much more new money in establishing a serious coastal patrol capability, not only in the Arctic but also along the east and west coasts. This, of course, will mean that the United States will have to take on increasingly the defence of the maritime approaches to North America. When the NORAD agreement was renewed earlier this year, the new agreement included expansion to the maritime domain. It occurred largely because we haven't been able to demonstrate the ability or the will to do the job ourselves. This will probably apply to our Arctic waters also, and to the Northwest Passage, which raises sovereignty concerns. The other thing that will happen increasingly is that our tight connections with the US forces and interoperability will make it more difficult for us to disagree with the Americans on particular policy decisions. We stayed out of the Iraq war and we stayed out of missile defence, but it is going to become increasingly difficult to do that, even though the Bush administration, with its policy of pre-emptive war, is perhaps moving in directions that we would not like to move ourselves.

In my paper on defence—in which I played a sort of proactive devil's advocate—I recommended a two billion to three billion dollar per year increase in defence spending. I focused on a number of neglected areas: improved training, salaries, and benefits for Canadian Forces personnel especially in the lower ranks; and a reversal of the privatization of many functions within the Canadian Forces. (We've all heard about the heavy use in the US military of private military contractors. It happens in Canada, too.)

The paper called for the accelerated creation of the five-thousand-person peacekeeping brigade—one or two years instead of five or six—and assurance that it is really combat capable, so that, if they end up like Romeo Dallaire's forces in the middle of an escalating genocide, they can do something about it instead of having to stand by helplessly and watch the massacre unfold. I recommended that we accept equipment procurement decisions already made. I happen to think that we do need new helicopters for the navy. I would have preferred the other ones, but so be it. Most of our equipment procurement decisions made so far are reasonably defensible, and, of course, we learned with the cancelled helicopter contract a decade or so ago that cancelling procurement contracts can be expensive.

We should properly support the Disaster Assistance Response Team (DART). It may be expensive, but it is a heck of a good way to wave the Canadian flag abroad and do good in crisis situations. It was embarrassing that it was not used for the five years leading up to the tsunami crisis.

We should address glaring equipment needs—Arctic ice breaking, heavy-lift aircraft. We should think seriously about putting armed personnel, either Canadian Forces or RCMP, on some of our Coast Guard vessels. It is not just terrorism that people worry about these days, but international crime, human trafficking, and other threats to Canadian society. And if we want to be truly radical, we could think about incorporating elements of the Coast Guard into the Canadian navy.

We should maintain our very strong and clear decision to stay out of missile defence, not just because it is a bad idea in and of itself, but also because it is very clearly linked to the eventual weaponization of space. We should not support American military planning decisions simply because they are American and the Americans are our closest allies. We should assess each option on its own terms and decide accordingly. Paul Martin didn't stay out of missile defence because he wanted to stay out of missile defence; he stayed out of missile defence because his argument was bad and our argument was good. And we should continue to make assessments on the basis of the arguments and advocate very strongly in favour of what is right. Let's continue to stay out of missile defence.

But I do recommend that we stay in NORAD, although we should resist the extension of NORAD to land and sea. The airborne threat—airplanes in particular—remain a real threat. We saw that on September 11, 2001, and we have a long-standing and I think perfectly appropriate relationship with the United States in terms of dealing with airborne threats, and that is not something that should lightly be abandoned. But the fact that we are in NORAD doesn't mean that we should expand to partnership in an extensive way with Northern Command, which happens to be run in direct parallel to NORAD. Nor, indeed, should we allow our agreement entered into a few years ago—to share information with NORAD and NORTHCOM for the purposes of missile defence—to become a back door into the expansion of NORAD and the building of missile defence facilities on Canadian soil, such as the X-Band radar that may end up in Labrador.

The summation of what I am saying is that it is possible to have a pro-military, pro-Canadian defence policy that focuses on doing Canadian tasks like peacekeeping and sovereignty assertion. It is possible for us to do things militarily that the Americans aren't very well equipped to do, in conjunction with a policy that deals with our responsibilities as the custodians of the northern part of this continent. It is possible to have all this and to have it so that it cannot be attacked by pro-American Canadians as somehow incompatible with a responsible and secure and vigilant approach to the defence of Canada and the world.

I say all this as someone who is acutely concerned with the future of this country and the future of the United States. One of the things I learned in my five years in Durham, North Carolina, is that there are more Americans who think like us than there are Canadians.

CHAPTER 5

Canada's Oil and Gas: Security, Sustainability, and Prosperity

DIANA GIBSON AND DAVID THOMPSON

W hy are fossil fuels so important in any discussion of NAFTA? Why are they so important in any discussion of deep integration? As vice-president Dick Cheney's National Energy Policy group notes,

US oil production is expected to decline over the next two decades. Over the same period, demand for natural gas will most likely continue to outpace domestic production. As a result, the United States will rely increasingly on imports of both natural gas and oil from Canada.[59]

The United States is a major consumer of fossil fuels but produces less than it consumes.[60] Canada is the number one supplier of US oil imports. And Canada provides "nearly all" of US natural gas imports, those imports having risen by 200 percent between 1987 and 2000.[61] It is obvious that a key objective of any US trade deals with Canada is access to Canadian fossil fuels.

Why does this matter to Canadians? It's about our *energy*

security. Fossil fuels are non-renewable resources, and Canadian conventional production has already peaked and is declining. This is not because we consume so much of it, though we do consume more per capita than even the United States. Rather, our declining reserves are caused primarily by our huge exports. In 2004, natural gas exports accounted for 56 percent of production, and oil exports accounted for 63 percent.[62] Export proportions of both have been on the rise for years. When our reserves run down, we will be at the mercy of global energy market prices, and we know how sharply those can rise on the heels of events outside our control, for example, a hurricane or an invasion. Moreover, Canadians pay the high environmental, social, and economic costs of this fossil fuel extraction.

This chapter reviews Canada's oil and natural gas outlook: remaining reserves and production; consumption, imports, and exports; and the unaccounted for and high costs of our current path. At the same time, it examines how we got here—the policy decisions that led to our excessive extraction rates and declining reserves.[63] It then takes a look at where deep integration with the United States might take us, and the likely impacts. Finally, it points out a policy alternative, a soft-path that will ease the pace of extraction, provide greater social benefits, and help protect our local and global environment.

Where We Stand and How We Got Here

Integration with the United States has had a major impact on Canada's energy sovereignty and security. The Canada-US Free Trade Agreement and the North American Free Trade Agreement dramatically affected citizens' democratic control over non-renewable and declining petroleum resources, along with other kinds of energy. These trade regimes, tied to the lack of an energy plan or an industrial strategy, have caused dramatic price increases, dwindling reserves, and loss of investment in value-added processing in Canada.

In the context of shrinking reserves and growing extraction, security of Canada's future energy supply is critical. And yet our provincial and federal governments have not created an energy security strategy. The United States has created one called the National Energy Policy.[64]

As the CD Howe Institute notes, "the United States' major energy policy goal is energy security."[65] And the United States' plan deals with a wide range of strategies to secure US supply in the future. It is clear from that policy that the United States has prioritized securing additional supply from foreign markets over conservation as their path to security. Canada features prominently in the US supply picture, and specifically the Alberta tar sands. And it is clear that the United States is not afraid of taking strong action when its interests are at stake: witness the Congressional move to reverse the CNOOC (Chinese oil company) bid to purchase Unocal in 2005.

Like the United States, our other NAFTA trading partner, Mexico, has an active energy strategy. It negotiated within NAFTA an exemption for its energy sector, maintaining the authority to determine export quantities (not to mention price, production, national ownership, and imports). Unlike Canada, Mexico has a nationalized energy sector and is not required to maintain export volume proportions.[66]

Canada negotiated the opposite of Mexico's position: we committed to a proportional sharing agreement guaranteeing exports to the United States, and we abdicated control over our energy sector. Article 6.05 of NAFTA prohibits Canada from reducing the proportion of our energy that we export. This prohibition would require Canada to reduce its own consumption if it wants to reduce exports.[67] Energy exports can go up, but they can't be brought down until there is an immediate shortage. This is the "ratcheting upward" nature of the proportionality rule.

Sovereignty Eclipsed

In 1994, NAFTA completed a process of energy deregulation in Canada that had begun with the signing of the Free Trade Agreement in 1989. These energy provisions of NAFTA fall into the following five key areas:

- "National treatment" rules by which foreign corporations must be treated as if they are Canadian.
- The opening of Canada's energy sector to foreign corporations.
- The prohibition of preferential pricing—having a lower domestic price than an exporting price for Canadian industries and consumers.
- The elimination of export taxes, impact assessments, requirements for export licences, and Canada's twenty-five-year vital supply safeguard.
- The introduction of the "proportional sharing" requirement whereby current export levels are guaranteed to the US .[68]
- Domestic reserve requirements weakened.

Prior to the implementation of NAFTA, there was a federal rule that oil and gas could not be exported unless there was a twenty-five-year supply for Canadians—the vital supply safeguard. However, when NAFTA cancelled this requirement and at the same time eliminated export limits and regulations, there was a dramatic increase in exports, and reserves began to decline more rapidly.

Historically, there was also an energy security policy in Alberta. R.J. Dinning, the grandfather of Jim Dinning (widely thought to be the next premier of Alberta), headed a commission in 1949 that recommended that Alberta retain fifty years' supply of natural gas before exporting from the province. The Dinning Commission recommended that, if there were surpluses, exports should go to other Canadians before going outside the country.[69] Alberta's Social Credit government implemented a rule that oil and gas could not be exported unless there was a thirty-year domestic supply.[70]

This thirty-year vital supply rule was eliminated by the current government of Alberta when NAFTA came into effect, and was instead replaced by a requirement that there be a fifteen-year reserve for Alberta consumption. But this protection is quite weak as it allows reserves to be calculated as "expected reserves," which include both proved reserves[71] and "anticipated reserves," and will soon include unconventional sources such as coal-bed methane. Thus, despite there being only 8.9 years of proven reserves of conventional natural gas remaining, the export limit has not been triggered.

Likewise, the National Energy Board replaced its previous supply safeguard, which was based on reserve life, with a weaker market-based rule.[72] The new rule requires prospective exporters to make their offer to foreign buyers available on roughly the same terms to Canadian buyers. Given that this merely places into policy the market reality of obtaining the best price for one's goods, it is no surprise that there has never been a complaint under this rule.[73] In any event, industry and the Board have largely circumvented this rule by replacing long-term licences with short-term export orders that do not even have this requirement.[74] Indeed, for gas exports, there hasn't been a long-term licence issued in over seven years; for oil exports all licences are for short-term orders.[75]

Production and exports increase dramatically.
Canada's oil and gas production has been on a steady incline, and exports have been making up a growing percentage of that production. From 1982 to 2002, natural gas consumption increased by 96 percent, while exports increased by 396 percent. Crude oil

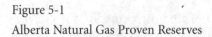

Figure 5-1

Alberta Natural Gas Proven Reserves

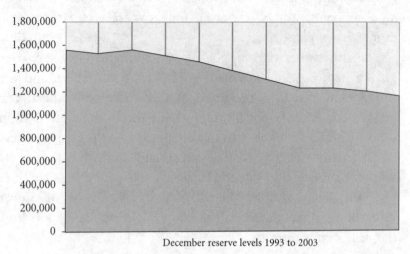

December reserve levels 1993 to 2003

Source: Statistics Canada, table 128-00041 – Petroleum and marketable natural gas, remaining established
reserves in Canada, annual (cubic metres x 1,000,000)

consumption increased by 29 percent, while exports increased by
595 percent.[76] Almost all Canadian natural gas exports, and over
99 percent of oil exports, go to the United States.[77] When former
prime minister Brian Mulroney signed NAFTA in 1992,[78] natural
gas and oil exports to the United States were 41 percent and 44
percent of production, respectively.[79] In just ten years, those
export percentages climbed to 56 percent and 62 percent, respectively.[80]

Though domestic consumption has also increased significantly and conservation is imperative, in order to substantially reduce
our rate of oil and gas extraction and extend our reserve life, we
will have to cut back on exports.

Reserves fall.
Not surprisingly, given the dramatic increases in production and
exports, proved reserves of conventional oil and gas have

declined despite increased exploration spurred by high prices. New natural gas finds have not been keeping pace with this high level of production and export growth, and we are eating away at our reserves. In 2003, about 8.9 years of natural gas production remained in Alberta, given proved reserves and production levels for that year (see figure 1).[81] Increased production has meant that the expected lifetime of Canada's proved gas reserves has declined by more than ten years over the past decade.[82] For conventional oil, there are reserves of less than ten years.

Non-conventional sources to fill the void.

Governments across Canada are confident that this shortfall will be addressed by controversial new sources such as offshore oil and gas, coal-bed methane, the Mackenzie Valley pipeline, and the tar sands. In addition to these "new" sources, as natural gas runs out, there is a plan to shift back to coal for power generation in Alberta. The Mackenzie Valley pipeline has not yet been approved and may still be scuttled, as happened the last time this pipeline was proposed. Even if the petroleum industry does push through the pipeline, much of the volume of the gas it will deliver is already allocated to fuel the extraction of oil from the tar sands.

Offshore energy exploration and development carry significant ecological risks. Tar sands and coal-bed methane development, because of their enormous potential reserves, will have very high environmental costs. The tars sands are generating large and mounting environmental costs in several areas: excessive demand for water and natural gas, permanent pollution of between one and three barrels of water per barrel of oil extracted, the accumulation of tailings, destruction of delicate boreal ecosystems, and air pollution and acid rain.[83]

Similar to the tar sands, coal-bed methane (CBM) will have higher environmental costs compared with conventional natural gas.[84] Most notably, experience with CBM in the United States

indicates significant landscape impacts from the higher intensity
of wells drilled and serious potential impacts on local water
tables where the coal is wet.

There are also serious climate change implications to these
trends. Canada's greenhouse gas emissions are already 24 percent
above our Kyoto commitments.[85] Our emissions have shot
upward, placing us at sixth worst of the forty developed Annex 1
signatories to Kyoto. Unless we take action, by 2010 our greenhouse gas emissions will be "about 36 percent above 1990 levels,
or about 45 percent above our Kyoto target."[86] Given that some of
the largest emitters in the country are in the energy production
sector, this shift to non-conventional fuels will take Canada in the
wrong direction. The move away from conventional oil and gas
to non-conventional sources to fuel high export levels requires
broader debate.

Securing Economic Benefits from Our Energy

Canada's energy resources are a tremendous endowment, and we
should be receiving the maximum economic benefits from them.
This is especially so in view of the increasing local, national, and
global environmental impacts, the fact that the majority of the
resources are going to foreign markets, not to mention the fact
that a significant portion of the extraction is being conducted by
foreign corporations for the benefit of foreign shareholders.
Canadians are receiving an economic benefit, but it is far short of
what it should be.

Jobs and value-added.

The rush to export our resources is fuelling boom-and-bust
cycles in the economy, with unsustainable pacing of extraction.
The Alberta tar sands are an excellent example. The targets range
from a tripling to six times the current rate of extraction for the
near future, most of which is destined for export. Already the

Figure 5-2

Canadian Provinces Collect Inadequate Rents (*average 1995–2002*)

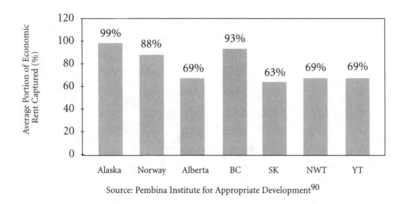

Source: Pembina Institute for Appropriate Development[90]

industry faces escalating labour and input costs, and inadequate infrastructure. At the same time, value-added processing of the natural resources is being sacrificed, and those high end value-added jobs are being sent south of the border with the raw resources. The government is suffering an embarrassment of riches. In the absence of an energy policy, provincially or federally, the provincial government continues the unnecessarily rapid pace of expansion, with shortsighted solutions such as offering "royalty holidays" to most operations, changing the laws to allow foreign workers to be brought in, and randomly throwing money at infrastructure and rebate cheques.

Rents, royalties, and selling off the family silver.

Another area where Canadians are not being guaranteed the maximum return is in resource royalties. *Rents* are the financial surplus available from the proceeds of selling the resource. They are simply the price obtained for the product minus the costs of finding, developing, extracting, and transporting it, and a "normal" level of profit (that is, a level of profit that assumes a

Figure 5-3

Alberta GDP vs. Average Family Income

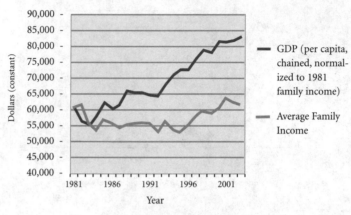

Sources: Statistics Canada CANSIM tables 384-0013 (GDP)
and 202-0403 (Family Income)

competitive market with other investments). *Royalties* are that portion of the rents collected by the government on behalf of the owners of the resource, the public. Technically, 100 percent of the rent available could be collected through royalties,[87] and resource corporations would still have enough money to cover all their costs and make normal levels of profit.[88]

Both the Parkland Institute and the Pembina Institute have done in-depth studies of royalty rates in Alberta and across Canada compared to other oil-rich regions like Alaska and Norway.[89] As figure 2 shows, all of Canada's provincial governments collect less in rents than they could. Canadian provinces are forgoing anywhere from 7 percent to 37 percent of available fossil fuel rents. Notably, Alaska and Norway, while collecting higher rents, still manage to attract private sector energy investment.

Where Have All the Dollars Gone?
Certainly, Alberta's GDP is high—the highest in Canada. And it

Figure 5-4

Corporate Equity: Oil, Gas and Coal Extraction Corporations in Canada

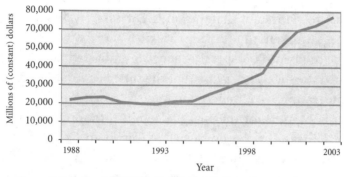

Source: Statistics Canada CANSIM table 187-00011 (Equity) and 326-00011 (Inflation)

has been going up, as has Canada's overall GDP. Energy extraction has been largely responsible. It's less clear, however, how much Alberta's citizens have benefited from this aggregate wealth. Figure 3 shows the strongly rising GDP, but also shows that family incomes have not risen significantly in over twenty years.

Clearly, the dollars from the bonanza have not been shared with the families who own most of the resource in Canada's most fossil-fuel-rich province. However, those dollars have been shared—amply—with energy corporations. As figure 4 shows, energy corporations have been socking away rising levels of profits and increasing their holdings dramatically. Given the high levels of foreign corporate ownership in the fossil fuel sector—not just multinationals and foreign-owned subsidiaries, but also foreign share holdings of "Canadian" publicly-traded corporations—it is clear that a significant portion of that energy wealth is flowing out of the country.

Where Are We Going?

The forces behind the deep integration agenda are strong, particularly in relation to energy. The US National Energy Policy, developed by a working group led by US Vice-President Dick Cheney, recommends that the United States "develop closer energy integration among Canada, Mexico, and the United States."[91] In a December 2003 speech, then US ambassador Paul Celucci repeated the message, saying that the time has come "to complete the integration of our energy markets."[92]

Nor is support for the energy deep integration agenda limited to the US side of the border. The Canadian Council of Chief Executives (CCCE), dutifully following the American lead, has been lobbying for the same energy deep integration agenda.[93] The Canadian conservative think tank, the C.D. Howe Institute, urges that Canada further open access to its energy in order to bargain for "customs-union- and common-market-like arrangements that achieve deeper integration."[94] In 2003, Stephen Harper, now prime minister, proposed the creation of a "continental energy strategy."[95]

What would deep integration for energy look like? There are already over thirty-five natural gas pipelines and twenty-two oil pipelines between Canada and the United States,[96] and the flow through those pipelines is guaranteed by the NAFTA proportionality rule. Some argue that integration can't get any deeper than that. They should think again: integration could be deeper on many fronts. Here are a few examples:

- More drilling and extraction (the CCCE, formerly the Business Council on National Issues, calls for full development of "continental" reserves).[97]
- More pipelines (the CCCE also calls for an expansion of energy infrastructure).[98] The US National Energy Policy proposes that Canada and the Unit-

ed States "expedite the construction of a pipeline to deliver natural gas to the lower 48 states."[99]

- Kyoto will likely be dumped.
- Already weakened strategic reserve requirements for exports and environmental assessment requirements would be further weakened or eliminated.[100]
- Taxes and royalties could be cut even further.
- Despite the obvious negative implications of NAFTA for Canadian energy supply, price, and sovereignty, as other chapters in this book describe, the Conservative and corporate political agenda is strongly geared toward further integration.

What to Do About It—Toward an Energy Security Strategy for Canada

If you don't change direction, you end up where you're headed.
— *Chinese proverb*

We are headed toward declining supplies, vulnerability to global price instability, climate change, local environmental damage, conflict with Aboriginal communities, job losses, future shocks to our stock market, and the long-term hollowing out of our economy. Deep integration is the continuation of this trend over the last twenty years.

If we want to avoid that destination, then it is up to us to map out an alternative route—to articulate a compelling vision, a soft-energy path that will ease the frenetic pace of extraction, extend our reserves, provide greater social benefits, help protect our local and global environment, add jobs, and stabilize and strengthen our economy. Such a strategy needs to guide government action at both the provincial and federal levels, and in both the net-producing and net-consuming regions of Canada.

The Parkland Institute of the University of Alberta is engaged in just such a process. It held a symposium in Calgary in the fall of 2005, inviting people and organizations from across the country to discuss energy security in Canada. Arising out of that discussion and other input, in December 2005 it released a discussion paper.[101] At the time of writing, this initiative is ongoing.

There is a window of opportunity for Canada to regain energy sovereignty and shift its economic relationship with the United States onto more balanced terms. An opening is available because high petroleum prices combined with peak oil have increased the bargaining power of citizens and governments in charge of energy-rich territories. Additionally, the US Bush administration has made it clear that it will be ignoring the recent NAFTA disputes tribunal decision on softwood lumber, and the agreement is not providing the market guarantees that Canada expected. The NAFTA agreement has provisions within it for signatory countries to exit the agreement, either because another country is not complying or for other reasons.[102]

The Principles to Govern a Canadian Strategy
The following are key elements that should constitute the basis for a Canadian energy security strategy. This list does not attempt to be comprehensive; the elements set out below are necessary but not sufficient.

Conserve.
We should manage our non-renewable resources as responsible stewards, carefully conserving their economic availability for future generations, "banking" more of them now, and selling and using them over a longer period into the future.

Canadian resources are for Canadians.
We should eliminate any trading arrangements that limit the ability of Canadian governments to protect domestic energy supplies for Canadians (such as NAFTA). We should create new arrangements that require governments to protect domestic energy supplies for Canadians with specific recognition or producing regions.

Democratic management.
We should question the model of foreign corporate ownership and instead increase the democratic management of the resource and its extraction. The organizations managing resource extractions should be doing so with the public interest as their primary, if not sole, allegiance.

Maximize the return to Canadians.
To ensure that maximum return is received for these finite resources, the maximum practicable royalties should be collected from our resource extraction. The pace should be slowed to one that ensures maximum jobs for Canadians over the long term rather than foreign workers in the short term. And value-added processing of the resources should be done within Canada.

Treat assets as assets.
We should ensure that the benefits from our fossil fuels are invested in other forms of capital that will ensure our future prosperity and energy security. We should create a long-term economic plan that explicitly takes into account the decline and depletion of the resource and contains realistic measures to ensure our future prosperity.

Environmental security.
We should ensure that the extraction and use of our resources

minimize the impacts on the planet, and we should cooperate with other jurisdictions in an effective global solution to climate change. Effective domestic policies to protect the environment should be created and enforced, including a mix of policy instruments designed to ensure that all sectors, regions, and people share the task of protecting our environment.

Putting First Nations first.
The benefits extracted from our massive extraction of the land's resources should be used for education, social and health services, land claims and land use settlements, and the elimination of poverty among First Nations peoples. Energy development should not occur where there are any outstanding land claims. First Nations peoples should be seen as full partners in negotiating the terms for proceeding where land claims have been addressed through treaty.

Protecting jobs and workers.
We should protect energy-related jobs and workers by developing an industrial strategy that includes pacing the development to maximize longer-term jobs for Canadians, investing in value-added processing, investing in renewable energy development, and just transitions for energy workers.

Protecting consumers.
We should use consistent, depoliticized policies to reduce the impact on low-income Canadians of both free-market price swings and the unavoidable costs of environmental protection.
Some examples of specific energy policies:

- Building on these principles, producing regions and the federal government must articulate specific policies for securing Canada's energy future—policies such as:

- Restructuring all royalty policies to ensure the maximum rent is recovered.
- Investing the increased proceeds of oil and gas sales in renewable energy.
- Placing a moratorium on any further oil and gas pipeline expansion for export, and re-introducing vital supply safeguards that secure Canadian energy supplies.
- Creating provincial and federal Crown corporations for extraction and value-added processing of gas and oil.
- Slowing and planning the pace of expansion such that skilled labour shortages will be avoided and jobs will be maximized for Canadians in the long term instead of being given to foreign workers in the short term.

Many more specific policies flow from these principles. The authors encourage readers to contact the Parkland Institute[103] with their ideas and policy proposals.

Conclusion

We hope that this chapter will help form the basis for public debates leading toward an alternative path of development provincially and nationally—one that prioritizes the interests of the majority of citizens, rather than those of a few large multinational corporations; one that aims to conserve non-renewable resources as much as possible, rather than selling them off fast; one that shifts away from burning them, and instead uses them to provide quality jobs that support families and communities over the long term.

CHAPTER 6

A North American Energy Policy Means a US Energy Policy

MARJORIE GRIFFIN COHEN

Canadians who care about the effects of US imperialism tend to associate it with the adamant positions the United States takes on trade deals and its aggressive measures related to security. The drama of these events—particularly the war in Iraq, the softwood lumber and beef disputes, border issues, and US surveillance of Canadians—overshadows less visible but equally insidious acts of US imperialism.

I refer here to the regulatory changes that the United States makes, by fiat, on matters like energy that affect Canadian economic security. These involve actions that are leading to a deep and permanent integration with the United States—to a form of continentalism with the United States firmly in control.

Canadians did not pay much attention to the 2004 US *Energy Policy Act*—aside, that is, from the warnings of environmentalists that the Act would likely intensify North American environmental destruction. I suspect the decision to ignore it by Canadian media and politicians is because the US point of view already firmly dominates the oil and gas sectors in Canada. And the federal government is anxious not to say or do anything that might give the impression it was contemplating another National Energy Policy. By adopting a head-in-the-sand approach to energy, however, Canada imperils its energy security for the future, particularly for one area of energy that is still mostly in public hands in Canada: electricity. But both the generation and sale of electricity in Canada are increasingly and rapidly coming under US control.

Official US policy is designed to create an integrated, competitive, privatized "North American" electricity market run by American rules and American players. The prevailing Canadian system is based on public utilities that engage in long-term planning to ensure sufficient supply of electricity and adequate transmission and distribution. The Americans plan to transform it into a competitive market-based model that will rely on the vagaries of the market to determine how much is produced and who gets it.

In Canada, the response of governments to US dictates has been surprisingly limp: rather than challenging US regulatory imperialism—as, ironically, many US states and state public utilities are doing—Canadian governments at both the national and provincial levels are readily acquiescing to US demands. All of this is occurring with virtually no public debate, government analysis, or media scrutiny.

The US plans for electricity restructuring assume that competition will bring about abundant supplies and lower prices. In the face of the rather monumental restructuring failures that have actually occurred in the United States, this approach seems more faith-based than reason would allow. The weird reluctance to face up to the problems of restructuring—inadequate supplies, transmission congestion, price escalation, and more government subsidies of private electricity development just to get more generation built—can only be accounted for by a government that is firmly in the control of the private energy companies, or one that follows a blind adherence to the myth that the market is always efficient—even when it clearly isn't. (Of course, there is always the possibility that both these factors are in play.)

One of the major problems for Canada is that our own energy regulatory body, the National Energy Board (NEB), is extremely weak, at least relative to the enormous powers of its US counterpart, the Federal Energy Regulatory Commission (FERC). And it is through FERC that the United States is implementing its plans. The new US *Energy Policy Act* ratcheted up FERC's powers considerably. According to FERC's chairman, Joseph Kelliher, these new powers constitute "the most important change in federal electricity and gas laws since the 1930s."

FERC has become decidedly imperialistic since George W. Bush came to power. The main drive is to pave the way for a seamless continent-wide marketplace for electricity through what it called a standard market design (SMD). This standardization would require breaking up integrated utilities to allow competition in the electricity market. This is a dramatic change in policy that amounts to a profound and thorough redesign of the entire US electricity market and, of course, the Canadian market as well. It affects Canada because the United States insists that any Canadian provinces that export electricity to the United States must adopt an identical system to that in the United States. This demand, by the way, flies in the face of NAFTA, and, if Canadian governments wanted to protect public systems of providing electricity, NAFTA would be the vehicle to do it.

One key feature of a private market is the separation of transmission systems (the large power lines that transport power from the generators to the distributors) from the control of public utilities. FERC is extremely aggressive in pursuit of this objective because, without access to transmission systems, private generators of electricity would have no markets. Since utilities usually own the transmission systems, removing utility control over transmission is crucial to privatization initiatives. The US FERC envisions very large transmission areas, or regional transmission organizations (RTOs), that would control the transmission activity in specific areas of the continent.

The creation of any RTO requires that all utilities give up the operation and control of their transmission systems to the new entity. Each RTO will be set up as a private company, and no utility will have a voice in its governance structures or its operations. The major change this makes for Canadian public utilities is that it will give a private US company control over the entire electricity system.

Any RTO will have authority to set prices, enact all interchange schedules, maintain system reliability and security, and plan for future expansion of the system. While the utilities may still own the assets—the transmission lines and control centres—the private RTO will be able to determine the extent of new investment, its nature, and, thereby, who gets the electricity.

Many state governments, utilities, and consumer groups in the United States, most notably in the west and the south, have reacted very negatively to FERC's invasion of their regulatory territory. Surprisingly, there was no resistance from any governments or consumer groups in Canada. This was such a sore point in the United States that, in an effort to have the Energy Bill passed, Congress forced FERC to hold off ruling on "standard market design" until the end of 2006. Nevertheless, according to FERC's chairman, the way that voluntary RTOs are proceeding means in effect that standard market design is already happening, so specific rulings aren't needed.

In sharp contrast to FERC, Canada's regulatory body, the

National Energy Board, has minimal powers, and even those it does have are seldom exercised. The NEB's location in Calgary ensures that it completely supports private energy—of any description. So it is not surprising that it has had no role in resisting US attempts to redesign the North American system in US interests.

The NEB's mandate on electricity is restricted to the regulation of exports and the construction of facilities related to international trade. Unlike FERC, the NEB does not regulate energy within provincial boundaries, interprovincial electricity trade, or energy emissions. But in recent years, even the NEB's close monitoring of exports, which in the past included public hearings on each application for an export permit, has been replaced by blanket export permits that last for up to ten years.

These permits appear to be given very easily, and certainly without public scrutiny. The result is that frequently export permits are given to companies that do not produce any electricity at all. For example, Duke Energy, headquartered in Charlotte, North Carolina, was given a ten-year blanket export permit to export electricity from B.C. even though it has no generating facilities. Big companies see their future in *trading* electricity— much in the way that Enron did—not in actually generating it.

All major electricity-exporting provinces in Canada have complied in some measure with FERC orders for breaking up the integrated nature of the utilities. While the provincial governments in Canada seem to realize the United States is encroaching on their regulatory areas, they are cooperating with FERC to a much greater extent than are many of their US state counterparts.

One of the major implications for Canada in the new design for the transmission market is that it will encourage the system to expand in order to increase the export and import of power, and to encourage private electricity generation. When increased access to US markets occurs, as is the intention of the RTOs, all new private energy generation in both countries will have the option of selling within the province *or selling in the United States.* This will result in domestic consumers competing with American consumers for power produced within Canada, very much as they already do for oil and gas. And, since the prices in the United States are higher, they will rise much higher in Canada too.

New investments in cross-border transmission lines could well turn out to be very expensive for provinces in Canada—particularly in view of the proposed large expansion of private generation and the relatively small proportion of electricity that can now be exported through existing transmission lines. Since for the most part the wires will still remain in the public sector in Canada, it will very likely be the public that will be paying for the expansion of the system—primarily to meet the requirements of the private sector and the export markets.

Developing a private electricity system within an integrated North American market creates huge problems. One is related to the relentless increase in the sheer size of the electricity markets and the distances over which electricity is transported. The electricity grids between Canada and the United States serve two main purposes: one is to ensure the reliability of the system, and the other is to permit trading of electricity. But the main issue in the creation of continent-wide markets is the extent that the objectives of trade itself will override other significant domestic objectives of delivering electricity: the social objectives of equity, low costs, regional development, Aboriginal rights, reliability, and conservation. As trading areas extend thousands of miles across the continent, efficiencies are lost, reliability of the system is compromised, and meeting local needs can be superseded by the lure of large incomes from exports.

A second problem created by the restructuring of the electricity sector is the startling increase in electricity trading by corporations that do not produce electricity, but buy and sell it to take advantage of different prices in different areas of the continent. While Enron's trading needs brought about the North American system redesign and the new rules to facilitate traders, its initiatives have taken a life of their own long after its activities have been discredited.

A third problem related to restructuring comes from the attempts to deregulate some parts of the electricity business (generation), while retaining the monopoly aspects of other aspects (transmission and distribution). The technology of transmission has not changed its characteristic as a natural monopoly, mainly because the construction of a transmission system is complex, expensive, and does not efficiently allow for competing transmission lines. The result is a hybrid system with a competitive market in electricity generation that encourages increased supply, coupled with a limited and monopolistic transmission system. The bottlenecks that are created then tend to limit the expansion of the generation market and thus increase the unreliability of the system itself. It is this problem that is most crucial in overcoming the barriers that now exist to a continent-wide electricity market.

The crucial decision facing Canadians is whether electricity systems should remain independent and controlled by Canadian governments, or whether they should be subsumed within the US system. Integrating the United States, Canadian, and Mexican electricity markets—which is the goal of FERC—will result in prices that are established by the US markets, and regulations that advance the energy objectives of the United States and private companies.

This does not need to happen. The North American Free Trade Agreement permits both trading and investment without instituting standard market designs. There is no requirement in international law that any entity in Canada has to completely change its system to export into the United States. This is a fundamental protection that has been retained under NAFTA. According to the NAFTA Commission for Environmental Cooperation in its assessment of the cross-border electricity trade, provincial decisions to acquiesce to FERC demands are voluntary—at least under NAFTA's legal requirements—and the United States has no right to insist on identical systems in order to trade. Under NAFTA, no province in Canada is required to have exactly the same kind of organization of its market or industry as exists in the United States. (Admittedly, Canada must grant "national treatment" to foreign firms. But, as long as a government treats private domestic and foreign firms in the same way, it is not contravening NAFTA.)

To use the protections of NAFTA, Canada would need to have a national government that is proactive in protecting Canada's electricity interests. The absence of a strong Canadian presence becomes glaringly evident in the negotiations with the United States over market design and transmission organizations. Each province is basically on its own in determining its relationship with the United States. This is unfortunate because the impression FERC projects in its drive to control the entire North American electricity industry is that Canadian electricity systems will have to mirror developments in the United States in order to have access to the US market.

Canada has a strong legal position to maintain public provision of electricity. Among some important actions that would need to take place are the following:

- Electricity, currently a provincial issue, needs to be treated as a national one. The increased internationalization of US regulatory design requires a strong national voice in negotiations with the US.

Electricity is no longer confined by provincial boundaries and, in the face of US regulatory imperialism, Canada can justify taking action in the design of future markets.

- The federal government should firmly resist the development of a "seamless North American electricity market," which requires the complete integration of provincial electricity systems with the US system.
- Canada should use the protections in NAFTA to allow public utilities and provincial governments to maintain integrated utilities in the public sector.
- The federal government should encourage greater integration of the Canadian electricity sector. Currently, each province has closer ties with the United States than it does with other provinces. This is partly a result of the regulatory vacuum at the national level. With the need for market reliability and for new investments in electricity generation, increased interprovincial planning would make a lot of sense. The United States has a regulator that deals with national and international issues. It is time that we in Canada had one, too.
- Canadian public entities should maintain control of transmissions systems and not surrender any part of these systems to foreign-controlled organizations (like the regional transmission organizations).
- All transmission systems should be owned and operated by public entities.
- Canada should prohibit private exports of electricity and private power trading.

- The federal government should have a strong regulatory role in electricity-related environmental
  issues. Related to this, it should do the following:
  institute a nation-wide electricity conservation
  program; require provincial governments to conduct system-wide assessments of all private power
  projects for their cumulative effects (currently
  they are assessed individually); and establish an
  institute for environmentally responsible energy
  development and invest heavily in green energy
  development in the public sector.

It is time for Canada to recognize that it needs a clearly defined energy policy. So far, there is no sense that energy security, which is much on the minds of the United States and other countries, figures at all in Canadian government policy. Canada gave up control over its oil and gas, and appears not to be rethinking this policy even with regard to the treatment of new reserves and new exploration. In this neglect of its national energy security, Canada is distinct from most other countries, where the largest oil companies and the largest reserves are owned by nation states.

If Canada begins to treat electricity as it has oil and gas, we can expect very similar results, and the loss of control of another vital resource. Canada is free to make its own decisions and need not adopt the US strategy for a deep integration of electricity markets. NAFTA allows both trading and investment across borders without having to establish identical market structures. But in order to pursue this route, the Canadian government would need, at the very least, to have a plan and become proactive in protecting the country's interests.

CHAPTER 7

Turning on the Tap? Water Exports to the United States

TONY CLARKE

In my judgment, water is the most critical area of Canada-US relations over the next 100 years ... How quickly this issue develops and how much attention is paid depends on how critical the American water shortage is.

–Simon Reisman
Canada's Chief Negotiator of the Canada-US
Free Trade Agreement

For more than half a century, Canadians have been wary about the United States running out of fresh water and, some day, coming knocking on the door of their northern neighbour. Well, in 2001, six months after he was sworn in as US president, George W. Bush made an offhand comment to journalists about growing water shortages in his home state of Texas and elsewhere in the country, saying he would like to begin negotiations with Ottawa on water exports from Canada. "In Texas," he said, "water is more valuable than oil. A lot of people don't need it, but when you head south and west, we need it." Bush added that he "looked forward" to discussing the matter with then Canadian prime minister, Jean Chrétien.

At the time, the reaction from Canadian officials was swift and blunt. "We're absolutely not going to export water, period," proclaimed David Anderson, then Canada's environment minister. Anderson's comment reflected what seems to be a general public consensus that water should not be treated like other natural resources (for example, oil, gas, minerals, timber) as a commodity to be bought and sold on the market. After Anderson's reaction, the issue seemed to fade from the news headlines until former US ambassador Paul Celucci revived the issue in the early stages of the 2005/2006 federal election. In a CBC radio interview, Celucci stated:

> Water is going to be, already is, a very valuable commodity, and I've always found it odd where Canada is so willing to sell oil and natural gas and uranium and coal, which are by their very nature finite. But talking about water is off the table, and [yet] water is renewable ... ?

The question now is whether Canada's new prime minister is willing to put water on the table in negotiating a new relationship with the United States. Although Stephen Harper's specific views on water exports are not known, he has called for more "economic and security integration" with the United States, highlighting the need for a continental energy strategy that would include "a range of other natural resources." As a new era of Canada-US relations opens up, Canadians would do well to take a closer look at the forces at work behind the scenes to turn on the taps for massive water exports to the United States.

Thirsty America

Today, the world's largest economic and military superpower is facing the problem of acute water shortages within its own borders.[104] More than 20 percent of farmland irrigation in the United States comes from the pumping of groundwater at rates that exceed the water's ability to recharge. In effect, this means that aquifers that are the country's source of fresh water are rapidly being depleted. A lethal combination of severe droughts and dried-up wells has become the plague of many American farmers. Every year now, it is estimated that more than US $400 billion is lost in America's farmlands because of the depletion of aquifers.

A prime example is the Ogallala aquifer, one of the world's most famous underground bodies of water. Covering more than 190,000 square miles (or a million-and-a-half square kilometres) in the American Midwest, the Ogallala is the largest single sub-surface water-bearing resource in all of North America. It is estimated to contain four trillion tons of water, 20 percent more than exists in Lake Huron, one of the Great Lakes. Yet today it is being drained mercilessly by over 200,000 wells irrigating 8.2 million acres of farmland—one-fifth of all the irrigated land in the United States. Every minute of every hour each day, 13 million US gallons of water are being pumped out of the Ogallala. At this rate, the Ogallala is being depleted fourteen times faster than nature can restore it. Every year since 1991, the water table in the aquifer has been dropping three feet, to the point where it is now estimated that more than half of the water is already gone.

Elsewhere in America, more water crises are looming. In California, the major aquifers are also drying up. With the Colorado River strained to the limit, the water table under California's San

Joaquin Valley has dropped nearly thirty-three feet (or ten metres) in some areas during the past fifty years. In the state's Central Valley, overuse of underground water supplies has resulted in a loss of over 40 percent of the combined storage capacity of all the human-made reservoirs in California. Unless vast new supplies of water are found, the California Department of Water Resources predicts that, by 2020, the state will be facing a freshwater shortfall that is nearly as great as the amount that all of the state's cities and towns are currently consuming.

The desert regions of the American southwest, largely barren of water, continue to experience population growth. Arizona, for instance, has gone through a ten-fold increase in population over the past seventy years. The city of Tucson, which had until recently relied solely on aquifers in the region for its water, is now having some of its water supplies imported from the Colorado River while buying up local farms for other water supplies. In the city of Phoenix, with urban development taking place at a rate of one acre every hour, water tables have dropped more than 390 feet (or 120 metres) in the eastern section. Meanwhile, in Albuquerque, New Mexico, if current levels of groundwater withdrawals continue, water tables are projected to drop another 66 feet (or 20 metres) by 2020, with other cities and towns in the region drying up over the next ten to twenty years.

In Bush's home state of Texas, water scarcity is also approaching a critical stage. All current sources of water in El Paso, for example, are expected to be dried up by 2030. In northeast Kansas, the water shortage has become so acute that state officials have been discussing plans to build a pipeline to bring water from the Missouri River, which is already overtapped.

Moving further into the American Midwest, the cities of Chicago and Milwaukee could be facing severe water shortages. The huge sandstone aquifer underlying the Illinois-Wisconsin border, which supplies these two major cities with their water supplies, is currently overtaxed and may well be depleted in the near future, say scientists, unless there are significant reductions in groundwater withdrawals. In May 2005, Southern Illinois State University published a report warning that the Chicago metro area water demand would increase an additional 30 percent over the next twenty years, requiring a major escalation in bulk water diversions from Lake Michigan. And, in 2004, more than half of Kentucky's 120 counties either experienced or came close to facing water shortages.

Similarly, the Florida aquifer system in the southeast is also being mined at a rate that is far faster than it can be naturally replenished. Although this aquifer covers a vast area (an estimated 76,000 square miles or 200,000 square kilometres), its water levels have been dropping to dangerous lows. Every minute, 1.7 million gallons (or 6.6 million litres) of water is taken out of this aquifer alone. Indeed, the water table has dropped so low in Florida that seawater is now said to be invading its aquifers. In what can only be described as a desperation tactic, Florida governor Jed Bush has championed a proposal to collect surface water and pump it back into depleted groundwater sources, untreated and contaminated by all sorts of impurities.

In short, the United States is becoming thirstier and thirstier as it reaches the danger point of running out of its own freshwater sources. When the US government surveyed the fifty states of the union in 2003, it found that more than two-thirds predicted they would face water shortages in one form or another over the next ten years. Nor does the US government seem prepared to confront this impending water crisis. In June 2004, the National Academies of Science (NAS) and the US Geological Survey reported that Washington is ill-prepared to deal with the water shortages emerging across the country. NAS reports have also shown that overall federal funding for water research in the United States has remained stagnant for the past thirty years.

As the water crisis intensifies, one proposed quick-fix solution is to tap into what is perceived to be Canada's considerable water wealth.

Canadian Sponge

In an *Atlantic Monthly* article entitled "Desert Politics," writer Robert Kaplan portrayed in dramatic terms how what he called "some visionary engineers" propose that the salvation of thirsty America is to be found in "that shivery vastness of wet, green sponge to the north: Canada." According to this scenario, Canada is a giant green sponge full of freshwater lakes and rivers—a massive reservoir of water that can be tapped to serve the insatiable thirst of people and industries in urban America. All it would take is the construction of a network of new dams, reservoirs, canals, tunnels, pipelines, and supertankers to transport water in bulk form from Canada to the United States.

There are a lot of myths floating around about this so-called Canadian sponge. For example, Canada is frequently portrayed as possessing between 20 percent and 25 percent of the world's freshwater supplies within its own borders. Yet studies conducted by the highly respected Russian hydrologist Igor Shiklomanov paint a quite different picture. According to his in-depth studies of countries containing large supplies of fresh water in the form of lakes, rivers, and glaciers, as well as underground aquifers, Shiklomanov concludes that Brazil has the highest proportion of freshwater sources—approximately 20 percent of global supplies. Following Brazil is Russia and the former Soviet Union countries at 10.6 percent, and China with 5.7 percent. Canada is rated fourth, with 5.6 percent of global freshwater supplies.[105]

While there is no doubt that Canada is blessed by Nature's endowment of numerous freshwater lakes and rivers, it should be noted that 60 percent of our rivers flow north into Hudson Bay and the Arctic region. As a result, 60 percent of Canada's fresh water flows in the opposite direction from the United States and is largely inaccessible. Even so, say politicians, engineers, and economists on both sides of the border, there are ways of overcoming these obstacles through technology and investment. In the meantime, it is argued that huge amounts of Canada's fresh water remain "unused" or "wasted" in various regions of the country. It has been estimated, for example, that British Columbia possesses 1,600 times more freshwater than it consumes. What's more, say the critics, a number of fresh water rivers in BC flow into the ocean, thereby wasting huge amounts of fresh water.

Of course, the largest freshwater system on the planet is the Great Lakes, lying between Canada and the United States, which contain no less than 20 percent of the world's fresh water. But the Great Lakes have also been a dumping ground for industrial wastes, contaminating much of the lake water and ground water in the region. Each year, between 50 and 100 million tons of hazardous waste is generated in the surrounding watershed, pesticides alone counting for 25 million tons. Although governments on both sides of the border have taken steps to clean up the Great Lakes over the past decade or so, studies show they are becoming increasingly polluted again and water levels are dropping due to growing demand. Indeed, the International Joint Commission declared in its 2000 *Final Report on the Protection of Waters in the Great Lakes* that there is no surplus water in the Great Lakes and emphatically warned against any new diversions. Yet in 2004, *Time* magazine reported, 28 billion litres of water was taken out of the Great Lakes, mainly for agricultural irrigation.[106]

According to one of Canada's foremost water experts, drought patterns are returning to the Prairie region. Studies conducted by Dr. David Schindler at the University of Alberta show that rivers and lakes in the Prairies are drying up. Schindler's studies reveal that, during the last century (between 1910 and 2002), the South Saskatchewan River has declined 80 percent. The Old Man and

Peace Rivers are down 40 percent, while the Athabaska River has dropped by 30 percent. At the same time, several lakes have dried up, including Lake Maglore near Grand Prairie, Alberta. Add global warming to the mix and Prairie drought patterns are likely to intensify. Already the glacier that feeds the Bow River in Alberta is melting so quickly that there may be no water left in it fifty years from now.

Meanwhile, Canada's wetlands are vanishing at an alarming rate. Like a sponge, the wetlands soak up excess rain and snow and help prevent flooding. The wetlands also function like the Earth's kidneys, filtering out dirt, pesticides, and fertilizers before water runs off into lakes and rivers. As well, the marshes in the wetlands serve as a storage house for purified water. In short, wetlands are a vital part of the ecosystem for the regeneration of water. In a study prepared for the Canadian Wildlife Federation, water specialist Jamie Linton documents how Canada's wetlands, which have traditionally covered only 14 percent of this country's land mass, have mostly been destroyed by urban sprawl and large-scale farming. Atlantic Canada, for example, has lost 65 percent of its wetlands, and southern Ontario has destroyed 70 percent of its wetlands, while the Prairies have lost 71 percent, and a staggering 80 percent of the wetlands have vanished in the Fraser River Delta of southern British Columbia.

Like Washington, Ottawa is also unprepared for the looming water crisis and the demands for water exports. In 2003, the National Water Research Institute published a major study, "The Threats to Water Availability in Canada." The scientists who conducted the study concluded that there were "substantial shortcomings" in governmental protection of Canada's freshwater sources. Declaring that fresh water is "inadequately resourced" and its protection "poorly coordinated," the scientists called on Ottawa and the provinces to put together a reliable inventory of Canada's lakes, rivers, glaciers, reservoirs, and aquifers and the threats they face. Meanwhile, Canadians remain wary of the demands being made by the United States and other thirsty countries. In a 2002 survey by the Centre for Research and Information on Canada, 69 percent of Canadians said they were opposed to bulk water exports.

Bulk Water Diversions

As Frederic Lasserre of Laval University points out, the call for bulk water diversions from Canada to the US dates back to the 1960s.[107] In a conflict between Arizona and California over water takings from the Colorado River, the US Supreme Court put a limit on the volume of water withdrawals from the Colorado. At that time, California was already withdrawing volumes from the Colorado in excess of the Supreme Court's limits. After searching for other sources to replace its water takings from the Colorado, California focused its sights on the Columbia River. However, four western states (Washington, Oregon, Utah, and Montana) were opposed to California taking water from the Columbia River, because the Columbia crossed over their jurisdiction and they depended on this source for their own water needs in the future. In 1969, the US and Canadian governments signed the Columbia River Treaty to buy Canadian water that would be transferred to the Colorado basin via the Columbia River.

Meanwhile, according to Canadian water specialist Richard Bocking, there have also been a number of other major bulk water diversion projects in the Pacific northwest of the United States to address pressing regional water shortages, notably in California and Arizona.[108] Before the Columbia River Treaty, three canals were built to divert water in California: the Los Angeles Aqueduct in 1913, the All-American Canal in 1940, and the Colorado River Aqueduct in 1941. Since the Columbia River Treaty, three more bulk water diversion projects have been built in this region: the California Aqueduct in 1970 covering Sacramento and the central part of the state, the second Los Angeles Aqueduct in 1970, and the Central Arizona Project in 1993 to divert water from the Colorado to Tucson. The largest bulk water diversion in the region is the Central Valley Project involving the Joaquin and Sacramento river systems.

Elsewhere in the United States, the Great Lakes have been tapped for bulk water diversion by the Chicago Diversion Plan. Every day, Illinois is allowed to take 2.1 billion gallons of water from Lake Michigan, largely to serve the water needs in metropolitan Chicago. The Chicago Diversion Plan is an exemption that was grandfathered into the Boundary Waters Treaty between Canada and the United States. Today, as we have seen, the International Joint Commission that oversees the Great lakes is now opposed to any more bulk water diversions. Yet, as recently as 1998, the Ontario government went so far as to approve a plan by a Canadian export company (Nova Group) to extract millions of litres of water from Lake Superior for export by tankers to Asia. The approval, however, was promptly rescinded after an outcry from the International Joint Commission, which oversees the Great Lakes on behalf of both the US and Canadian governments. Madeleine Albright, then US secretary of state, also issued a declaration to the effect that, since the United States held joint jurisdiction over the Great Lakes, no decision on bulk water exports from Lake Superior could be made without US approval.

The state of Alaska in the far northwestern region of the continent provides the United States with another option. Alaska's potential for bulk water transfers is reported to be enormous. According to the *Alaska Business Monthly*, a one-million-gallon tanker in Sitka could be filled every day and it would still represent less than 10 percent of the region's current water usage. In Eklutna, Alaska, it is estimated that the bulk water potential could be as high as 30 million gallons (113 million litres) per day. Moreover, the political authorities in Alaska are committed to selling bulk water, becoming the first jurisdiction in the world to permit bulk water sales. But there are constraints. Bulk water shipment by supertankers down the Pacific northwest coast may not prove to be cost-efficient, since they would have to operate year round on tight schedules, moving through very treacherous seas and tortuous coastal waterways. What's more, most of the transport companies to date are unable to comply with the provisions of the *Jones Act*, which requires that shipment of goods from one US port to another in the United States make use of US vessels crewed by US sailors.

More recently, the state of North Dakota's decision to drain Devils Lake poses another kind of bulk water diversion problem between the United States and Canada. To prevent flooding, the project is designed to drain Devils Lake into the Cheyenne River, which is a tributary of the Red River that flows northward into Canada. Devils Lake, however, has become a cauldron of toxic chemicals from industrial runoffs and is now so polluted that its water is unsuitable for irrigating agricultural crops. The Devils Lake diversion has been strongly resisted by the people of Manitoba, who fear that it will destroy the Red River system, including Lake Winnipeg. Although a last-minute deal was struck between the Martin and Bush governments in August 2005, requiring the construction of a rock and gravel filter, the non-binding agreement is not sufficient to prevent chemical contaminants from spewing into the Red River system.

Mega Diversion Schemes
The implication of the 1963 US Supreme Court decision to restrict water takings from the Colorado River is that massive bulk water imports from Canada would increasingly become the preferred option. In 1968, the American Association for the Advancement of the Sciences concluded that mass transfers from water-rich to water-poor regions was inevitable, and that Canada

was the only possible source. By 1970, the US secretary of the interior, Roger Morton, declared that the United States must make plans to import water from Canada and the Arctic. Between the 1960s and the 1980s, a series of mega diversion schemes were planned for massive bulk water transfers from Canada to the United States.[109] In retrospect, these mega-projects can be categorized in terms of three major water corridors.

Western corridor.

The centrepiece of the western water corridor flowing from Canada to the United States is the North American Water and Power Alliance (NAWAPA). Originally conceived in 1964 by a Los Angeles engineering firm, Ralph M. Parsons Co., NAWAPA was designed to bring bulk water from Alaska and northern British Columbia for delivery to thirty-five US states. By building a series of large dams, the northward flow of the Yukon, Peace, Liard and a host of other rivers (Tanana, Copper, Skeena, Bella Coola, Dean, Chilcotin, and Fraser) would be reversed to move southward and pumped into the Rocky Mountain Trench where the water would be trapped in a giant reservoir approximately 500 miles long (or about 800 kilometres). A canal would then be built to take the water southward into Washington state, where it would be channelled through existing canals and pipelines to supply fresh water for customers in thirty-five states. The annual volume of water to be diverted through the NAWAPA project is estimated to be roughly equivalent to the average total yearly discharge of the entire St. Lawrence River system.

Although the NAWAPA plan lay dormant for over fifteen years, it was revived again in the early 1980s. Still, the prohibitive costs of the project (estimated to be between $100 billion and $300 billion) put the project back on ice. Meanwhile, other less ambitious schemes, like the Western States Water Augmentation Concept, were proposed in 1968. Like NAWAPA, this mega-project was designed to divert water from the Liard River basin south into the Rocky Mountain Trench, where it would then be transferred through tunnels and canals into the Fraser, Columbia, and Kootenay rivers for flowing directly into the United States. During this period, however, neither of these mega-projects was publicly promoted for water exports to the United States. Instead, Canadians were repeatedly told that the damming and diversion of so many rivers was needed to augment hydroelectric power at Niagara, provide irrigation for the Canadian prairies, and establish something called the Canadian Great Lakes Waterway.[110]

Central corridor.
Another water corridor consists of a series of water diversion schemes proposed from the Northwest Territories (NWT) through the Prairies into the United States. In 1968, the Washington State Resource Center developed plans for the Central North American Water Project (CeNAWAP). The plan calls for a series of canals and pumping stations linking Great Bear Lake and Great Slave Lake in the NWT to Lake Athabasca and Lake Winnipeg and then to the Great Lakes for bulk water exports to the United States. A variation on the CeNAWAP is the Kuiper Diversion Scheme, which proposes to link the major western rivers into a mega water diversion scheme involving the Mackenzie, the Peace, the Athabasca, North Saskatchewan, Nelson, and Churchill river systems. Both the Kuiper and the CeNAWAP are designed to transport water for export to the United States.

The central water corridor includes other diversion projects. The Magnum Diversion Project, for example, proposes to divert water from the Peace River Basin in northern British Columbia through the Athabasca, North Saskatchewan, Battle, South Saskatchewan, and the Qu'Appelle rivers into the Souris River which flows naturally into the United States. Another proposal coming out of the Western States Augmentation Concept calls for diverting waters from the Smokey, Athabasca, and Saskatchewan rivers through the Qu'Appelle River to Lake Winnipeg, where they would flow south into the United States. And then there is the Saskatchewan–Nelson Basin project of the Prairie Provinces Water Board, which proposes to divert water from the Mackenzie River into the Churchill River and the Saskatchewan River for storage in Cedar Lake, where it will be delivered south through canals into Lake Manitoba and then pumped into the Assiniboine River and the Souris River into the United States.

Eastern corridor.
The centrepiece of the eastern water corridor is known as the GRAND Canal—the Great Recycling and Northern Development Canal. As originally conceived, the GRAND Canal plans called for the damming and re-routing of northern river systems in Quebec in order to bring fresh water through canals down into the Great Lakes, where it would be flushed into the American Midwest. A dike would be built across James Bay at the mouth of Hudson Bay (whose natural flow is northward), thereby turning the bay into a giant freshwater reservoir of about thirty thousand square miles from James Bay and the twenty rivers that flow into it. Through a system of dikes, canals, dams, power plants, and locks, the water would then be diverted from the reservoir and re-routed southward down a 167-mile canal, at a rate of 62,000 imperial gallons a second (about 282,000 litres) into two of the Great Lakes—Lake Superior and Lake Huron. From there, the water would be flushed through canals into markets in both the American Midwest and the US Sun Belt.

From the outset, the GRAND Canal enjoyed considerable political favour in Canada. It was widely promoted in the mid-1980s by then Québec premier, Robert Bourassa, who also presided over the construction of the massive James Bay hydro project in the 1970s, and by Simon Reisman, Canada's chief negotiator for the US-Canada Free Trade Agreement in the late 1980s. A key player and partner in the GRAND Canal scheme was the Bechtel Corporation, the US construction and engineering giant that had close ties with the Reagan administration through secretary of state George Shultz, who served on the Bechtel board of directors. Bechtel still owns the project's blueprints. Still, the GRAND Canal project did not go ahead, largely because the US need for bulk water imports in the 1980s was not as acute then as it is today, and also because the more than one-hundred billion US dollars in capital required to build it was not forthcoming at the time.

Canadian Sovereignty
Given all of these grandiose plans for bulk water exports from Canada to the US, the question remains as to why none of these mega-projects has been implemented over the past four decades. From the US side of the equation, there are at least three plausible answers. One reason is that America's thirst has been temporarily quenched as regional water demands have been mitigated by mostly internal bulk water diversions like the California Aqueduct, the second Los Angeles Aqueduct, and the Central Arizona Project. A second reason has to do with the fact that these mega water diversion projects require an immense amount of capital to develop, and the prospects of investment by either the public or private sector were hampered by the absence of urgent and acute demand in the United States. A third reason may have to do with the lack of adequate engineering and construction technology to satisfactorily build some of these mammoth water diversion projects.

From a Canadian standpoint, however, there are other key factors having to do with public opinion and national sovereignty. Polls showing more than two-thirds of Canadians (69 percent) opposed to bulk water exports have made it difficult for governments to support any mega water diversion scheme. But the challenge is even more complicated. Historically, Canadians seem to have garnered a special (if at times ambiguous) relationship with this country's freshwater heritage. Our poetry and music are often sprinkled with water images. So the very idea of exporting our last frontier of natural resources to the United States is repugnant to most Canadians. It's like selling our national birthright. And so the very idea of bulk water exports becomes a thorny political issue of national sovereignty when it comes to Canada-US relations.

Seven years ago, the Canadian government began to more actively assert its national sovereignty over the management of freshwater basins that exist within its own boundaries and the export of water in bulk form. By 1998 the prospect of bulk water exports from Lake Superior in Ontario and Lake Gisborne in Newfoundland had become a hot political issue. Given its thirsty neighbour to the south, the question of how Canada was to manage the abundant supply of freshwater within its jurisdiction became a major concern in Parliament. On February 9, 1999, the House of Commons passed a motion (introduced by the NDP) calling on the federal government to ban the export of water. In response, however, the Liberal government of the day chose not to formally issue a ban on the export of water. The prime reason? A water export ban would contravene Canada's international trade obligations.

Instead, the Chrétien government adopted an environmental approach to the issue of water sovereignty by asserting its right to protect "water in its natural state" and prevent the "bulk removal of water" from major water basins. Bulk removal of water, the government argued, causes environmental damage to water basins. Preserving our natural waters is "the most comprehensive and environmentally sound way to protect our water basins from environmental damage that can be caused by bulk removals." In

other words, water is to be protected in its natural basin before
the issue of its export arises. For these reasons, the government
maintained that prohibiting bulk water removal from water
basins is a better approach than an export ban because it is "consistent with Canada's international trade obligations," is "more
comprehensive and environmentally sound," and "respects constitutional responsibilities."[111]

There were three components of the Canadian government's
water strategy that were launched in February 1999: (1) amend-
ing the *International Boundary Waters Treaty Act* to grant the
minister of foreign affairs the authority to prohibit bulk removals
from boundary waters, principally the Great Lakes, within Canada's jurisdiction (enacted in February 2001);(2) calling upon the
International Joint Commission—the bi-national commission
responsible for preventing and resolving disputes over shared
waters—to study the effects of water consumption, diversion,
and removal from boundary waters (including for export), especially from the Great Lakes; and (3) a Canada-wide Water Accord,
initiated by the federal minister of the environment and
endorsed by the environment ministers of the provinces and territories, designed to prohibit bulk water removals from all major
Canadian water basins. The provinces were expected to put in
place legislation and/or regulations to accomplish this goal within their respective jurisdictions.

Asserting sovereignty over bulk water transfers on ecological
grounds certainly has merit. There are mounting concerns about
the ecological dangers of large-scale extractions from water
basins. While comprehensive independent studies are needed,
there is sufficient evidence that draining massive amounts of
water from lake and river basins disrupts local ecosystems, dam-
ages natural habitat, reduces biodiversity, and dries up aquifers
and underground water systems. During inter-basin transfers,
parasites, bacteria, viruses, fish, and plants from one water body

would be carried into another. Mercury contamination from the flooding required for water diversions would bio-accumulate in the tissues of mammals, thereby having a potentially damaging effects along the food chain. Large-scale structures required for the storage of exported water would also disrupt ecosystems in remote areas.

Although Ottawa's strategy was designed to respect the constitutional responsibilities of the provinces, legal experts differ on whether it will prove to be effective. According to a legal opinion prepared by international trade lawyer Stephen Shrybman, the Water Accord itself would "do nothing to actually prohibit export initiatives that might be undertaken by provincial governments, municipalities, Crown agencies, corporations, or even private parties." This would require nothing less than federal legislation. While jurisdiction over Canada's water resources is shared between various governments, only the federal government has the constitutional authority to regulate exports. Nor is the accord reached in Parliament legally binding on the provinces, meaning that a subsequent change in political administration could result in an abandonment of the obligations to ban bulk water exports.[112]

NAFTA Handcuffs

Ottawa explicitly chose to develop an environmental approach as the basis for asserting sovereign control over bulk water exports in order to avoid constraints imposed by international trade rules, which Canada has already enshrined and implemented. Labelled as a "watershed strategy," its aim was to protect water in its natural state. Prior to signing the North American Free Trade Agreement in 1993, Canada, along with Mexico and the United States, issued a joint statement declaring that water, which has not entered into commerce and has not become a good or a product, is not subject to NAFTA rules. Despite these clever manoeuvres, argues Shrybman, Canada's watershed strategy is still vulnerable to an international trade challenge for several reasons.

First, Canada's strategy of avoiding its international trade obligations by treating water in its natural state rather than as a tradable good is weak on several grounds. Under both US and European law, water in its natural state (as in, groundwater) is considered to be a "commercial good" because it is capable of monetary valuation and of being the object of commercial transaction. Even if one accepts, says Shrybman, the dubious proposition that water becomes a tradable good only when it has "entered into commerce," a very large proportion of Canadian water resources are already considered subject to commercial use, either because it has been allocated to various users or because it is subject to proprietary claims through licences—to be used for public consumption, agricultural irrigation, industrial production, hydroelectric power, and bottled water. As a result, says Shrybman, the joint statement designed to exempt bulk water exports from NAFTA rules "would not, under international law, be binding on a panel or tribunal called to resolve a dispute concerning water export control measures."

Second, Canada's obligations under both the World Trade Organization (WTO) and NAFTA impose serious limits on our ability to exercise sovereignty over water exports. Under Article 11 of the GATT (now the WTO rules), the use of quantitative export controls, such as a ban or embargo, on any product "destined for the territory of any other contracting party" is prohibited. While Canada could impose a tax or duty for water conservation purposes under the WTO, it surrendered this option for exports to the United States under NAFTA.[113] Under Article 315 of NAFTA, Canada would also be obliged, once the export tap is turned on, to provide the United States with a proportional share of its water resources in perpetuity. Flows could only be reduced if Canada's water is being proportionately rationed to Canadian consumers and companies at the same time. Furthermore, Article 301 of NAFTA would require Canada to apply the "national treatment" rules to water as an export commodity, since water bound for export would have to be treated in precisely the same way as water used for domestic consumption. In short, all of these trade disciplines would impose severe limitations on what Canada can and cannot do in regulating the export of our water to the United States or elsewhere.

Third, water is not only considered to be a "good," but is also becoming recognized as a "service" in the new trade regimes. Under new rules currently being negotiated at the WTO in the General Agreement on Trade in Services (GATS), everything is on the table, *including water.* The European Union has made recognition of water services a top priority in the GATS negotiations. In NAFTA, water is already recognized as a service and therefore subject to rules for cross-border trade in services outlined in Chapter 12, including measures respecting the production, distribution, marketing, sale, and delivery of water as a service. Any US-based water service company, or a US-based subsidiary of a European water service provider, would be entitled to the benefits of the "national treatment" provisions outlined in Article 1202 of NAFTA and the "standard treatment" provisions of Article 1204. As a result, Canada's intent to exercise sovereignty over the management of its water resources could be further constrained by new as well as existing rules governing cross-border trade in services.

Fourth, water is not only recognized as a good and a service, but also as an "investment" under international trade rules, and therefore subject to investor rights provisions. In NAFTA, the disciplines outlined in Chapter 11 on investor rights would allow foreign investors to sue Canadian governments directly if they are denied guaranteed access to Canadian water resources, including water in its natural state. Once Canadian governments allow water to be withdrawn from its natural state for domestic purposes, as it does regularly for large-scale agricultural, industrial, and personal consumption, then the national treatment clause would require that foreign investors be accorded the same rights. As Article 1102 of NAFTA states, Canada must "accord to investors of another party *treatment no less favourable than it accords, in like circumstances, to its own investors*" [italics added]. Moreover, Article 1110 of NAFTA, which contains a broad definition of what constitutes expropriation, could conceivably be used by a US investor seeking to exercise its "rights of establishment" for bulk water exports from Canada to claim substantial compensation for "expropriation" of its investment.

In short, when it comes to trade regimes like NAFTA and the WTO, it is transnational corporations rather than governments that have sovereign control. Since the establishment of these new trade regimes in the late 1980s, governments have become increasingly hobbled in terms of exercising national sovereignty and regulatory controls over the operations of corporations. Given that bulk water exports are big business for foreign-based corporations, the NAFTA and WTO rules will definitely put severe constraints on what Ottawa can do. What's more, these rules are reinforced by binding enforcement mechanisms such as NAFTA's Chapter 11 provision allowing corporations to sue governments directly for violation of trade rules. In British Columbia, for example, Sunbelt Water Inc. is suing the BC government under NAFTA because the province's ban on water exports has prevented the company from doing business and making future profits. "Because of NAFTA," declared Sunbelt's CEO, "we are now stakeholders in the national water policy in Canada."

US National Security

Perhaps the most dangerous threat to Canada's sovereignty over its water resources and control of bulk water exports would be if the United States were to declare water to be a matter of national security. To date, the Bush administration has not made such a move.[114] But, if the US agricultural and industrial demands for fresh water continue to grow, and if water shortages become more acute in California, Arizona, New Mexico, and various states across the farm belt of the American Midwest, then there will be increasing pressure on the president and Congress to make water access a priority of national security. If that were to happen, then the powers of enforcement would be much more than legally binding trade rules. The full weight of the US empire's military as well as economic power would be applied to ensure the superpower's water security.

Ever since the 9/11 attack on the World Trade Center in New York and the Pentagon in Washington, national security has become America's number one priority. Not only has "security" become the buzzword in public policy making circles, but it has also rapidly become the defining metaphor and paradigm for a whole new era of domestic and foreign policy in the United States and in its operations around the world. One year after 9/11, President Bush outlined a new National Security Doctrine for America in its ongoing war on terrorism. In addition to pronouncing the US right to exercise pre-emptive strikes against its enemies and take unilateral action where and whenever it thinks necessary, Bush also declared that trade and security matters would be interlinked to the point where security would trump trade in terms of priority. Moreover, in carrying out its mandate in fighting the war on terrorism, the Department of Homeland Security has put a priority on water security, protecting reservoirs and freshwater basins against possible bacteriological or chemical attacks.

In this context, Canada's leading big business coalition, the Canadian Council of Chief Executives (CCCE), has been vigorously promoting the idea of a "resource security pact" between Canada and the United States as a new phase of the free trade arrangement between the two countries. Although NAFTA contains a clause on "proportional sharing" of resources, the CCCE insists it is essential to go beyond this to create "a zone of resource confidence in North America" at a time when the United States faces the prospect of "disruptions in global supply chains," by ensuring "unrestricted flows" of natural resources. To date, this "resource sharing pact" has been mainly focused on energy resources (oil, natural gas, hydro power). While the CCCE maintains that water is "off the table" in these negotiations, leaked minutes from meetings of the Task Force of the Future of North America (co-sponsored by the CCCE) show that water is very much on the agenda. Noting that the issue of water is "invested with a great deal of emotion in Canada," the task force minutes recommended that it be handled with care in crafting the North American Resource Pact.

Meanwhile, the new Annex agreement on the Great Lakes contains provisions allowing the eight bordering states to grant permits for bulk water diversions. This is a legally binding compact outlining the terms and conditions for new water diversions from the Great Lakes. It gives the governors of the eight states the legal authority to license the extraction and diversion of unlimited quantities of water to communities that are either partially or entirely outside the Great Lakes Basin. Neither Canada, nor Ontario and Quebec, which border the Great Lakes, would have a say in, or a veto over, these decisions, even though the lakes are interlinked in a common ecosystem. Nor would these water diversions have to be approved by the International Joint Commission, which oversees the Great Lakes. In effect, the eight state governors alone would have the authority to grant companies and communities outside the Basin legal rights to the water of the Great Lakes.

Yet, as Maude Barlow warns, the demands for Canada's water may come sooner than many think, with or without the new Great Lakes Annex and a formally negotiated North American Resource Pact.[115] In January 2005, Agence France Press reported that Lake Powell on the Arizona-Utah border and Lake Mead, which serves as a reservoir for the Colorado River, may soon run out of the volumes of water needed to power the turbines at the Glen Canyon and Hoover dams. Since 2000, when severe drought conditions hit the US southwest, there have been growing concerns that the water levels will drop below the minimum power pool of 1,063 metres required to rotate the eight turbines in the generating room. The prospect of the Glen Canyon and/or the Hoover dams shutting down within the next three years has sent shock waves across the land and put Washington on the alert.

It is critical events like this that could trigger the making of water a national security priority for the United States. If this occurs, then the full apparatus of the *USA Patriot Act* and the Department of Homeland Security, reinforced by the US Marines, would come into play. Since 9/11, the Bush administration has been committed to building a continental security perimeter that would encompass both Canada and Mexico, largely governed by Washington's Homeland Security agency. In many ways, Ottawa's new Ministry for Public Safety and Emergency Preparedness has been established to carry out Canada's role in this continental security perimeter. Under these conditions, if Canada were to resist US claims to Canadian freshwater sources, it could be viewed as an act of terrorism. Even if Canada were to put a quota on bulk water exports for conservation purposes, it could be challenged not only as a violation of NAFTA or the WTO, but also as a denial of water security for the United States and its national security doctrine.

Conclusion

In its cover story on November 28, 2005, *Maclean's* magazine declared that "America is Thirsty: Let's Sell Them Our Water Before They Take It." Well, as we have seen, the issue is not as simple as that. It is true that Canada is faced with the option of selling and exporting our water in bulk form to the United States, on the one hand, or the option of having an increasingly thirsty America coming and taking our water from us. But neither of these two scenarios constitutes a satisfactory solution as far as the majority of Canadians is concerned.

Today, most Canadians would probably agree with Simon Reisman's view that "water is the most critical area of Canada-US relations over the next 100 years." There may even be widespread consensus that water is potentially a major bargaining chip when it comes to negotiations with Washington. But Canadians would more than likely add that what we urgently need is a comprehensive water policy in this country before any decisions are made regarding water exports to the United States. According to a 2005 Ipso-Reid poll, a whopping 97 percent say that Canada needs a comprehensive water policy.

The time has come for Canada as a water-rich nation to develop a clear and comprehensive water policy based on sound principles of sovereignty, ecological responsibility, and democracy. In our view, such a policy must include a nationwide ban on bulk water exports. Furthermore, a comprehensive water policy of this nature should be grounded in federal legislation and ratified by the provinces. As a democratic society, this can only be done, of course, by engaging Canadians in a nationwide debate about our collective rights and responsibilities with regard to our freshwater resources. Indeed, a national debate on water could do more than anything else to define who we are as a people and a nation, as well as our destiny in the twenty-first century.

CHAPTER 8

Deregulation and Continental Regulatory Harmonization

MARC LEE AND BRUCE CAMPBELL

Deregulation has been de facto federal policy for more than two decades. Driven almost entirely by corporate interests, it has not been subject to any meaningful public debate in spite of major potential impacts in areas such as environmental policy and health protection. While lip service is paid to protecting the public interest, the federal government appears much more interested in reducing the costs of regulation to business in the name of competitiveness.

The recommendations of the business-friendly External Advisory Committee on Smart Regulation[116] are now being implemented in federal departments under the direction of the central bureaucratic agencies (Treasury Board and the Privy Council Office)—that is, outside the purview of Parliament. Under the Orwellian-sounding moniker of "smart regulation," the initiative is targeting approval processes in controversial areas such as pharmaceuticals and biotechnology, while promoting greater use of "voluntary approaches" and "self-regulation" in place of actual regulation.

In addition to the smart regulation initiative, deregulation at the federal level is being twinned with "regulatory cooperation," another Orwellian term referring to greater harmonization of regulations with the United States (and to a lesser extent with Mexico) in the interests of reducing allegedly high costs for businesses engaging in North American trade. Harmonization of regulations is a principal component being encouraged by corporate Canada for deeper economic integration with the United States.

It does not take long to figure out who will be doing the harmonizing. Cooperation implies, incorrectly, that Canadian regulations might be raised in certain areas where US levels are higher, such as environmental standards for the disposal of hazardous waste. But any such examples are never made in federal documents. The reality of asymmetric power imbalances between Canada and the United States means that the real issue is whether Canada should unilaterally deregulate to US levels. For the United States, the notion of a common regulator for both countries is simply unthinkable unless it were their regulator; and there is good reason to suspect that "mutual recognition," another variant on the cooperation theme, would not be palatable down south either (consider the US Food and Drug Administration's claims, in response to Canadian Internet pharmacies exporting to the United States, that imported drugs from Canada were unsafe for Americans).

Because the Bush administration has been moving the yardsticks through its own deregulation initiative, harmonization is tantamount to importing US deregulation. While corporate Canada has claimed that economic integration will not produce a race to the bottom, this is indeed what is being set in motion.

Harmonization is also viewed by government as a cost-saving measure. The idea that federal budget surpluses might be used to reinvigorate the capacity of federal regulators to ensure reasonable standards is not on the table in this exercise. Rather, Ottawa's current program review is aiming for further reductions in federal spending (building on large government downsizing in the mid-1990s).

Yet federal spending on regulation is a relatively small part of the federal budget. According to calculations done by Statistics Canada, the federal government spent $3.4 billion on regulatory activities in 1997/1998, the last year for which data are available.[117] While this number sounds large, it represents only about 3 percent of program expenditures. Relative to GDP, federal regulatory expenditures amounted to about 0.4 percent of GDP.

It is an article of faith among proponents that deregulation will be beneficial for the Canadian economy. Certainly, it will enable companies that find regulatory measures intrusive and costly to externalize more of their costs to increase profits. But beyond the narrow self-interest of companies, there is not a solid economic case to be made for deregulation. Instead, there is good reason to believe that this is a policy initiative that exclusively benefits corporate Canada, largely hidden from public view by deceptive language, and ultimately paid in greater risks borne by average Canadians. And because of the international context of harmonization, it has profound implications in terms of whether governments in the future will be able to enact and enforce regulations in the public interest.

Foxes and Henhouses: Recent History

Like its counterpart in the United States, Canadian business has crusaded for decades for large-scale reduction or elimination of regulations. It has been aided and abetted by legions of lobbyists and right-wing think tanks like the Fraser Institute. By and large, they have been successful in pressing for deregulation. And, like tax cuts and debt retirement, the work of deregulation is an ongoing process that is never quite finished to the satisfaction of corporate Canada.

Federal governments responded to the business deregulation agenda with the Neilson Task Force in the mid-1980s and the Prosperity Initiative in the early 1990s. The Mulroney government established a formal regulatory policy in 1986, which has since undergone several reviews and modifications, the latest in 1999. As part of the Chrétien government's Growth and Jobs Agenda, a deputy ministers' committee was set up in 1996 to advance regulatory reform.

In 1998, a regulatory affairs secretariat was established in the Privy Council, the central agency responsible for approving regulations. Regulatory control was further centralized with the transfer to the Privy Council of control over regulatory policy oversight of the regulatory implementation process. (This mirrors the centralization of US regulatory control within the Bush White House.)

In 2000, the deputy ministers' committee recommended a regulatory reform agenda focusing on "promoting Canada's international competitiveness," risk management approaches, alternative instruments such as voluntary codes, and regulatory compliance measures that ensure transparency and (business) stakeholder engagement.

The 2002 Speech from the Throne announced that the government would undertake a "smart regulation" initiative—an apparent reincarnation and repackaging of its failed 1994 *Regulatory Efficiency Act* (C-62), which proposed giving companies non-regulatory options in meeting policy objectives. The initiative's stated purpose was to contribute to innovation and growth by reducing the regulatory burden on business. It would also bring regulatory regimes into line with the government's trade and investment policies.

As part of the initiative, the government also asked the Organization for Economic Co-operation and Development (OECD) to review Canada's regulatory regime. The OECD concluded that a reduction in the regulatory burden (it is always seen as a burden) would substantially increase productivity growth and foreign investment. Free trade proponents have been mystified by the failure of NAFTA to close the productivity gap with the United States as they had forecast. Regulatory harmonization (along with the ever-popular tax cuts) became the new panacea for the productivity problem.

Harmonizing regulations with the United States has been a goal since NAFTA's inception, though progress has been slow. However, like the deep integration agenda overall, regulatory harmonization gained new momentum with the arrival of the Bush administration—especially after September 11, 2001.

The External Advisory Committee on Smart Regulation

In 2003, the federal government created the External Advisory Committee on Smart Regulation (EACSR), dominated by business representatives, to advise it on how to implement its smart regulation strategy. After fifteen months of deliberations and consultations with (primarily business) stakeholders, but no public hearings, EACSR submitted its 150-page, seventy-three-recommendation report to the government in September 2004.

The Committee strongly supported—over the objections of citizens' groups and public preferences—flexible, or non-regulatory, approaches such as voluntary codes, self-regulation, and tax incentives. It recommended further centralization and control of the regulatory process at the Privy Council Office (departments were deemed to be resistant to change) and creation of external (business-dominated) "swat teams" to examine and, presumably, as implied by the military jargon, obliterate unnecessary existing regulations.

The smart regulations committee also placed a major emphasis on "regulatory cooperation," especially with the United States. Its key recommendations were: eliminate small regulatory differences and reduce regulatory impediments to an integrated North American market; capitalize on the greater resources of the US regulators by accepting their procedures and outcomes in many areas; move toward a single review and approval of products and services for all jurisdictions in North America; and put in place integrated regulatory processes to support key industries.[118]

In principle, there is nothing wrong with regulatory cooperation at the international level, provided that sufficient space for democratic decision making is maintained. To this end, Canada has been involved for many years in all kinds of international regulatory cooperation and standards-setting bodies. Regulators share information, knowledge, and expertise and participate in a vast array of informal agreements and protocols with United States and other foreign regulators. Canadian scientists and officials have been at the forefront of developing international regimes and protocols for global health, safety, and environmental threats.

What the smart regulation committee recommended went far beyond the usual meaning of cooperation to include joint decision making and unilateral adoption of US regulations. "Cooperation" is a user-friendly term that masks what it is really advocating: handing over Canadian decision making in many areas to US authorities.

Michael Hart, one of the original FTA negotiators, wrote in a paper commissioned by the committee that giving up sovereignty is in fact an exercise of sovereignty: "a readiness to accept increasingly more stringent limits in the scope for autonomous decision-making, particularly in relations with the United States, in return for increased discipline on our foreign partners."[119] But we know from experience—most recently from the softwood lumber debacle—that the United States does not accept limits to its sovereignty. This begs the questions: how much of this one-sided surrender of policy autonomy is acceptable before democracy is seriously compromised, and should these decisions be left in the hands of those for whom concerns of independence take a back seat when they clash with the efficiency imperatives of continental economic integration?

Canadian business enthusiastically embraced the smart regulations committee report. Tom d'Aquino, President of the Canadian Council of Chief Executives (CCCE), said in a news release: "The Committee has provided the government with a superb blueprint." He singled out international regulatory cooperation recommendations for immediate action.

His colleague, CCCE vice-president David Stewart-Patterson, in testimony before the Commons Industry Committee, argued for eliminating "the tyranny of small differences" in regulations between Canada and the United States, asking: "Is the health of Canadians better protected because we define 'cheddar-flavoured popcorn' as having less than 49 percent real cheese instead of 53 percent as in the United States?" But, while a clever and colourful quip, this difference is merely a labelling issue that has essentially no cost implications for popcorn makers.

Given its appearance in pro-harmonization speeches, the notion that there is a "tyranny of small differences" undermining Canada-US trade has become a point of mythology. Certainly, to the extent that small differences do pose extra costs to business without much in the way of benefit, these issues are likely to be uncontroversial and could be addressed without much difficulty. As noted above, however, corporate Canada has had ample opportunities to make any such cases since the advent of Canada-US free trade, and the Canadian government regularly solicits the input of business when making decisions.

Instead, the "tyranny of small differences" is like smart regulation: a catchy, uncontroversial PR term that diverts attention from the real issues that matter to corporate Canada and that *are controversial* to most Canadians. What is really of public interest is the promotion of a continent-wide deregulated zone of economic activity that is of benefit to corporations but that sets aside reasonable standards to protect health and safety, the environment, workers, and consumers.

Regulatory Harmonization and Deep Integration—
The Security and Prosperity Partnership

The North American Security and Prosperity Partnership agreement (SPP) has replaced NAFTA as the framework under which the regulatory harmonization agenda is moving forward. The SPP was signed by the NAFTA leaders in March 2005. Under the heading "Improve Productivity" of the Leaders Statement, the first bullet point reads, "regulatory cooperation to generate growth," followed by, "lower costs for North American businesses, producers and consumers and maximize trade in goods and services across borders by striving to ensure compatibility of regulations and standards and eliminating redundant testing and certification requirements." Though the standard PR cover phrase "while maintaining high standards for health and safety" was inserted in the press release, it was absent from the Leaders Statement. This editorial slip reinforces the point—if it were not clear enough already—that cost cutting, not protection, is the priority.

The SPP established nine ministerial working groups with concrete implementation targets—amongst them a deadline of 2007 to set up a North American Regulatory Cooperation Framework agreement. Three months later, the first SPP implementation report released work plans for nearly one-hundred initiatives—many of which are regulatory in nature—to be implemented by trilateral working groups on an ongoing basis with regular progress updates. Many of these initiatives cover regulatory harmonization of goods and services including financial services, motor carrier regulations, energy infrastructure, pesticides, biotechnology, and pharmaceutical products. What this indicates is a two-track approach to regulatory harmonization—one comprehensive and the other sectoral. (It should be noted that public information about the SPP is almost nonexistent.)

The energy sector was singled out as a priority for regulatory harmonization to facilitate US access to energy resources from both Canada and Mexico. The SPP update reported that the three national energy regulators were establishing a tri-national regulators expert group to coordinate regulatory efforts and, among other things, to collaborate on ways to increase Alberta tar sands and natural gas production by examining infrastructure and refining bottlenecks, regulatory issues, and environmental impacts.

In their second SPP meeting in March 2006, the NAFTA leaders (with Stephen Harper as prime minister) reasserted energy as a top priority, announcing a North American Energy Security Initiative. Accompanied this time by big business representatives, the Leaders also announced the creation of a North American Competitiveness Council (NACC), composed of CEOs from each of the three countries, to give direction and advice to the politicians.

These initiatives mirror the Smart Regulation Action Plan, which references the goal of the North American Regulatory Cooperation Framework: "to reduce the compliance burden and duplication for business and create a division of labour allowing regulators to specialize in areas where they have expertise." (The PCO and International Trade Canada are the lead players here.)

The handprints of Tom d'Aquino and his big business colleagues are all over the SPP. The Canadian Council of Chief Executives (CCCE) has been aggressively pushing its Security and Prosperity Initiative—the name is almost identical—since January 2003. He also spearheaded a tri-national business task force on North American integration, which released its final report, *Building a North American Community*, in May 2005, less than two months after the NAFTA leaders accord.[120]

Like the SPP, it called for the rapid implementation of a North American Regulatory Action Plan "to eliminate existing regulatory differences as quickly as possible." Consistent with the 2004 EACSR smart regulation report, it identified "regulatory efficiency as an important way to improve North American competitiveness and [also with the standard PR cover clause] find new ways of enhancing protection of people and the environment…" It called for analysis of the cost of regulatory differences and the benefits of regulatory convergence, though costs are framed as business costs of unnecessary regulatory differences and delays in product approval, and benefits are framed as quicker access by consumers and higher profits by companies. It also proposed—like the EACSR report—a North American default principle: no country-specific regulation unless an international or North American standard does not exist, where there are unique national circumstances, or where there is a lack of trust among the partners.

Citing the Policy Research Initiative's research showing the corporate benefits of such a policy, the business report proposed that governments immediately adopt a "tested-once" policy for biotech products and pharmaceuticals whereby a product tested in one country would automatically be accepted as meeting standards in the others. The need to speed up regulatory approval of energy infrastructure projects (for example, the Mackenzie Valley natural gas pipeline) and a North American alternative to Kyoto was also identified.

What is most striking is how tightly coordinated the deregulation agenda is—among business, politicians, and bureaucrats—between the domestic and the continental initiatives. Big business is driving the process and providing the policy direction, political leadership is providing the precise shape and pace of policy change, and the bureaucrats the policy implementation. Absent from the process is parliamentary oversight and citizen input—in short, democratic accountability.

For Canadians, it should not take long to figure out who will be doing the harmonizing. "Cooperation" implies (incorrectly) that Canadian regulations might be raised in certain areas where US levels are higher, such as environmental standards for the discharge of waste by the cruise ship industry. But any such examples are never made in federal documents. The reality of asymmetric power imbalance between Canada and the United States means that Canada would sacrifice its policy autonomy and regulatory philosophy, and unilaterally adopt US regulatory standards and approaches. And that is what "smart regulation" proponents want—a backdoor way of achieving their deregulation objectives when the front door approach meets with resistance.

Harmonizing regulations to US levels is even more of concern because the Bush administration has been moving the yardsticks through its own deregulation initiative. Harmonization in this context is tantamount to importing US deregulation, even as American public interest lawyers and citizens groups have decried these moves that blatantly favour corporate interests. While corporate Canada has claimed that economic integration will not produce a race to the bottom, this is indeed what is being set in motion.

Policy Research Initiative Studies
Regulatory harmonization with the United States is receiving a big push from deep inside the federal government. The source is a group called the Policy Research Initiative (PRI), a think tank until recently housed in the Privy Council Office. Reading its publica-

tions on regulatory cooperation, it appears that the PRI's role is not to make a balanced assessment of the pros and cons of greater regulatory harmonization, but rather to manufacture the economic case for an agenda that has already been approved further up the line. The PRI has geared its research to supporting its contention that positive net benefits will accrue from increased regulatory harmonization with the United States. There is a glaring absence of critical or skeptical perspectives in all its publications.

The basis of the PRI's claims comes from two internal, unpublished studies, by Ndayisenga and Downs,[121] and by Blair,[122] the findings of which have been elaborated in a number of spin-off publications such as the PRI's *Horizons* magazine, proceedings of a conference organized by the PRI, and the *December 2004 Interim Report*. The two studies have been used to support the proposition that regulatory convergence with the United States is the best path forward for Canada. These studies have also been used to bolster arguments coming from industry lobbyists for further deregulation.

On closer inspection, there is good reason to be skeptical of the PRI's evidence. There is no empirical link between deregulation and higher productivity or improved rates of economic growth—a point conceded by the PRI. In fact, prominent authors such as "competitiveness guru" Michael Porter have argued that regulations—particularly environmental regulations—can have a pro-competitive impact. The PRI studies make some extraordinary assumptions and use questionable methodologies to arrive at their conclusions in support of regulatory harmonization.[123] Such approaches may make for interesting discussion at an academic conference, but in no way do they justify the astonishing claim made by the PRI in its 2004 *Interim Report* that "a reduction in the level of economic burden of Canadian regulations to the level of the United States would substantially increase productivity growth."[124]

The danger is that numbers and results from these studies (absent any kind of peer-review process) become truth when translated into ministerial briefing notes and government documents, such as the PRI's *Interim Report*, without any of the nuances and caveats that come with the original research, much less a rigorous critique of their methodology.

Outsourcing Legal Responsibilities

As stated previously, one of the priority areas identified by both the Canadian and US governments for regulatory harmonization is drug testing and approval—the idea of a "tested once" policy for North America recommended by business, the smart regulations advisory committee, and the Privy Council research arm—to forgo its own testing and simply accept those of the US Food and Drug Administration.

But how wise would it be to entrust such a vital government responsibility to a US body that has been widely criticized as under the sway of the US pharmaceutical lobby? How can government be accountable to its citizens when its vital role is being outsourced to a foreign government? It is especially disturbing in light of the unprecedented politicization of the regulatory process under the Bush administration.

Consumer groups in the United States are already concerned about the FDA's safety record in the context of a number of high-profile drug recalls that have occurred as approval times have been reduced. Concerns include the FDA's relationship with industry, which since 1992 has paid user fees to the FDA in exchange for faster approval times. During the Clinton administration, a survey by consumer group Public Citizen (1999) of FDA medical officers found that many felt pressured to approve new drugs, and that standards had been lowered such that safety was compromised.

For example, drug companies managed to keep the FDA from

taking PPA, a decongestant and appetite suppressant, off the shelves for two decades despite strong evidence that it caused strokes—two-hundred to five-hundred a year, according to the FDA. Another example is the FDA approval of the pain reliever Vioxx in 1999, despite independent evidence and evidence within the company that it had increased the risk of heart disease. Its producer, Merck, after five years, finally took it off the market in September 2004 when a trial reported that users had twice as many heart attacks as non-users.

Senior FDA analyst David Graham estimated that Vioxx caused between 88,000 and 139,000 heart attacks—30 to 40 percent of them fatal—in the five years it was on the market. Graham testified before a US Senate committee in November 2004 that the FDA is incapable of protecting the public against another Vioxx disaster.[125] He said the corporate culture of the agency "views the pharmaceutical industry it is supposed to regulate as its client, overvalues the benefits of drugs it approves, and seriously undervalues, disregards, and disrespects drug safety." Moreover, he added, "the scientific standards it applies to drug safety guarantee that unsafe and deadly drugs will remain on the US market."

These controversies led the *Journal of the American Medical Association* in 2004 to call for the creation of a new independent agency to monitor drugs already approved by the FDA to avoid conflict of interest between those approving drugs and those monitoring them in the marketplace.[126]

When it comes to the drug approval process, there is good reason to have redundancy built into the system by having reviews by multiple bodies. As Raymond Woosely, MD, and vice-president of the University of Arizona's Health Sciences Center, remarks, "when a drug goes on the market, only about 3,000 patients have ever been given that drug. We will never know the toxicity that can occur, especially at the one-in-ten-thousand or the one-in-twenty-thousand that could be seriously harmed. Our detection of that will only happen after the drug is on the market and exposed to huge numbers of patients."[127]

In making its case for faster drug approvals by adopting FDA rulings in Canada, the EACSR report emphasized the benefit to consumers from access to new drugs. The report, however, appears to have sidestepped the numerous controversies surrounding the FDA in recent years. It is notable that the terms "recall," "side-effects," and "death"—the potential downsides to faster approvals—are each mentioned precisely zero times. Yet the drug approval process in Canada is only about six months slower than in the United States,[128] and the principal reason for this is that half of the FDA's budget for drug approvals now comes from the companies seeking approval. Again, it begs the question: why is this such an important policy issue when the only benefit would appear to be increasing drug company profits?

The EACSR also cited economic gains from new innovation in pharmaceuticals that would be in Canada should approval processes be faster. This is a puzzling claim provided without any evidence, especially since they note, a couple of paragraphs later, that Canada represents only 2 percent of the world pharmaceutical market. Why, then, would the approval process in Canada have any impact whatsoever on the location for research and development investments made with a view to global markets?

What Are We Harmonizing To? The Bush Assault on Regulation

The perils of harmonizing regulations to US levels are not limited to drug approvals. In other major areas where there is a substantial public interest, developments south of the border have been troubling. Corporate interests have been successful in undermining the public interest, even though research by the Office of Management and Budget (part of the Executive Office of the President of the United States), in an annual study of the costs and benefits of regulation, estimated that the benefits of regulation exceeded their costs by a factor of three to six times.[129]

The Bush administration has been a dream come true for the decades-long corporate deregulation drive. Bush stacked his regulatory agencies with former corporate lobbyists and prominent anti-regulatory crusaders to an unprecedented degree. Years of corporate propaganda have created fertile ground among legislators that the costs of regulation are excessive. With the foxes more than ever in charge of the henhouse, the deregulation assault has moved into high gear.

The Union of Concerned Scientists concluded in a February 2004 report, *Scientific Integrity in Policy Making: An Investigation of the Bush Administration's Misuse of Science*—signed by sixty renowned scientists, including twenty Nobel Laureates: "There is significant evidence that the scope and scale of the manipulation, suppression and misrepresentation of science by the Bush administration is unprecedented."

David Michaels, former assistant US secretary of energy for environment, safety and health, wrote in the June 2005 issue of *Scientific American*: "Never in our history have corporate interests been as successful as they are today in shaping science policies to their desires."[130]

Robert Kennedy Jr., in his 2004 book *Crimes Against Nature*, charged that "the Bush administration has so violated and corrupted the institutional culture of government agencies charged with scientific research that it could take a generation [after Bush] for them to recover their integrity."

Two American non-governmental organizations (NGOs)—the Centre for American Progress and OMB Watch, a group that monitors the White House's Office of Budget Management, within which the regulatory affairs office is located—produced a report, *Special Interest Takeover*, in May 2004, documenting the dismantling of public safeguards by the Bush administration. The report identified 123 examples of White House rollbacks, weakened standards, problems ignored, enforcement undermined, information withheld, and science thwarted. It says there are many more.

Conclusion: Regulatory Diversity, not Harmonization

Closer integration has already had an impact on regulation in Canada. The dearth of environmental regulations since the 1989 Canada-US Free Trade Agreement suggests an unwillingness to introduce new regulations that might be perceived as undermining our competitiveness or that might provoke the ire of US investors (in spite of environmental regulations often being viewed by some prominent academics as pro-competitive). There is growing evidence that provisions in NAFTA such as the investor-state dispute mechanism—which allows companies to sue governments—have imposed a chill on new regulations.

The danger is that policy makers are being swayed by economic arguments that smart regulation and regulatory cooperation will close the gap between average income levels in Canada and the United States. This promise echoes that of the original FTA, and is likely to have as little success. In taking such a leap of faith, Canada risks falling into the chasm, as corporate cheerleaders gain at the expense of ordinary citizens.

Canada and the United States are different countries, and the cultural, social, and environmental context in which regulations are developed, and the issues they are meant to address, are different. Laws and regulations, as a result, will differ, reflecting the democratic choices made in those differing contexts. For example, regulatory differences lie at the heart of the long-standing trade disputes between Canada and the United States such as agriculture and softwood lumber. Diversity of regulations, then, should not be dismissed as something to get rid of in the name of harmonization, but something to be encouraged. Indeed, such differences may create comparative advantages that enhance the gains from trade.

The issue is really about what the proper role of government is in shaping/influencing the economy and society, regulation being one of many tools to that end. There may be good reasons for regulations to differ across jurisdictions to reflect local or national circumstances and priorities. Diversity of policy responses is a good thing; at the least, there is a trade-off between diversity and harmonization that must be recognized.[131]

One-size-fits-all regulation and regulatory structures may lead to policy failures that cascade across borders. Longer drug approval times in Canada mean that Canadians can learn from what happens in the US market when new drugs are approved, and can avert disasters when drugs are recalled. Due diligence is required on the part of Canadian regulators to ensure that products in the Canadian marketplace are safe. We should not aim to free-ride off work done in the United States (in light of issues around quality due to the extensive corporate presence).

Furthermore, surrendering regulatory decision making to the United States forecloses on independent policy responses in the future. A current example is that Canada is a signatory to the Kyoto protocol, and one of the main instruments for meeting the Kyoto targets is regulation. But in a harmonized regime, Canada would essentially forgo one of the most effective means of achieving the targets. It is impossible to say how many future issues will demand a different response in Canada than in the United States. Suffice it to say, lots. Why would our federal government willingly tie its hands to preclude responding as Canadians would like it to respond in the face of future threats and challenges?

Canadian regulators have long shared information, knowledge, and expertise and participated in a vast array of formal and informal agreements with US and other foreign regulators. Canadian scientists and officials have been at the forefront of developing international regimes and protocols for global health, safety, and environmental threats. There is no reason why we cannot continue to cooperate with other countries' domestic regulators to ensure better protection for Canadians while raising the floor of environmental and health safety standards globally.

There is room for international cooperation among regulatory authorities, but Canada should not get involved in any harmonization initiatives with countries that do not share the basic regulatory principles of precaution and primacy of protection. Nor should Canada be outsourcing this vital public function to other jurisdictions. Canada needs to strengthen its regulatory and scientific capacity to provide a check on the political might of business in both the US and Canadian regulatory processes. This is especially important in light of the unprecedented damage inflicted by the Bush administration on the US regulatory system.

Cooperation should be considered where it makes sense. When proceeding with regulation, it only makes sense that Canada look first to international standards and what other key trading partners are doing. But meeting the objectives of regulation may require that Canada go beyond these minima. A multilateral approach to raising standards in key areas would be welcome rather than harmonization with the United States based on private economic interests.

Canada should be looking at places where it can harmonize its regulations *upwards.* One example is emissions standards for the cruise ship industry. Another is California's auto emission standards. We should not be afraid of being leaders—there may even be competitiveness advantages to being first movers in, say, environmental technologies.

As the economy becomes more complex and more global,

stronger and more effective regulation is required. Regulation works, while voluntary approaches by themselves do not. Guidelines not backed by the force of law and penalties for non-compliance are not regulations. And conflicting goals for regulators—assessing health and safety impacts at the same time as "enabling" and competitiveness—should be eliminated so that they can do their jobs effectively.

CHAPTER 9

Canadian Workers and Contradictions of Deep Integration

ANDREW JACKSON

Introduction: Not With a Bang, But a Whimper

The drive for deeper Canada-US integration reflects the deeply supine character of Canada's governing class, of our dominant corporate, political, and media elites. Their views span the narrow range from taking the path of least resistance against external imperial power, and falling in line with US demands after the September 11 "paradigm shift"; to willing acquiescence in the further entrenchment of the neoliberal economic and social model embodied in NAFTA; to a very conscious and enthusiastic desire to be valued allies in building the "New Rome on the Potomac" (to use Tom d'Aquino's own admiring expression for American Empire).

The North American Security and Prosperity Initiative of the Canadian Council of Chief Executives and the "Big Idea" of Wendy Dobson of the C.D. Howe Institute envisage a strategic bargain. They say we should deliver on what the United States wants in return for some kind of customs union and formal "protection from US protectionism." The basic proposition is that Canada should fall into line with US Bush administration demands—especially regarding continental and global security, and access to Canadian energy (and water) resources—in return for the "holy grail" of secure access to the US market.

Our business elite are pushing forward an incredibly wide-ranging—and incredibly arrogant—policy agenda. The report of the so-called Independent Task Force on North America launched by the CCCE calls for a common tariff; a permanent trade tribunal; negotiated elimination of NAFTA exclusions (unspecified, but which can be safely assumed to include water and public services); common regulatory standards for biotech, pharmaceuticals, and food; a common security perimeter, including a joint military command for North American defence going well beyond the existing joint air command under NORAD; joint visa and asylum rules; interoperability of intelligence agencies; a "regional alternative" to the Kyoto treaty; and a North American Resources Accord.

This agenda has morphed into the less ambitious but official post–2005 NAFTA summit "Security and Prosperity Partnership," which envisages incremental, below-the-radar integration across a number of fronts—intelligence, security, resources, regulation—but no "big bang" new deal. It is notable that Canada's 2005 International Policy Statement gives clear priority to "Canada in North America" and "Revitalizing the North American Partnership," and is almost completely silent on contextual realities such as aggressive US demands to uncritically fall into line with US military unilateralism and new missile defence projects, to adopt US security standards, and to limit civil liberties.

Narrow incrementalism reflects the reality that big deals are a non-starter in Washington and potentially politically explosive here at home. The official discourse on North America is silent on the impacts of continental integration on social and environmental policy, and on civil liberties. It is almost silent on the context of US repudiation of multilateral and continental trade rules in deference to powerful US lobbies. The operative political elite assumption is that, if we act nice to the United States, don't provoke them, and do most of what they want, they'll leave us alone. They think that they can say one thing to voters, and do another thing out of their sight. In the final analysis, incrementalism recalls a line of T.S. Eliot's: "This is the way the world [read Canada] ends: not with a bang, but with a whimper."

Contradictions of the Corporate Deep Integration Agenda

There are at least four major contradictions of the corporate deeper integration agenda, which create a space within which it is possible to resist and to advance alternatives.

Contradiction #1. The search for more effective trade remedies vs. the reality of US unilateralism

The FTA and NAFTA have clearly failed to deliver on their key goal of secure access to the US market. The reality is US-managed trade in politically sensitive sectors, and the continued hard fact of the border as a major factor in corporate investment and production decisions. Softwood lumber is a key case in point of US rejection of NAFTA/WTO rules, but the Byrd amendment was an even clearer signal. Countervailing duty revenues collected by the US state and then paid to the complaining industry are in flagrant violation of liberal trade rules and make a complete mockery of Chapter 19—dispute settlement—under NAFTA, as well as WTO rules. Even the most fanatically free-trade, international trade lawyers are aghast.

Deep integration proposals represent Canadian corporate over-reach and hubris, in the sense that their power to influence the Washington trade agenda is very limited. It is notable that,

while the Task Force on the Future of North America was front-
ed in Canada by the likes of Tom d'Aquino, John Manley, Michael
Wilson, and Alan Gotlieb (urged on behind the scenes by Brian
Mulroney), the US participants included no prominent corporate figures, and involved no politician of higher standing than
Bill Weld, a long-retired former governor of Massachusetts. The
lead US organization was the Council of Foreign Relations, a last
holdout of Republican multilateralists and not exactly a core
Bush constituency.

There is no serious backing in Washington for a deeper continental relationship, as opposed to unilateral assertion of US
hegemony, and there is little prospect of winning the holy grail of
a seamless Canada-US border short of outright political union.

If there were any possibility at all of reversing aggressive US
trade unilateralism, it would instead arise from a tougher-mind-
ed Canadian policy stance of the kind proposed by NDP leader
Jack Layton (and denounced by much of the media). For example, energy could be used as a powerful bargaining chip. But Tom
d'Aquino and the deep integration crowd are quite prepared to
give with no take. They are enthusiastic proponents of a continental energy pact, common regulatory standards, and common
security and defence policies. The dominant wisdom of our corporate and political elites repudiates the idea of "linkage" in
favour of not rocking the boat. But why should the Americans
give us what we are too supine to demand as our right, namely,
rights of market access as conceded (and already paid-for) under
the current trade rules?

Contradiction #2. Democratic expression of Canadian public opinion vs. the goals and values of the Bush administration

Corporate hegemony is usually successfully maintained by mut-
ing class differences, but the deep integration project heightens
class-based ideological cleavages.

Our obsequious elites steadfastly ignore the political part of the Canadian political economy: the fact that the majority of Canadians embrace our national distinctiveness and are hostile to the steady rightward shift to market fundamentalism and social conservatism south of the border. The reality of this clash is hidden from sight to some degree by the non-reflective nature of much of our corporate media, but the political process in Canada means that the governing party must at least balance corporate goals with popular values and demands, as they have always done.

Opinion polling over the years by EKOS has highlighted a growing divide between elite and mass views on what kind of Canada we want to live in, and Michael Adams has detailed some key differences between the centre of gravity of public opinion in the United States and Canada. As Ed Broadbent has noted, a large minority—or even majority—of Canadians endorse broadly social-democratic goals and values, and a majority clearly favour secular liberalism in the non-economic realm.

Most Canadians want action to deal with environmental sustainability and global warming through the effective implementation of the Kyoto Accord, in implicit and explicit conflict with the accelerated development of continental energy resources and attachment to hard energy paths. Most Canadians want to secure and enhance not-for-profit public services. Cleavages on issues of war and peace and national security are fundamental. Canada lined up with "old Europe" in defence of multilateralism, and Canadians are attached to expansive notions of citizenship rights, cosmopolitanism and diversity, and are certainly not prepared to jettison them in the name of "national (let alone continental) security."

The key point is not that Canadians and Americans are fundamentally different. The United States is sharply polarized, and progressive Canadians and Americans can find common ground on at least as many issues as our respective corporate elites. But the respective centres of gravity in our two political systems are quite distinct and distant, and this seems likely to persist so long as right-wing Republicans dominate US politics while their Canadian soul-cousins struggle to appeal to the mainstream. This means that there will continue to be flashpoints on specific policy issues, and continuing political tensions. In short, even incremental integration is likely to periodically surface, arouse concern and controversy, and to be actively resisted by Canadian citizens.

An important part of Canadian distinctiveness flows from the fact that the left is stronger in Canada. Our labour movement is much stronger, and social democracy has some (perhaps increasing) political clout. While we need to maintain linkages with US progressives and share their hope of a shift in US politics, this reality also means that we cannot afford to surrender our capacity to influence Canadian politics by acquiescing in the weakening of the Canadian democratic state.

Contradiction #3. Continental economic integration vs. the living standards of Canadian workers and working families

Deeper integration has to be sold—and is being sold—as a "Prosperity Initiative." But the record of the FTA/NAFTA era has been one of stagnant real wages; increased income insecurity for many working families; more stress at work; and declining union protection, especially in the most integrated and exposed sectors, such as manufacturing. One of the most notable features of the past fifteen years has been a very sharp increase in earnings inequality, driven by a major shift of income to the top 1 percent. (The share of the top 1 percent of tax-filers earning at least $170,000 per year jumped from 9 percent to 14 percent of total income over the 1990s.) Labour's share of national income is today at its lowest level in the post-war era, while corporate profits are at a record high. In short, any gains from deepening economic integration with the United States have gone massively to capital and the elites and have not been shared with working people.

It is, of course, true that trade and investment integration is only one part of the broader neoliberal agenda which shifts power and income away from labour. But it is *directly* implicated in the upward convergence of Canadian corporate elite income to US levels and is the major driver of competitive downward pressures on wages and unions in closely integrated sectors. Continental integration also helps fuel the relentless and largely successful corporate drive for lower corporate, capital, and high-end personal income taxes. The alleged imperative of competitiveness is constantly invoked by business and governments to bludgeon Canadians into moving towards the low tax / low social standard US model.

The dominant corporate argument on "policies for prosperity" is deeply contradictory. They deny pressures to downward harmonization of social standards, but advocate tax cuts which erode the fiscal base for the somewhat more progressive Canadian social model. They claim that trade and investment liberalization bring better jobs and higher wages, while simultaneously downsizing, outsourcing jobs, and demanding concession after concession from workers.

As importantly, integration has not been a successful "national economic development project." Free trade was about creating a more sophisticated, productive, and diversified economy in place of the old Canada of hewers of wood and drawers of water, plus manufacturing branch plants. It is true that exports have grown strongly, but the productivity and innovation gap between Canada and other advanced capitalist countries has widened. Our economy remains highly dependent on the export of resources (especially energy) and basic commodities, such as minerals, wood, and pulp and paper. As Statistics Canada recently revealed, more than 60 percent of value added in the export sector is resource based. Our capacity in sophisticated machinery and equipment manufacturing and high-end services remains very weak.

The talk has been of shifting to a high-skill, "knowledge-intensive" economy—which is indeed what we need to do to benefit from the new global division of labour—but business investment in research and development, workplace training, and new machinery and equipment has been inadequate to do the job. Indeed, far from investing in our productive capacities here at home as profits have soared, Canadian capital has been massively dis-investing, shifting resources to investments outside the country.

Through the 1990s, a low dollar protected us from weak investment and weak productivity. But the underlying weaknesses of a market-driven, continentalist economic policy agenda are now being exposed. A much higher Canadian dollar and the rise of China are driving a major new round of industrial job losses and restructuring, and marked divisions of regional economic fortunes.

With relatively low unemployment and continuing growth, it would be too much to say that current economic problems are serious and dramatic enough to force a major change in policy direction. But one-sided distribution of the fruits of growth and emerging structural issues are quite capable of sparking a renewed debate over continentalist and neoliberal policies, and certainly provide a space to build support for alternatives. Moreover, the return of energy and resources as central drivers of the economy points the way to new linkages between the left and the environmental movement.

Contradiction #4. Deeper North American integration as a development strategy in the context of relative decline in US economic hegemony

United States consumption remains a key driving force of global demand (and a major driver of Canadian growth and job creation), but global production (including by United States transnational corporations) is rapidly shifting to China, India, and developing Asia. The result is a huge, chronic US trade and current account deficit, a slide in the US dollar against floating currencies, and growing potential for a "hard landing" for the domestic US economy. At some point in the not-too-distant future, the United States is likely to face increased difficulty financing its twin public and trade deficits and will have to respond through some combination of higher interest rates and fiscal restraint.

Deepening our already extreme dependence on the US market is not the smartest strategy in the world, especially at a time when there is some potential to broaden markets for Canadian resources, capital goods, and high-end services. Again, it is time to at least think about alternatives.

Economic Alternatives to Deep Integration

We have to start from a careful analysis of where we are now, not where we were more than fifteen years ago when the FTA was signed. Ongoing restructuring has meant that some key sub-sectors of our economy are very deeply integrated within North American economic space. Complex cross-border supply chains exist in auto, aerospace, and high-tech. Disentanglement would be complex and highly disruptive, implying that we do not want to return to pre-FTA tariffs and rules of origin.

A very significant (though routinely overstated) share of Canadian production is driven by US demand. International trade is also important to our economy in the sense that there are indeed important economies of scale and scope to be achieved. There are good jobs to be preserved and gained by producing high-value goods and services for export, and there is such a thing as mutually beneficial patterns of trade. In short, we want to regain more national control of economic development, rather than return to greater national self-sufficiency.

This observation does not mean that we stay with, let alone deepen, the NAFTA status quo. As noted above, dispute settlement under NAFTA has proved an empty gain, and reliance on WTO rules is now just as effective (or ineffective) a way to deal with trade disputes with the United States. We have much more leverage vis-à-vis the United States than our supine elites think. Customers buy our exports because they need them, or because US transnationals directly profit from the continental division of labour, not to do us a favour. This is especially true with respect to our exports of energy and other resources, which are currently in high demand in global markets.

A determined government could challenge NAFTA constraints to regain some policy space. At the top of the list should be getting rid of Chapter 11—which acts as an impediment to regulation in the public interest and makes privatization potentially a one-way street—and the energy provisions, especially proportional sharing. It makes sense to be assertive in terms of re-regulating energy exports by imposing a Canadian needs test, and regaining the ability to impose export taxes.

But changes to trade arrangements must be part and parcel of a broader alternative economic strategy. Some of the key elements were sketched out in the paper "Good Jobs and Wealth Creation" passed at the June 2005 Canadian Labour Congress Convention, echoing and building upon many of the points made in recent Canadian Centre for Policy Alternatives (CCPA) Alternative Federal Budgets.

The CLC has called for much higher rates of public investment—especially in infrastructure, research and development, education, and skills—to create a more attractive climate for private investment, and to compensate for the failures of the private sector in terms of building innovative productive capacity. Given corporate under-investment, we need to invest in the innovation programs of the National Research Council and our universities and colleges, rather than leave it all to tax breaks for corporate research and development.

The CLC paper calls for public sector procurement programs (for example, by the pan-Canadian health care system) as a tool for industrial development. It also calls for new institutions— involving labour and the community—to develop sectoral job strategies, supported by targeted public investments. Rather than broadly based corporate tax cuts (which have not worked and have eroded our fiscal base), it calls for financing of keystone new investments by low-cost loan and equity capital from a national sector development bank prepared to accept lower than market rates of return.

This alternative strategy supports a review of foreign investment to maximize Canadian benefits, and to retain Canadian control of and capacity to regulate our financial, cultural, and communications industries.

Last, but not least, it calls for a green industrial and jobs strategy as part of Kyoto implementation, with aggressive investments in public transit, building and industrial process retrofits/conversions; and research and development of renewable energy and high-energy efficiency vehicles, all of which are potentially a major source of new jobs and productive capacities.

In sum, we need a national economic development and sustainability strategy that also gradually opens up ways to democratize economic decision making: a strategy that pushes against the limits of and challenges NAFTA and the current economic model, and could open up further space for exploring alternatives. To get there, we need to deepen democratic debate on economic alternatives and to engage in an energetic "Battle of Ideas" with the corporate elite and their political and media allies.

CHAPTER 10

Modelling North American Integration: Pushing the Envelope of Reality

JIM STANFORD [132]

F ew ideas are as sacred in conventional economics as faith in the mutual benefits of free trade. Economists learn from an early age, starting in Economics 101, to appreciate the counterintuitive beauty of the principle of "comparative advantage": the notion that every region will benefit from free trade, by specializing in producing those products that they can produce relatively most efficiently. In policy debates, too, the predisposition to support trade liberalization is strong, and most economists readily endorse trade liberalization initiatives. The predictions of traditional neoclassical Hecksher-Ohlin trade theory indicate the potential and mutual welfare gains from liberalization and comparative advantage specialization—although even they imply potentially difficult trade-offs regarding the impact of free trade on income distribution *within* countries (an aspect of the theory which is mostly ignored by free trade proponents).

More complex modern theories, such as those which incorporate increasing returns to scale in production, are not quite as unambiguous in their conclusions (under certain conditions in these theories, free trade can be harmful), yet their conclusions also generally suggest that freer trade will almost always be mutually beneficial. Attaching numbers to these theoretical models allows economists to predict, with seeming scientific certainty, the scale and distribution of predicted benefits.

The experience of North American free trade (considering both the Canada-US Free Trade Agreement in 1989 and the NAFTA in 1994, and now proposals for deeper continental integration) provides an interesting opportunity to compare the predictions that economists made regarding the benefits of trade liberalization, with the subsequent real-world economic results. Indeed, North American trade liberalization probably constitutes one of the most "simulated" policy initiatives in economic history. The consecutive continental trade talks have spawned a cottage industry of quantitative economic models, each exploring the various routes and transmission mechanisms by which free trade should work its economic magic.

The popularity of this modelling activity reflects both geography (focused in North America, with its preponderance of neoclassical economic thinkers) and timing—with the trade liberalization initiatives coming on the heels of interesting innovations in the techniques of quantitative policy modelling, in particular the growing use of computable general equilibrium (CGE) models. These models are theoretically authoritative and allow for unprecedented modelling detail, even if their quantitative parameters are admittedly ephemeral. The application of new CGE techniques, together with the use of more traditional macroeconometric models, generated dozens of quantitative predictions regarding the impacts of North American free trade—the majority of them optimistic.

And economists and their models also played an important role in the intense political debates that have accompanied North American trade liberalization in all three countries. Their quantitative models seemed to put hard numbers on the predicted benefits that economists have traditionally expected to result from freer trade. Fifteen years later, however, there remains lingering disappointment (in all three countries) regarding the real-world record of continental free trade in delivering those promised gains.

In Canada, the improvements in productivity and inflows of investment predicted by the key quantitative models have definitively not materialized.[133] In the United States, the long-run weakness of manufacturing and the persistence of large trade deficits (including large and sustained bilateral deficits with both of its NAFTA partners) have sparked popular concern about the impacts of globalization generally, and NAFTA in particular, on US jobs and incomes.[134] Even in Mexico, predicted almost universally to be the biggest "winner" under NAFTA, the economy—after growing rapidly in the run-up to NAFTA—has not met expectations since the agreement came into force.[135] In each case, economists sympathetic to free trade can point to various mitigating factors in trying to explain this disappointing performance.[136] But this does not negate the general perception that the promised economic benefits of free trade have been difficult to identify in practice.

This chapter will introduce non-specialist readers to the theory and practice of CGE modelling. It will survey and reconsider the major predictions of CGE models regarding the effects of free trade in North America. It will compare those predictions to economic performance since liberalization. It is difficult to conclude decisively that the models were either right or wrong in their specific *quantitative* predictions, since even the more optimistic of the models expected gains from trade liberalization that would be too small to distinguish over time from normal fluctuations in economic data.

For example, the most influential CGE models of continental free trade predicted long-run gains from trade for Canada equivalent to under 5 percent of starting GDP, experienced over a period of at least a decade. This implies annual effects of less than half of 1 percent of GDP: smaller than normal year-to-year fluctuations in GDP growth.

What is obvious, however—at least in the Canadian case—is that the most important *qualitative* shifts that were supposed to be motivated by trade liberalization have clearly not occurred; and those swings in economic and export performance (both positive and negative) that are measurable in the wake of free trade are clearly explained by phenomena not directly related to trade liberalization. In this case, the real-world economic experience since 1989 might not indicate conclusively that the models were wrong, but rather that they were beside the point. The models simply missed the most important determinants of Canadian economic performance in a global world.

Finally, the chapter will review the findings of a number of CGE models that have been developed to highlight the still further potential economic gains allegedly waiting to be reaped as a result of *deeper* North American integration, including proposals to eliminate rules of origin on trade within NAFTA,[137] and/or form a North American customs union. The fact that earlier predictions of significant economic gains from continental free trade have been unsubstantiated at best has not stopped economists within the CGE tradition from applying their sophisticated tools to develop seemingly concrete predictions of economic gains from further, deeper integration.

And we can expect a similarly politicized use of those findings in coming debates over further continental integration. While very few policy makers could ever hope to understand the questionable methodology and highly speculative nature of these models and their findings, they will repeatedly invoke the apparent "proof" provided by these models to justify their continuing integration agenda. Both the dubious record of past modelling efforts, however, and the particularly questionable practices embodied in this new crop of CGE models of deep integration, should give Canadians ample warning to discount these optimistic findings.

What Is a CGE Model?

Mainstream or neoclassical economics attempts to describe the complex interactions that occur in the various markets that make up an economy: markets for produced goods and services, the market for labour, and the markets for other "factors of production" (such as natural resources, land, or produced capital goods). Neoclassical theory rests on a faith that competitive market forces will ensure that every market tends to settle at an "equilibrium" position, where supply equals demand. Usually it is the action of flexible price signals (rising under excess demand, falling under excess supply) that tends to "push" each market toward its equilibrium position. When every market in the economy reaches its equilibrium point (both goods markets and factor markets), then the economy is said to be in a state of general equilibrium. Neoclassical theorists believe that all markets (even the labour market) tend to clear (at least in the long run), and hence that the whole economy can be described by a set of equilibrium conditions applied to each of those markets.

A CGE model is simply a numerical representation of a system of equations describing supply and demand forces, and equilibrium conditions, in all of those individual markets. Economists can "solve" very simple general equilibrium systems (usually involving no more than two factors of production and two different industries), using geometric or algebraic techniques, in order to study and understand how the various market forces interact with each other, and how changes or "shocks" in the economy will affect final equilibrium levels of income and prices.

But the system gets very complicated as the number of industrial sectors or factors is increased, the number of complicating variables (such as taxes or technological change) is increased, or more than one region is introduced into the model. In these cases, the only way to solve the model is to build a numerical representation of the general equilibrium system, consisting of a large number of mathematical equations—one for each supply, demand, technology, or equilibrium condition which the modeller wants to consider. Modern CGE models typically contain hundreds of such equations. By attaching actual numbers to the equations, the modeller can then solve the system (as long as it is properly specified, with the number of equations equal to the number of variables) to replicate the actual state of any particular economy—in as much sectoral or regional data as the modeller cares to build in.

Numerical parameters are attached to each equation in the model using a process of calibration: typically, benchmark values for certain key elasticities[138] are assumed (sometimes based on more pragmatic empirical or econometric studies reported in economics journals), and then other parameters (called scale parameters) are selected such that the model's equations exactly replicate a benchmark data set. It is important to note that any CGE model can be calibrated to precisely replicate the outcome of any national economy. This does not mean that the CGE model is empirically accurate, only that the mathematical formulae built into the model are sufficiently flexible that the modeller can precisely fine tune the model's output.

In this sense, while CGE models allow for considerable structural detail and theoretical precision, they are quantitatively ungrounded: *any* CGE model can be calibrated to precisely replicate *any* real-world economic data set, and hence their quantitative predictions are highly ambiguous, completely dependent on both the theoretical specification and quantitative calibration that have been performed by the modeller. CGE modelling is thus a "quasi-empirical exercise,"[139] at best; the quantitative detail that these models produce in their results should not be misinterpreted as empirical reliability.

The model is typically used to describe an initial "base case" solution: that is, a snapshot of the economy before any assumed policy change or shock is applied. Then the modeller changes some parameter in the model to simulate the policy change in question, and re-solves the model. The difference between the base case solution and this simulated "counterfactual" solution is then taken as the potential economic impact of the policy change. But this estimate is 100 percent contingent on the modeller's specification of the model: both its theoretical and behavioural structure, and the precise parameter values that were assigned to its numerous equations.

A CGE model cannot prove anything. Its quantitative results are essentially the output of a grand, numerical "if-then" experiment. *If* each of the equations and assumed equilibrium conditions in the model is an accurate representation of the real-world economy, *then* the model's estimate might be interpreted as an approximation of what would actually occur after the policy change in question. Moreover, since different economists will have different views regarding both the theoretical underpinnings of the model and its numerical specification, different CGE models will produce different results—and none is more correct than any other. The relative credibility of each model, rather, depends on the relative realism of the assumptions and relationships that are built into it. And an apparent consensus of estimates from different models simply reflects a prior consensus of opinion amongst the corresponding modellers regarding those theoretical and numerical inputs—not evidence of any robustness in the model's predictions.

In this regard, it is worth pointing out that CGE models do not necessarily have to incorporate standard mainstream assumptions regarding the workings of supply, demand, and markets. It is possible to develop numerical equations to simulate the workings of any theoretical system. Alternative CGE models can be constructed to reflect different views regarding whether or not markets (such as the market for labour, in particular) really do clear; whether prices really are determined purely by cost; whether investment is an active, independent decision by companies, or merely the passive result of the clearing of a market for capital; and whether an entire country can be meaningfully described as a single "representative household." Lance Taylor was a pioneer in developing these alternative modelling approaches, and a few of the models adopt broader or more critical assumptions regarding the workings of the real-world economy.[140]

CGE models have been applied to many different policy issues, but trade liberalization scenarios have been perhaps the most commonly analyzed in the CGE tradition. In part this reflects a commonality of perspective between the inter-sectoral, productive efficiency preoccupation of free trade theory and the faith in market-clearing equilibrium embodied in the (neoclassical) CGE models. In addition to the models of North American free trade surveyed below, CGE models have also been used extensively to model WTO liberalization scenarios and other regional or bilateral trade initiatives.[141]

Typical Assumptions of CGE Models

Most CGE free trade models incorporate a very dubious mix of assumptions that essentially predetermine their optimistic findings—but that can hardly be interpreted as a realistic depiction of the workings of any real-world economy. Here are some of the most important standard assumptions of the neoclassical models:

Full employment of all factors (including labour).
The models require that all labour be employed, both before and after trade liberalization. So there is no worry that anyone can lose their job as a result of shifting competitive pressures after free trade.

Uniform factor pricing.
Competitive market forces also require complete equality in factor pricing. In this sense, there is never an issue of attempting to attract (or protect) a larger share of good jobs—since all jobs pay the same, anyway.

Demand and macroeconomics do not matter.
Competitive market-clearing pressures ensure that all of a country's economic resources will always be fully occupied. Therefore, a country can never experience aggregate job loss or macroeconomic downturn (such as a recession) from any economic change.

Society can be described by a single "representative" household: Most CGE models summarize all the economic behaviour of a country's citizens through equations describing the tastes, purchasing habits, and factor supply decisions (including labour supply decisions) of a single representative household. No explicit consideration is given to the impact of trade liberalization on income distribution among different groups of households: every family is assumed to share equally in all the income, wealth, and consumption of the whole nation. (A few models, following the "structuralist" tradition initiated by Taylor, describe all of these factors separately for different groups or classes of households, and hence provide a much richer portrait of the real economy. But these models are the exception.)[142]

Constant income shares.
CGE models must include "production functions" that describe the process by which factor inputs (labour, capital, resources, and intermediate goods) are transformed into finished goods and services. The most common such function is called a Cobb-Douglas production function, which has one peculiar but important feature: the final distribution of aggregate income in this equation between labour and capital is always *constant*. Thus there can be no impact of trade liberalization on the distribution of income among *classes*.

No capital mobility.
Neoclassical CGE models describe the process of investment in a very odd manner. In most cases, there is simply a national stockpile of capital (described as if it were fully malleable "putty") that can move seamlessly and painlessly between industries. There is no explicit process of investment (or disinvestment), just a shift of capital from one industry to another, based on wherever it can be utilized most profitably. In a few cases, the decision of the representative household to save out of their personal income (thus generating additional putty-like capital for the national economy) is also modelled. Most models allow for no capital mobility between countries. In this case, again, one of the major fears of free trade opponents—namely that liberalization will allow profit-maximizing companies to shift capital to low-cost jurisdictions—is simply assumed away, by virtue of the modeller's specification.

Balanced trade.
A corollary of the capital mobility assumption is that each country's overall trade will remain balanced (or, if it was unbalanced in the base case, then that imbalance will not change in the counterfactual simulation). With full equilibrium in the model

between income and expenditures, the model enforces that a country's representative household can only buy in international markets exactly what its earnings in international markets will allow it to. Thus, free trade can never undermine an economy's balance of payments or its overall competitive position—no matter how inexpensive may be the products imported from competing jurisdictions.

Products are differentiated by place of origin.
Most CGE models incorporate some version of what has come to be known as the "Armington assumption."[143] This odd assumption was developed to explain an anomaly in world trade patterns: contrary to the predictions of orthodox trade theory (that countries would specialize in products reflecting their comparative advantage, and hence their relative endowments of capital, labour, or other productive resources), in practice there is a great deal of *two-way* trade within broad classes of commodities. For example, Germany and Denmark export beer to each other, and Canada and the United States export cars to each other (this phenomenon is often called intra-industry trade). To allow CGE models to capture this two-way trade pattern, the Armington approach assumes that every product is inherently defined or distinguished by the nation where it is produced. A car produced in one country is inherently different from a car produced in another (even if it is produced by the same company). The consumer will be willing to try the car from the other country, but somewhat unwilling to buy it (because they sense that it is different, and hence an "imperfect substitute" for their home-grown car).

The modelling impact of this assumption is also odd. Any country's share of any industry is, to some extent, inherently protected, since it is the only place in the world that can produce that *precise variety* of the product in question. This also gives every country a certain degree of monopoly power in pricing its unique, home-grown products. But once again, this approach—while mathematically convenient—mis-portrays the true issues at stake under free trade. Most products are differentiated not by the country where they are produced, but by the company which produces them. When multinational corporations are able to shift location of *their* variety of a product to whatever jurisdiction offers them the highest profits, then the Armington assumption ceases to be realistic.

Imagine if average Canadians could be assured, in real life, that each of these assumptions actually prevailed in the economy that they live and work in. They will always be employed—and they don't need to worry about holding an inferior job, since all jobs pay the same wage rate. They hold an equal share of the country's entire wealth and income and will share equally in all wages, profits, and other income generated. The overall distribution of income between wages and profits cannot change. Capital cannot flee the country. And Canada is the only place in the world that can produce unique Canadian varieties of goods and services that are demanded by consumers all over the world.

This sounds more like some utopian form of "socialism" than an idealized free-market economy. Yet those are the assumptions that fundamentally determine the behaviour of the CGE free trade models that are held up to "scientifically" verify that continuing trade liberalization will indeed generate the mutual (and equally shared!) benefits predicted in neoclassical economic theory. If these assumptions actually prevailed in the real world, then it is unlikely that many Canadians would ever question the wisdom of trade liberalization and other market-enhancing economic reforms. Unfortunately, however, they most clearly do not.

Previous CGE Models of North American Free Trade

Table 1 summarizes the central results (gains in national welfare or GDP, in both cases expressed as a share of starting GDP) of fourteen different CGE models that estimated the economic effects of various North American trade liberalization scenarios. Most of the models are static: that is, they simply provide before and after snapshots of the long-run effects of trade liberalization; in some cases,[144] the models attempt to explicitly describe the adjustment process to that long-run position. Trade liberalization is simulated by eliminating the tariff mark-up in equations that determine selling prices for domestic and imported varieties of products in each market.

Table 10-1

CGE Estimates of the Economic Effects of North American Trade Liberalization: Summary Results, Change in Welfare or GDP

(percent of GDP)

	Canada	US	Mexico
Bachrach and Mizrahi (1992)		0.04	4.64
Brown, Deardorff, and Stern (1992)	0.7	0.3	5.0
Cox and Harris (1992)	4.67		
Hamilton and Whalley (1985)	0.60	-0.04	
Hinojosa & Robinson (1991)		-0.2	6.8
Levy & Wijnbergen (1992)			0.60
McCleery (1992)		0.51	11.39
Roland-Holst, Reinert, & Shiells (1992)	10.57	2.07	3.38
Sobarzo (1992)			8.0
Spriggs (1991)		-0.62	8.21
Stanford (1993)	-1.47	0.04	13.10
USITC (2003)		0.1	
Wigle (1988)	0.7	0.1	
Young and Romero (1992)			8.1

Source: Author's compilation from sources indicated. Where modelling groups simulated different trade liberalization scenarios, the scenario corresponding most closely to the actual negotiated NAFTA, measured relative to a pre-CUFTA baseline, is reported.[145]

In the traditional neoclassical CGE models, the typical assumption of fully employed factors (including labour) before and after liberalization essentially predetermines that welfare gains will result from factor reallocation and specialization. But in standard constant-returns CGE models,[146] those gains are typically very small—so small that one wonders why any government would undertake the political fuss and risk of negotiating trade agreements in the first place. And in models that incorporate the Armington assumption of national product differentiation, free trade can potentially result in a deterioration in the "terms of trade" (that is, the ratio of the prices of a country's exports to the prices of its imports) that can, in some cases, overwhelm the welfare benefits of trade-induced specialization.

A crucial innovation that became central to discussions of the Canada-US FTA in the latter 1980s was to incorporate increasing returns to scale: that is, the notion that firms become more efficient when they become larger. The influential Cox-Harris model[147] utilized a theory of imperfect competition in which domestic producers use tariff protection to reduce output and collect excess profits. Tariff reduction reduces this protection and hence stimulates an increase in the scale of output; this in turn leads to productivity gains, which considerably amplify the expected gains from trade. Those CGE models that incorporated increasing returns[148] generally predicted that the welfare or GDP benefits of North American free trade would be significantly larger.

Another crucial modelling choice involves the treatment of international capital mobility. The relationship between trade policy and international investment flows is central to the economic history of both Canada and Mexico. In the Canadian case, one might expect that the reduction of bilateral tariffs with the United States would have implications for flows of incoming foreign investment that were traditionally motivated by tariff-jumping. In Mexico, a dominant rationale for participation in the NAFTA was precisely to signal to foreign investors that pre-NAFTA liberal reforms in economic and investment policy were permanent and reliable. In both cases, one would assume that the treatment of the impact of continental trade liberalization on international capital mobility would be a topic of central concern to the economic modellers. Yet this was not always the case—and even those models that did incorporate foreign investment flows, typically did so in a rather one-sided and optimistic fashion.

Several of the models[149] allowed for no international capital mobility whatsoever. Some of the one-country models[150] allowed for incoming foreign investment, which boosted the resulting predicted gains from liberalization; in the Cox-Harris case, the boost in productivity, resulting from the shift in the imperfectly competitive price-quantity equilibrium of goods producers, motivated (via enhanced profitability) a substantial inflow of foreign capital that further boosted domestic growth. Some of the multi-country models[151] modelled a foreign capital inflow to Mexico following a NAFTA, without allowing for any possibility of a capital *outflow* from the United States or Canada (implicitly or explicitly assuming that all new capital entering Mexico came from jurisdictions outside of North America). Given the investment location flexibility that firms enjoy in a liberalized context, and the importance of intra-firm investment and trade decisions in the North American setting, this approach seems especially dubious. Models that allowed for the possibility that some or all of the new investment in Mexico is diverted from its North American trading partners[152] were significantly less sanguine about the predicted impacts of liberalization, which could turn out to be negative in those countries that were the source of capital for the new investments in Mexico.

One model summarized in table 1 also allows for the possibility of international labour migration.[153] Migration flows are assumed to reflect some initial equilibrium based on starting international wage differentials; in a counterfactural simulation, net migration increments will depend on the evolution of that wage differential. In this case, since NAFTA leads to strong growth and hence wage increases in Mexico, it is predicted to stimulate a net migration from the United States back to Mexico, thus enhancing the overall positive effect of the agreement for Mexico. This prediction seems dubious, however, in light of more grounded, multidisciplinary theories of international migration,[154] which indicate that incoming foreign investment to a developing country such as Mexico tends to be associated with continuing or even increased outflow of migration.

I will invoke the privilege of authorship to draw attention to my own entry in the North American free trade CGE modelling sweepstakes. I constructed a multi-country CGE model that incorporated assumptions quite distinct from the standard supply-constrained practice of mainstream models—and that consequently generated less mutually beneficial results.[155] This model described a demand-constrained, investment-driven macroeconomic general equilibrium. In this context, the impact of trade liberalization on absolute competitiveness (and hence on the demand constraint regulating overall output and employment) becomes relevant—unlike in the supply-constrained neoclassical system, in which full employment is maintained and demand is not a problem.

Trade liberalization in this context can have positive or negative effects, depending on whether it expands or contracts the demand constraint. Bilateral tariff reduction alone is found to have relatively little impact in either direction (the model assumed constant returns to scale); but investment mobility (simulated by a NAFTA-induced reduction in an implied risk premium associated with investment in Mexico) is found to generate negative impacts for Canada and the United States. In the US case, this effect is offset by positive trade impacts resulting from stronger Mexican growth, but in the Canadian case it is not (since Canada's share of Mexican demand is infinitesimal).

As indicated in table 1, the models generated a relatively wide range of estimates of the impact of the NAFTA, although in most cases the results were found to be positive. For Canada, some models predicted very small positive effects (under 1 percent of GDP), while others (those incorporating increasing returns) predicted larger gains (up to 10 percent of GDP in the model of Roland-Holst, Reinert, and Shiells[156]). Note that even the more optimistic projections would be hard to "find" in the normal ups and downs of economic fluctuations, given that they would take many years to be realized. For the United States, all the models predicted near-zero effects from the NAFTA of well under 1 percent of GDP (and potentially negative, in three cases); this begs the question again as to why US policy makers would have any interest in North American trade liberalization (unless this policy was pursued for non-economic, strategic reasons). For Mexico, the predicted gains were larger—between 5 and 13 percent of GDP for almost all the models.

Comparing Models to the Real-World Experience of North American Free Trade

The more optimistic of the quantitative models invoked in the North American free trade debates predicted small economic effects for the United States, significant gains (in the order of 5 percent of GDP) for Canada, and potentially larger gains in Mexico (driven by inflows of foreign investment and even, in some models, returning migrant labour). This was the general scale of impact predicted by those CGE models that allowed for increasing returns to scale, and modelled foreign investment flows in a "win-win" manner (that is, allowing for an inflow to some countries but no outflow from the other countries).

In practice, there has been no visible impact of continental trade liberalization on overall economic growth rates in the three NAFTA member economies (see table 2). Growth rates in the wake of the Canada-US FTA and NAFTA are not measurably different than they were before liberalization. Indeed, for the two countries most impacted by these initiatives—Canada and Mexico—growth initially declined in each respective case in the immediate wake of liberalization (following the 1989 FTA for Canada, and following the 1994 NAFTA for Mexico). This may have reflected an initial period of adjustment to the new continental economic reality.

Table 10-2

Real GDP Growth, NAFTA Countries, 1980–2003

(*compound average annual rate, percent*)

	1980-1989	1989-1994	1994-2003	1980-2003
	(pre-FTA)	(FTA)	(NAFTA)	
Canada	3.0	1.2	3.4	2.8
United States	3.0	2.3	3.2	2.9
Mexico	1.7	3.9	2.5	2.4

Source: Author's calculations from Statistics Canada, *Canadian Economic Observer, Historical Statistical Supplement*, 2004; Council of Economic Advisors, *Economic Report of the President 2004*; Organization for Economic Cooperation and Development, *Economic Outlook*, July 2004.

Macroeconomic developments in all three countries during this period have clearly been dominated by factors other than North American trade liberalization. The US economy performed strongly in the latter 1990s, partly thanks to macroeconomic spin-offs from the dot-com stock market bubble. But the US economy then weakened in the wake of the 9/11 terrorist attacks and the high-tech stock market implosion. Mexico's economy grew strongly in the lead-up to that country's entry into the NAFTA free trade area, benefiting from a large inflow of capital as investors anticipated new export opportunities opened up by Mexico's NAFTA membership. Following NAFTA's creation in 1994, however, Mexico experienced a financial and exchange rate crisis as some of the "hot money" that flowed into Mexico subsequently exited; more recently, Mexico's economy has performed sluggishly in the wake of the US slowdown and the reallocation of global foreign investment toward China.

In Canada, meanwhile, uniquely tight monetary policy conditions at about the same time as the FTA was implemented contributed to a painful recession, including a dramatic contraction in the country's export-oriented manufacturing sector (which shed up to one-quarter of its total employment in the four years following the FTA). Most economists agree that the FTA was at most a secondary contributor to this painful period,[157] and manufacturing employment subsequently recovered later in the 1990s, exceeding its pre-FTA peak by 2001.

Indeed, swings in the Canada-US exchange rate were clearly the dominant influence on the performance of Canadian manufacturing throughout this period (figure 1). The dramatic appreciation of the Canadian currency from 1988 through 1991 sparked a relocation of manufacturing employment from Canada to the United States, while the subsequent and equally dramatic depreciation through the next decade sparked an even greater relocation of employment back to Canada. More recently, the Canadian dollar has risen again (by 40 percent versus the US dollar from late 2002 through early 2006); it remains to be seen what the impact of this dramatic appreciation will be on Canadian manufacturing, but the strong historical evidence summarized in figure 1 does not lead one to be optimistic.

From the Canadian perspective, the FTA was associated with a strong rise in the export share of GDP (figure 2), entirely due to an increase of exports to the United States.[158] (Canadian exports to Mexico and to non-NAFTA trading partners have not grown relative to GDP since 1988.) At the same time, however, Canada's share of total US imports has actually declined since the FTA came into effect, suggesting that the growth of Canadian exports to the United States was primarily driven by the same macroeconomic factors (strong US aggregate demand conditions through most of the 1990s, its large trade deficit, and the strong US dollar) that sucked in imports even more quickly from the rest of the world than from Canada.

Sectorally disaggregated studies find that the growth of Canadian exports to the United States was proportionally greater in those sectors that experienced the largest reductions in US tariffs;[159] similarly, a proportionally greater growth in Canadian imports was associated with those sectors that experienced larg-

Figure 10-1
Exchange Rates and Manufacturing Employment Performance:
Canada, 1980–2003
(Canadian dollar in cents US, Canadian share of combined Canada-US manufacturing employment in percent)

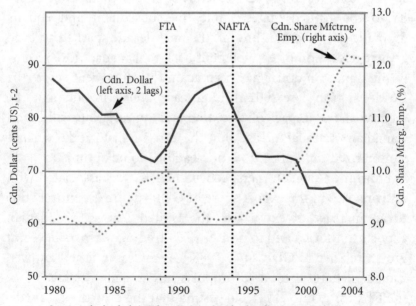

Source: Author's calculations from Statistics Canada, *Canadian Economic Observer,*
Historical Statistical Supplement, 2004, and Council of Economic Observers,
Economic Report of the President 2004.
Canadian exchange rate (left axis) lagged two years. 2004 data for first ten months.

Figure 10-2
Trade Shares of GDP Canada, 1980–2003 (percent)

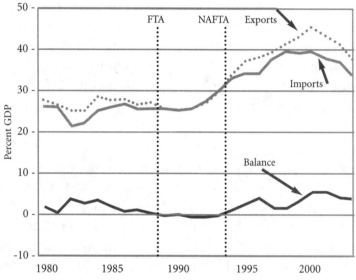

Source: Author's calculations from Statistics Canada, *Canadian Economic Observer
Historical Statistical Supplement, 2004.*

er reductions in Canadian tariffs. At the same time, however, the growth in exports from sectors that were already liberalized prior to the FTA (such as automotive products, pulp and paper products, and energy products) accounts for most Canadian export growth since the FTA. The conclusion is hard to deny that most of the growth in Canadian exports since 1989 would have been experienced even without the FTA; at the same time, the dramatic rise in the overall export share of Canadian GDP since 1989 does seem to indicate some type of structural shift as a result of continental integration—in both intermediate supply patterns and the disposition of final Canadian output.

The more optimistic (and influential) estimates of the impacts of free trade on the Canadian economy relied on the faith (embedded in the increasing returns to scale assumptions of several of the CGE models) that tariff reduction would spark an increased scale of production and hence a gain in efficiency and productivity. An associated result predicted that the resulting expansion in output and profitability would draw in substantial amounts of foreign capital to the Canadian economy, further boosting the aggregate positive impact of the liberalization. Unfortunately, neither of these results has been attained. In practice, the productivity gap between Canada and the United States has actually widened considerably during the post-FTA period (figure 3).

Canadian foreign investment experience since the FTA is another source of intense disappointment, compared to the optimistic pre-FTA predictions of most of the quantitative economic models. Tariff-jumping foreign direct investment (FDI) has played a long and crucial role in Canadian economic history, and so on this basis alone it seems strange that economists would have been so sanguine about the impact of tariff removal (even though those tariffs had already declined substantially by the time of the FTA, relative to earlier decades) on foreign investment flows. The FTA has led to an increase in both inflows and outflows of FDI to and from Canada, as corporations on both sides of the border adjusted their operations to reflect the newly integrated continental market. But Canada has been a net loser in this process: since the FTA, direct investment outflows exceeded inflows by a cumulative total (to the end of 2003) of seventy-five billion dollars (or an annual average of about two-thirds of 1 percent of Canadian GDP).

In general, therefore, Canada's international economic links have exerted a varying impact on its overall economic performance in the fifteen years since the FTA was implemented. Initially, in the context of dramatically restrictive monetary policy and a soaring currency, that impact was clearly negative—with the result that Canada endured a uniquely painful, and probably

Figure 10-3

Canada-US Productivity Comparisons: Output per Hour Worked, Business Sector, 1980–2003 (national indices, 1980=100)

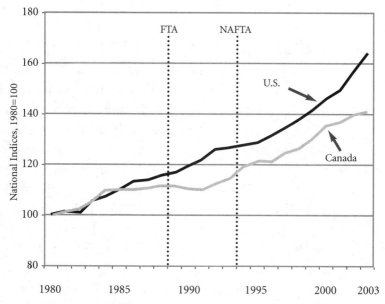

Source: Author's calculations from Centre for the Study of Living Standards (2004).[160]

unnecessary, recession in the early years of the FTA's existence. Subsequently, as the currency declined and domestic macroeconomic policy became more expansionary, strong growth in net exports to the United States (not primarily due to the FTA per se) became a central source of growth and dynamism in the Canadian economy. More recently, the external sector has been a net drag on Canadian growth and employment. Foreign investment flows to and from Canada reflect a complex mixture of structural and cyclical factors, but on the whole have worked against Canada since the FTA. And the country's productivity performance—which ultimately reflects a complex set of historic, structural, and market determinants, not just the relative efficiency of factor allocation and specialization—has lagged.

Clearly the optimistic conclusions of the CGE models regarding the measurable, positive impact of economic openness on economic performance have not been supported by the real-world evidence.

Recent CGE Models of Deep Integration

One would think that the questionable assumptions and dubious predictive record of CGE free trade models would spark a much more cautious approach to the use of this interesting but disembodied economic tool—on the part of both the modellers themselves and the policy makers who rush to use their predictions in the next political skirmish over trade policy. Unfortunately, the reverse seems to be true. The failure of the post–free trade economy to validate the predictions of CGE models seems to have encouraged some modellers to push the envelope even further in search of elusive trade gains. This pattern is evident in recent CGE models that have been developed to simulate the impacts of deeper continental economic integration in North America. The findings of three such models are summarized in table 3.[161]

The most cautious of the models was developed by an American team.[163] They simulate the establishment of a common external tariff by the three NAFTA members. They assume that the three countries set a common tariff on imports from outside of NAFTA equal to an average of the three countries' existing tariff rates (with that average calculated according to different methods: simple mean, trade-weighted, and production-weighted). This common external tariff is held to reduce the "diversion" of trade under NAFTA, and produces very small gains in welfare in most scenarios (although in the Canadian case welfare losses could occur, depending on exactly *how* the tariffs were averaged). The model, like most in the CGE tradition, assumes full employment, national product differentiation, and no international

Table 10-3

CGE Estimates of the Economic Effects of North American Deep Integration: Summary Results, Change in Welfare or GDP *(percent of GDP)*

Modellers	Scenario	Canada	US	Mexico
Brown, Deardorff, and Stern (2001)	Common external tariff	-0.11 to +0.26	+0.01 to +0.15	+0.16 to +0.64
Ghosh and Rao (2005)	Common external tariff and removal of rules of origin	+1.07 to +1.09	+0.11 to +0.12	+4.24 to +4.25
Papadaki, Merette, Lan, and Hernandez (2006)	Common external tariff and removal of unobserved trade costs	+5.94 to +7.15	+0.19	

Source: Author's compilation from sources indicated.[162] Each modelling group simulated multiple trade liberalization scenarios, and hence the range of estimates corresponding to the indicated scenario is reported.

capital mobility. It allows for imperfect competition and increasing returns to scale. The model does not explicitly attempt to simulate the elimination of rules of origin. This model seems to indicate that, economically at least, deeper North American integration is a non-event.

Canadians with a desire for closer economic ties with the United States have criticized this model for its infinitesimal predicted effects.[164] And conveniently, more ambitious gains from deep integration initiatives are predicted by two modelling groups associated with federal government agencies. One model developed at Industry Canada makes a novel effort to capture the predicted economic gains resulting from the removal of NAFTA's rules of origin.[165] It is a standard CGE model incorporating full employment, constant returns to scale, and a Cobb-Douglas production function (with constant factor income shares). It explicitly models the economy's adjustment path (and finds that adjustment is mostly complete after just two to three years). It even allows for a very limited, counterintuitive form of capital mobility: each country's single representative household is allowed to borrow on international markets if it determines that it wants to invest more (in malleable putty capital) than its current savings allow. But the model does not explicitly model business investment decisions, nor does it allow for international capital mobility at that level.

The model begins by estimating the impact of moving to a common external tariff—in this case not by averaging the tariff, but by moving either to the lowest level (of the three countries, within each tariff category) or to the US level (which, on average for Canada, is also equivalent to a tariff reduction). This reduction in NAFTA tariffs against offshore imports sparks a slight boost in trade and hence a tiny improvement in GDP (equal to less than one-tenth of 1 percent of Canadian GDP).[166] The more interesting feature of this model is its effort to estimate the costs of NAFTA's rules of origin. Here the authors simply assume that an "upper bound" to those costs might be the prevailing most-favoured-nation tariff rates; any higher than that, and traders would not bother applying for the preferential NAFTA rate (since it would cost more to apply for those rates than would be saved by qualifying for the special NAFTA rate). The authors provide no direct evidence for the proposition that rules of origin might actually impose costs that high; in fact, the actual administrative burden of NAFTA rules of origin is certainly far smaller than this assumed upper bound.[167]

Eliminating this burden results in an average tariff reduction of 2.1 percentage points for Canada, 0.6 points for the United States, and 5.7 points for Mexico. (It is worth noting that Canada's actual trade-weighted effective tariff rate on imports from within NAFTA, as implied within this model's database, is only about 0.7 percent;[168] this simulation therefore is equivalent to assuming that Canada's remaining small tariffs on intra-NAFTA imports are reduced to *less than zero*.)

This simulation sparks a relatively large increase in trade within NAFTA. Combined (in a full customs union) with the reduction in Canadian external tariffs to a harmonized lower level, this results in an increase in Canadian GDP of over 1 percent. This is as large as the gains that several of the earlier (constant-returns) CGE models predicted to result from NAFTA itself—implying either that CGE modellers are now "double-dipping" on a grand scale (predicting gains from the elimination of remaining marginal trade-related costs that are as great as the ones that were originally predicted from free trade itself), or that NAFTA's imposition of rules of origin wiped out most or all of the purported gains from that agreement. Either way, the model's predictions are exaggerated—a fact the authors themselves admit when they warn that their estimates should be interpreted, with caution, as an upper bound—and entirely contingent on the unproven claim that rules of origin within NAFTA impose costs on exporters equal to as much as 2–3 percent of their total shipments.

The simulated sectoral impacts of the elimination of a North American customs union in this model are also surprising. Canada's hard-pressed auto industry receives the largest boost in total output: a 28 percent gain in sectoral GDP, and major increases in employment and investment. Other manufacturing and technology industries also enjoy sizeable benefits, while the food and beverage industry contracts. These sectoral effects are driven by the curious interplay of the large assumed reductions in apparent rules of origin costs, the starting trade shares, and the Armington modelling assumption.

In the case of autos, the modellers have assumed that the "elasticity" of consumer choices with respect to national varieties is much stronger than in other sectors.[169] Thus the assumed reduction in rules of origin costs sparks large shifts in consumer preferences. Since in the base case Canada exports more autos to the rest of NAFTA than it imports from them, and those exports to the NAFTA market are large (relative to domestic Canadian purchases), this effect sparks a dramatic boost in our automotive production and net exports, and a shift of labour and capital from other, less productive sectors into the auto industry. But this prediction does not at all jive with the reality of North American automotive trade. This industry has been continentally integrated since 1965, with an extensive continental supply chain; almost all producers readily qualify for NAFTA's rules of origin; and the notion that those rules of origin could impose actual costs on exporters equal to NAFTA members' most-favoured-nation tariffs (2.5 percent for US imports, or 6.1 percent for Canadian imports) is not remotely credible.[170]

A second federal government modelling initiative takes this speculative effort to identify unexploited trade efficiencies to an even higher level.[171] This model is very traditional: it is static, incorporates full employment, constant returns to scale, fixed factor income shares, no capital mobility, and a fixed trade balance. It breaks Canada into three regions for the modelling (Canada East, Ontario, and Canada West). Like the Industry Canada model, this one begins by simulating the implementation of a common external tariff (again considering both a harmonization at the US level and a harmonization at the minimum NAFTA level), and the effects are similar (impact on Canadian GDP of about 0.01 percent—with a potentially negative impact in eastern Canada). The bigger effects occur when the modellers simulate the elimination of what they call "unobserved trade costs."

Their argument is that remaining trade frictions (including rules of origin, but also including many other factors—such as consumer preferences, border costs and delays, and the lack of a common currency) are inhibiting trade between Canada and the United States at levels below what would normally be expected, given the size and proximity of these two economies.[172] The authors postulate that this reflects the impact of unobservable trade costs, which could be eliminated under a full economic union between Canada and the United States (including a common currency).[173] To simulate this union, the modellers calibrate a tariff equivalent of the unobserved costs (based on the two-way structure of existing trade flows relative to what would be expected under gravity models, and the assumed strength of the Armington assumption). In the Canadian case, these unobserved "tariffs" range from 3 percent for non-electrical machinery to 45 percent in the case of wholesale trade. Unobserved US tariffs are somewhat smaller, ranging from 3 percent for transportation equipment to 17 percent for wholesale trade.[174] Then the model is re-solved with these unobserved tariffs set to zero.

Not surprisingly, the elimination of such large (but unobserved) tariffs sparks a dramatic surge in trade. Canadian exports grow by between 45 and 57 percent, and output grows by 1.3 to 2.8 percent of GDP. "Welfare" (measured by the inherent satisfaction that consumers attain from consuming the products they buy) grows by 6 to 7 percent. These are very significant positive effects. Remember, this model assumes constant returns to scale; it predicts economic benefits from "perfecting" integration between Canada and the United States many times larger than the predicted effects (in constant returns models) of Canada-US free trade in the first place. Again, these very optimistic findings are entirely contingent on the methodological choices of the modellers—who warn that their estimate reflects an upper bound estimate of the true impact of the unobserved trade costs.[175] Unfortunately, this expressed caution will not prevent those with a political interest in deep integration from citing these results with glee.

The sectoral impacts of the assumed removal of unobserved tariffs are strong but curious. Remember, in this model a small trade flow is interpreted as existence of an unobserved trade barrier. In a standard Armington world, every country produces its own varieties of each product; in the absence of trade barriers, we would expect roughly proportional two-way intra-industry trade flows in every sector. But where traditional "comparative advantage" (or what economists call inter-industry trade) specialization occurs, this should not be the case.

Consider, for example, exports of petroleum products from Western Canada. Western Canada exports a lot of petroleum products to the United States and imports very little. This simply reflects Western Canada's abundance of petroleum resources. Yet the International Trade Canada model interprets this relatively unbalanced trade flow as evidence of assumed but unobserved trade barriers that limit the *inflow* of petroleum products into Western Canada. In the counterfactual simulation, these barriers are removed—stimulating a dramatic (and utterly unbelievable) increase in petroleum imports to Western Canada (which grow by 263 percent in the simulated customs union).

Other resource-based industries, in which trade flows reflect natural specialization more than trade policy, also experience this seemingly perverse "anti-specialization" in the customs union scenario, running counter to what would normally be expected in comparative advantage specialization. Value-added industries (like transportation equipment, machinery, and other manufactures) experience less dramatic but still impressive gains in total trade, in response to the assumed reduction in (unobserved) trade costs. Canada is reducing its unobserved tariffs far more than the United States (since those tariffs were assumed to be significantly higher in the initial starting point in Canada). But in a full-employment model that asymmetry is not a problem, since the boost in Canada's imports due to its relatively greater tariff-reduction must be offset (in general equilibrium) by an exactly equivalent boost in our exports.

Both of these Canadian CGE models of deep integration incorporate interesting but extremely speculative and empirically unfounded assumptions regarding the nature of North American trade barriers which remain even under NAFTA. These assumptions are essential to their finding that significant economic gains will result from the removal of those remaining barriers (even the ones that we can't observe). The authors themselves are fully honest and transparent in reporting their methodology and warning readers clearly about the contingent nature of their findings. Yet it is not difficult to imagine that others will be less cautious in interpreting and promoting those results, in the politically charged debates regarding deep integration that are likely to occur over the coming years. References will be made (as they were during the earlier debates over the FTA and NAFTA) to an apparent consensus among economists that the gains from deeper integration will be "substantial." The true nature of these CGE exercises, and the far-fetched assumptions that they embody, will never make the newspaper headlines—but the apparent proof that deep integration will be significantly beneficial for Canada's economy likely will.

Conclusion

The predictions of economists, supported by the output of quantitative economic models (mostly CGE models), played an important role in the public debates that preceded the implementation of the FTA and the NAFTA. Those models were rooted in assumptions regarding the efficient, competitive behaviour of factor markets, the determinants of productivity, and the behaviour of foreign investment within an integrated continental economy that were unrealistic and one-sided. This tradition of modelling the impacts of trade liberalization in a one-sided and misleading manner continues in North America; indeed, the CGE models that have been developed to estimate the purported benefits of deep integration incorporate assumptions and methodological choices that are generally more unusual and questionable than those that were reflected in the initial NAFTA models.

A more balanced modelling approach would recognize that integration can have negative as well as positive economic impacts, depending on the interplay of demand, supply, and structural factors—and that the distribution of costs and benefits *within* a country (across different households) is an important variable. When demand-side issues (like unemployment) are considered in the model, then whether integration helps or hurts an economy depends on its absolute competitiveness in generating net exports and attracting net investment.

Policy makers and citizens alike would be better served if future trade liberalization initiatives were analyzed with the help of quantitative models that reflected a more open minded and situational perspective, guided by economists who are more even-handed in their treatment of international economic integration. Unfortunately, based on the experience of the initial CGE models designed to analyze deeper North American integration, this hope seems far-fetched. It will require a willingness by more economists to engage critically with the underlying assumptions of those models, and their uncertain real-world empirical relevance, before a more balanced and nuanced understanding of the impacts of trade liberalization will ever be constructed.

CHAPTER 11

Another Path for Canada

MAUDE BARLOW [176]

The world of geopolitics is in flux and facing four great questions: (1) how to deal with the proliferation of weapons, particularly nuclear weapons, and the stated intent of the Bush administration to weaponize space; (2) how to deal with deepening global poverty and injustice, particularly in the Third World; (3) how to end fundamentalist extremism, violence, and terrorism; and (4) how to acknowledge and deal with the ecological limits of the Earth, particularly climate change, and the coming energy and freshwater crises.

Each of these four great questions can be reframed as a question of security. In its war on terror, the Bush administration has adopted the narrowest possible definition of security. A world divided into good and evil can only be dealt with by identifying possible terrorists through massive data collection and border security in order to stop acts of terrorism before they occur. Scant attention is given to the fact that poverty and injustice, rampant in our world, are the breeding ground for fundamentalism and violence. The challenge before the world community now is to recast the notion of security to include the fundamental right to health and education, clean air and water, and peace and justice.

The heart of the deep integration debate is this: How will Canadians answer these great challenges? Will Canada take different positions than the US administration has taken? How much sovereign control will Canada have left at the end of the harmonization process now underway or as it is envisaged by the Canadian Council of Chief Executives? Are the answers of George Bush and his neoconservative hawks to these questions the answers most Canadians would choose? Will Canada help or hinder the call of the global civil society move to redefine security as the fundamental right of all peoples to economic, social, and environmental justice?

Global Security

The unprecedented escalation of nuclear weapons and preparations for the weaponization of space, coupled with the first-strike policy of the Bush administration, has set the stage for a new superpower conflict that threatens global security. Bush foreign policy now clearly rejects the constraints of collective security, the most effective vehicle for global security, in favour of the unilateral use of warfare.

Hardliners in the Bush administration are sounding the alarm about the growing economic and military power of China, leading some to believe that the United States could soon be entangled in conflict with the world's most populous nation.

Russia is rearming as well. In a November 17, 2004, speech to top-ranking commanders of the Russian armed forces, President Putin confirmed that Russia is "carrying out research and missile tests of state-of-the-art nuclear missile systems" and will "continue to build up firmly and insistently our armed forces, including the nuclear component." It is unreasonable to think that, as long as the United States maintains the legal right to presumptive strike, China and Russia would disarm. In fact, both have said that, if the United States builds toward weapons in space, their countries have no choice but to follow.

Many nations around the world are deeply concerned with this situation. The ending of the cold war presented the world with an opportunity for a new start. The Union of Concerned Scientists warns of the cooling of US-Russian relations and says that, by neglecting opportunities to negotiate with North Korea, choosing instead to deploy weapons aimed at that country, the United States is undermining the hopes of peace. The International Atomic Energy Agency warns that there has never been a more dangerous time. "An atomic war draws near." The Canadian ambassador to Moscow, Christopher Westdal, says the world is in "a race with catastrophe" and that the very survival of humanity is at stake.

The good news for the planet is the emergence of a massive civil society peace movement that brought out the biggest street protests in history in the run-up to the US invasion of Iraq. This movement has had a profound effect on governments around the world, including in Canada, where it forced Prime Minister Paul Martin to change his mind about joining the US ballistic missile defence program. The International Relations Centre predicts a new resolve by foreign nations, large and small, to confront US agendas that diverge from or intentionally undermine international law and multilateral rule.

Gradually, we can expect a more unified and clearly articulated counter-agenda by countervailing blocs of nations that insist on the importance of international treaties, reassert the primacy of diplomacy in settling security issues, and forge policy consensus around solutions that address the precarious state of the international economy and the impoverishment of many nations and communities.

Canada's role

This is a place where Canada could shine. It is unthinkable, given Canada's long history of promoting global security and disarmament, that it would be a party to the development of a system that is bleeding resources from health care, education, protection of children, and environmental defence around the world to build a dizzying array of horrific new weapons of mass destruction. Because of its tendency always to fall in line with the US agenda, Canada is missing the opportunity to assume a leadership role. The time is ripe for Canada to present a whole new global vision and make nuclear disarmament and the abolition of all weapons of mass destruction the top priority of its defence and foreign policies.

This would necessitate Canada taking on its own weapons industry. Canada is the seventh largest arms producer in the world, with annual sales of its ten largest contractors in the $2.5 billion range. Most are subcontractors to the US military, making Canada directly complicit in America's wars. A Canadian company, for example, manufactures the bullets used by US soldiers in Iraq. Project Ploughshares and the Canadian Council of Churches argue that Canada's military export control system must be improved by returning the management of the program to Foreign Affairs from Trade where it now resides; subjecting military exports to the United States to the same export permit requirements that apply to military exports to any other destination; tightening up export controls to states that are in violation of UN Security Council sanctions; fully disclosing information on the "end-users" of Canadian military exports; and taking leadership in promoting effective, legally binding international standards for the control of international military trade.

The war in Iraq clearly demonstrates that unilateral aggression and military might are not the way to stop terrorism or to promote world peace or good government. Nobel Laureate John

Polanyi says that Canadians are not comfortable with the aggressive military stance of the Bush administration because Canada is historically committed to the rule of international law. "This is the key to Canadian attitudes on both missile defence and the weaponization of space. One should not claim this as pure virtue," he writes. "It's to be expected that the weak will favour law. It was not King John but the nobles who insisted on the Magna Carta." Polanyi says the only global answer to this new arms race is restraint, but to have recourse to the restraint called law, one must acknowledge the supremacy of law. This is our global security challenge.

Social Security

Although economic globalization has recently been adopted by Europe, Canada, Japan, and some newly industrialized countries, it has really been a US-driven initiative from its inception. Having outgrown their domestic market, American corporations sought new global rules to limit the power of national governments to regulate trade and investment policies. They wanted a "level playing field" as they moved around the world in search of new business. Under the free-market doctrine known as the "Washington Consensus," countries around the world liberalized trade and foreign investment, deregulated their internal economies, and privatized public services, lowering social standards for many millions of their citizens in the process. United States–based globalization has been the primary instrument used by corporate America to dismantle and deregulate nation-state authority around the world.

The economic legacy of the Washington Consensus has been devastating. Its legacy in Latin America is unsustainable debt, feeble economic growth, and increased poverty. In 1980, 136 million Latin Americans suffered from poverty, of which 62 million suffered from extreme poverty. By 2003, reports the UN Economic

Commission on Latin America and the Caribbean, the number of Latin Americans living in poverty increased to 226 million, of which 100 million were living in extreme poverty. *The Economist* (November 6, 2003) was puzzled that twenty years of liberalization had failed to narrow the income gap in Latin America, where the richest tenth hold 48 percent of the wealth; the poorest tenth just 1.6 percent. And in Mexico, the number of people living in poverty has grown from 28 percent in 1984 to 50 percent in 2002, and those living in extreme poverty grew from 7 percent to 20 percent in the same years.[177]

Economic globalization has also created a wealthy consumer class in much of Asia, but has caused the majority to sink into deeper poverty. The *China Daily* reported that the income gap in China, once almost non-existent save for the ruling party, continues to widen dramatically, with the top tenth owning 45 percent of the wealth and the bottom tenth left with just 1.4 percent.[178]

Signs of the failure of globalization and US hegemony abound. Successive attempts to launch a new round of negotiations at the World Trade Organization—the principal institutional vehicle used to enforced globalization—were rejected by angry Third World delegates in Seattle in 1999 and again in Cancun, Mexico, in 2003; and the Free Trade Area of the Americas, intended to extend NAFTA to all of Central and South America, is all but dead. Latin America, in fact, is turning against US-style market capitalism as a failed experiment. Beginning with Venezuela in 1998, governments in Latin America's most important countries, including Brazil, Argentina, Uruguay, Bolivia, and Chile, have elected leftist governments. Mexicans could very well elect the popular leftist mayor of Mexico City, Andres Manuel Lopez Obrador, as their next president in the 2006 federal election. Citizen movements in Bolivia, Ecuador, Nicaragua, Costa Rica, El Salvador, and several other smaller countries of Latin America have literally taken over the streets, demanding justice and basic public services; and indigenous peoples in the region are becoming highly mobilized across nation-state borders in their demand for more political power.

The last five years have also witnessed the flowering of a civil society movement to provide alternatives to economic globalization and the military might that keeps it in place. The World Social Forum was created as a symbolic and political counterweight to the World Economic Forum where, every year, the CEOs of the world's one-thousand largest global corporations meet with heads of state in the town of Davos, Switzerland, during the last week of January. Where the World Economic Forum serves as an occasion for corporate and government elites to promote economic globalization, the World Social Forum, whose motto is "Another World Is Possible," brings literally thousands of grassroots civil society groups together to put forward alternative policies in the spheres of economics, international affairs, cultural diversity, human rights, social justice, and environmental stewardship.

Canada's role

Canadian governments appear untouched by this growing opposition to neoliberal economic policies. Starting with the Mulroney Conservatives, consecutive Canadian governments have increasingly not only adopted US economic globalization polices at home and abroad, but have taken the lead. Canada is now a leading advocate for unregulated free trade at the WTO and in the Americas, where its policies are virtually indistinguishable from those of the United States. Our Department of Foreign Affairs and International Trade has grown in power and now vets all potential new legislation for its implications on trade, creating what some call "policy chill." Canada's hard-earned former reputation as a force for good in the world is tarnished now by its positions on human rights, food security, and the privatization of essential social services in the Third World.

Canada supports World Bank and IMF policies to privatize essential social and public services such as health care and water in developing countries, much to the distress of many Canadian aid and development groups. While it is naïve to think the Harper minority government is going to do an about-face on these issues, Canadians wanting to define security in a broader context are going to have to work harder than ever to counter policies that are literally killing people in poor countries.

Canadian support for IMF/World Bank "structural adjustment" programs must end, and Canada must work as a force in the global community to reinstate essential public services around the world. This, of course, means fighting for them at home, and there is no more urgent domestic agenda for Canadians than preserving publicly funded health care. While all Canadians deplore the long waiting lists for certain surgeries, it is imperative that energies go into the fight to reduce these wait times and not into destroying Medicare. Unless Canadians fight now and fight hard for public health, US health corporations are going to move into Canada and there will no longer be American health care and Canadian health care; there will be North American heath care built on the privatized two-tier American model.

Finally, Canadians must demand a review of trade policy. The US government refuses to abide by the terms of NAFTA, and this gives Canada the opening to rewrite it and remove the most egregious provisions—or, failing that, to abrogate the agreement. At the very least, water must be exempted from NAFTA and all other trade agreements; Chapter 11, which allows corporations to sue governments, must be removed; and the energy provisions of the deal must be rewritten or removed altogether. Canada needs to take a thorough assessment of what twenty years of neoliberal policy and trade agreements have done to Canadians and to people around the world. Fundamental to this assessment should be a commitment to finally bring labour, social, and environmental groups into the process instead of playing lip service to civil society while listening only to the big business community. As well, the right of each nation to develop and protect its own institutions and standards must be respected.

Human Security

Fundamentalism, extremism, violence, and terrorism are on the rise around the world. The world community must ask now not only how to protect innocent people from random acts of terror, but why there are people who would kill like this and who are even prepared to give their own lives in the service of killing. The first, most important step, however, is to be clear about the nature of the problem.

First, the current spate of terrorist attacks are not the result of a conflict between Muslims and Christians or between East and West, as it is so often characterized. The conflict that results in such attacks is between moderates and fundamentalists. Terrorists are not obeying some basic tenets of Islam; rather, they have distorted the teachings of their religion. These acts of violence have been committed by an extremely small group of people and are contrary to the values and faith-based beliefs of the great majority of Muslims. The fact is that there are fundamentalists in the West, as well. While it is true that Christian evangelicalism does not teach its followers to go out and kill, it does divide the world into sinners and believers and almost joyfully awaits the fate that will befall those who do not accept faith on its terms. What can be said of the sects of evangelical Christianity who believe that, at Armageddon, the entire population of Israel will be forced to choose between accepting Jesus Christ as their personal saviour or perishing in horrible ways?

Fundamentalist movements in both the Middle East and the United States work in mutually enforcing ways to resist peaceful solutions as they share a world-view of absolutes. Adopting a Christian versus Muslim, or East versus West, analysis creates an atmosphere of us versus them. For the vast majority of Muslims who are moderate, these are terrible times and their sense of isolation in North America and Europe is growing. This is not the way to stop the spread of the fundamentalism that breeds the violence.

Second, terrorism is not an act of war; it is a criminal act and must be treated as such. A war needs a clearly defined enemy. Calling its military aggression a "war on terror" allows the Bush administration to characterize whole countries and peoples as evil and justify its military interventions. That is how Bush and Cheney got buy-in for the invasion of Iraq. They falsely connected Saddam Hussein to al-Qaeda and convinced the American people that they were officially at war with Iraq and that invasion was just the next logical step.

Third, there are indeed root causes of some of the hate that fuels these crimes. It is possible, indeed imperative, to detest the crime and respond to it in the strongest possible way, while at the same time still seeking to find ways to change the conditions that breed such hate. It is not something that the Bush/Cheney team wants to hear, but the anger raging in so many poor and troubled parts of the world can be traced back to economic and military policies that have deliberately allowed some individuals and corporations to reap the wealth of the world while billions live in poverty and ecosystems crash.

William Shultz, executive director of Amnesty International, reports that the gross product of all Arab countries together is less than that of Spain. One in five Arabs lives on less than two US dollars a day. In Arab countries, unemployment averages around 20 percent; in Egypt, it reaches 55 percent, and in Saudi Arabia, nearly 60 percent. No wonder millions of poor unemployed young Arab men "look with sympathy" on political and religious extremists. Feminist scholar Peggy Antrobus points out that, when governments are forced to get out of the business of looking after the needs of their people, either because they are poor or because of IMF-enforced structural adjustment programs, religious institutions often move in to fill the void and provide religious teachings along with food, education, and health care. Young people in these situations are particularly vulnerable to fundamentalist and extremist teachings and become a ready supply of soldiers and suicide bombers.

The good news for humanity is that many governments seem to finally understand the need to broaden the definition of security if they are to counter terrorism. At a mid-July 2005 Toronto conference of international security and emergency experts from more than fifty countries, officials called for a dramatic rethinking of the global strategy on terrorism. Experts said that the world hasn't done a good enough job of understanding and tackling the "disenchantment that is the root cause" of terrorism. They argued that the morphing of al-Qaeda into a global movement that is increasingly attracting new recruits warrants a "challenge on the assumption of the war on terror." Former Scotland Yard anti-terror expert Peter Power said that the West must embark on a new campaign for the hearts and minds of Muslims, especially the young, and to critically re-examine government policies to find out if they are feeding the fires of hatred in the Muslim world.

Canada's role

This is another opportunity for Canada to take a stand. There is clearly a new openness in the world once again to a fresh definition of security and a new way of understanding terrorism. Canada has taken leadership in this arena before. During the 1990s, reports Steven Staples of the Polaris Institute, Canada helped shape the post–cold war environment by promoting the rule of international law. Canada was instrumental in the creation of both the International Criminal Court and the United Nations Landmines Treaty. Then foreign affairs minister Lloyd Axworthy attempted to redefine security by promoting peace-keeping skills in the Canadian Forces and developing the doctrine of human security, which places people and their human rights at the centre of security policy, rather than states.

It was always hard slugging to try to get the United States onside with such an agenda, Staples notes, but it became impossible after George Bush was elected. He points to a post-9/11 Department of National Defense (DND) document that correctly predicted a global shift away from "championing poverty eradication and human rights." The report foresaw that the rule of international law would be cast aside in the war on terror, adding, "The international system will be re-ordered into allies or enemies in the fight against terror." The predictions made in the DND report were chillingly accurate, and the results of returning to the hard military solution are now clear for all to see.

The question for Canada, once again, is one of independence. Will Canada have the courage to reject the hard US model of military security and take leadership in the global community in redefining the fight against terrorism in a broader context? If it is true that US hegemony is making the world more violent and less stable, does Canada not have an obligation to take a different path? Roch Tasse of the International Civil Liberties Monitoring Group, which, like many groups in Canada, has urged a rollback of the new laws in Canada that threaten the civil liberties of Canadians, is very clear in his counsel: "Canada's response to terrorism must be rooted in the rule of law, with an emphasis on international law and the use of multilateral institutions, including the Criminal Court; in democratic development and good governance; in respect for human rights and civil liberties; and ultimately in social justice and the eradication of poverty as the only way to truly confront terrorism."

Ecological Security

If anything is going to limit the supposedly infinite possibilities of economic globalization, it will be the Earth itself. Humans have destroyed more forests, wetlands, and wild spaces in the last hundred years than in all of history put together. The highly regarded journal *Science* reports that recent extinction rates are 100 to 1,000 times higher than before humans existed, but says that, with the exponential extinction now being experienced, that rate could increase to between 1,000 and 10,000 times higher by the end of the century. Smithsonian Institution biologist Jonathan Coddington predicts a "biodiversity deficit" within this century, whereby species and ecosystems will be destroyed at rates faster than Nature can create new ones. Eighty percent of the oceans' large fish are gone. The United Nations Environment Program reports that only one-fifth of the planet is still covered with sustainable forests and that few of those are protected by governments. Over half of the world's wetlands have been lost over the last century; in Asia alone, more than 5,000 square kilometres are destroyed every year to make way for industrialization.

And greenhouse gas emissions are due to reach double pre-industrial levels by 2080, enough to lead to an increase in warming similar to the increase that melted the Ice Age. Phasing out fossil fuel use would require a different model for the Earth than the current model of unrestricted, unregulated growth. Even if humanity does not voluntarily phase out fossil fuels, it is soon going to be facing major limitations due to coming energy shortages.

The world is also running out of clean water. With every passing day, our demand for fresh water outpaces its availability, and thousands more people are put at risk. Per capita water use doubles every twenty years—and we will add another 2.6 billion people to the planet in the next quarter century. As well, technology and advanced sanitation systems in the global north have allowed people to use—and waste—far more water than they need, while lack of funding for sanitation in the Third World ensures that 90 percent of the sewage and wastewater is poured untreated into waterways.

The legacy of factory farming, flood irrigation, the construction of massive dams, toxic dumping, wetlands and forest destruction, and urban and industrial pollution has damaged the Earth's surface water so badly that we are now mining underground water reserves far faster than Nature can replenish them. Using massive new technology, ancient aquifers are being drained or destroyed by pollution.

Finally, the model of unlimited growth is destroying food and biological diversity in the name of science and profit. Genetically engineered foods are contaminating local seeds and crops, invading wild species, and destroying biodiversity. Transnational corporations, using the intellectual property rights of the WTO, are plundering the biological heritage of the Third World. Indian activist and physicist Vandana Shiva calls this practice "biopiracy" and compares it to the conquest and colonization of the New World by Spain and the other powers of Europe five-hundred years ago. "The land, the forests, the rivers, the oceans, and the atmosphere have all been colonized, eroded, and polluted. Capital now has to look for new colonies to invade and exploit for its further accumulation. These new colonies are, in my view, the interior spaces of the bodies of women, plants and animals."

If nothing else will do it, surely these stunning realities will wake up a sleeping elite. Right now, the system of economic globalization and the ecological limits of the planet are on a collision course. The only way to cope with current and impending ecological crises is to change our economic systems and political models and build new ones around the dictates of the natural world. Richard Heinberg teaches sustainable ecology at New College in Santa Rosa, California. He has been warning about what he calls the "petroleum plateau" for several years and describes two paths to deal with the coming energy crisis: Plan War and Plan Powerdown. By merely maintaining its current course, says Heinberg, the world is heading toward Plan War in which some parts of the world will start to run out before others, and those with military might will use their wealth and power to protect supplies for themselves, wasting precious resources that could have been used for conservation.

Plan Powerdown obviously calls for an international effort toward conservation and cooperation in reducing non-essential energy use, which will need political will at the highest level. Alternative energy sources that are not currently competitive with fossil fuels would have to be subsidized, and the use of fossil fuels taxed to encourage their conservation. Economic processes would have to be localized and downsized.

Canada's role

While Heinberg is only referring to energy here, there is little question that the world is on a Plan War footing environmentally. What is clearly needed is "Plan Rejuvenation" for the Earth, and most Canadians would be thrilled to see their country lead or join such a campaign. But this would require Canada to address its own severe shortcomings.

First and perhaps foremost, Canada must abandon the Smart Regulation initiative and commit to a regime of rules and standards to ensure the safety of Canada's food and drug supply, as well as clean air and water for generations to come. Cathy Holtslander of Beyond Factory Farming says that regulations are the "nuts and bolts" of sovereignty and are designed to create fairness, protect people's health and safety, and set limits on unacceptable behaviour. To give them up is to give up the right to self-determination. All of the policies now being drafted that would undermine the safety of Canada's supply of food, seeds, and drugs must be abandoned, and the precautionary principle must be placed at the centre of the rules governing these sectors. The National Farmers Union says that Canadians need a publicly funded, publicly controlled plant breeding system to protect their food supply. Shiv Chopra says simply that Canada must immediately rid the food supply of hormones, antibiotics, Genetically Modified Organisms, rendered protein, and pesticides.

Canada also must do better in honouring its Kyoto commitment, which also means that Environment Canada must abandon its Smart Regulation–inspired "Framework" project and return to its role as the most important protector of Canada's ecosystem. It is a potential mistake of monumental proportions for the department to exchange its monitoring and enforcement role for a voluntary "partnership" with big business, including, or perhaps especially, with the energy sector. Plans for the Mackenzie Valley pipeline should be scrapped, and a moratorium placed on further development of the Alberta tar sands while a full assessment is made of both the environmental impacts of tar sands development and the political and economic ramifications of American control of these resources. A fixation with the energy and military needs of the United States has limited Canada's vision and potential.

As Sierra Club Canada's Elizabeth May says,

> Canada has a place in the world distinct from our proximity to the United States. Our geographical placement alongside the declining and decaying empire to the South has the magnetic force of economic clout, but the True North for Canada is to the pole. Our destiny

lies far more in our planetary role as a circumpolar nation. We must increasingly make common cause with the other Arctic nations. We must be a voice for radical reductions in North American dependency on fossil fuels, or we risk losing ice cover at the North Pole altogether. We risk losing the polar bear, the permafrost, the Peary caribou, the way of life of the traditional peoples, the Dene, the Inuit, the Gwich'in— indeed, we risk destroying life on Earth. We cannot have our SUVs and polar bears, too.

Similarly, Canada must take action to protect its freshwater supplies, and this must happen soon. Canada needs a National Water Policy, which would include an exemption for water from NAFTA and all other present and future trade and investment treaties; recognition of the human right to water; binding rules to stop corporations and factory farms from abusing fresh water; a moratorium on all new diversions from the Great Lakes and other shared boundary waters; a prohibition against the privatization of public water; and rules to protect Canada's groundwater sources. As well, the Boundary Waters Treaty must be revised to include all waters of the Great Lakes Basin, including groundwater and tributaries; increase bi-national control over use and diversion of the Lakes; adopt ecological integrity and the precautionary principle as the cornerstones of the Treaty; and establish the priority of that agreement in the event of conflicts with international trade agreements. If the United States does not want to enter into these kinds of negotiations, Canada should reassert its sovereign right to its own energy resources and withhold or reduce energy exports.

Finally, to become eligible to take international environmental leadership, Canada must clean up the disgraceful practices of its mining industry in other countries. Canada is the world's leading mineral exploration nation and the leading supplier of capital for the mining industry worldwide. MiningWatch Canada reports that 64 percent of the world's mining companies are based in Canada and that Canadian companies hold interest in a portfolio of almost 2,800 mineral properties located outside of Canada. Almost half of the $12.7 billion in equity financing raised for mineral exploration and development projects every year is for companies listed on Canadian stock exchanges. "The expansion of Canadian mining overseas has been accompanied by some of the world's worst environmental disasters, the forced relocation of indigenous peoples, and numerous human rights abuses," says the watchdog group. The irresponsible mining practices of Canadian companies are facilitated by financial polices and practices in Canada. Tax credits and subsidies enabling the write-off of foreign exploration and development expenses against income and corporate tax are some of the most generous in the world.

The Export Development Corporation provides export credits, loans, and political risk insurance, with no human rights framework, no disclosure, and ineffective environmental policy. Canadian stock exchanges have no environmental or human rights requirements. Says MiningWatch, "Action is needed to hold Canadian mining companies and the Canadian government to account. Mining companies are too often the 'ugly Canadian' in their complicity in human rights abuses and environmental disasters when they operate abroad."

How the government of Canada answers these great questions of our time depends on whose counsel it seeks. So far, it is listening almost exclusively to the Canadian Council of Chief Executives and its think tank allies. The CCCE does not speak for Canada. It speaks for the interests of its members, many of which are branch-plants of American corporations. It is past time for the Canadian government to seek the counsel of other sectors in society. Civil society organizations concerned with human rights, health care, social justice, poverty, working people, education, international development, cultural diversity, conservation, and the environment would have a very different set of priorities. They would tell the prime minister that they want to be good neighbours and help secure safe borders. But they would warn him to back away from this process of deep integration with the Bush administration and get on with the job he was elected to do: protecting the lives and livelihoods of Canadians.

Joining the Bush Revolution would be a terrible mistake for Canada. A far better choice would be seeking out and working with the many millions of Americans who are equally appalled at their government and the triumvirate who brought George Bush to power. They are hard at work forming an effective opposition to the Bush administration and need support in building a different base for a future North America.

This is not a call to put up borders around Canada or to claim moral superiority. The world has some very serious problems that need to be addressed. Canada must decide if it is going to forge deeper economic, foreign policy, social, and resource ties with the world's superpower under its most aggressive government in modern history, or if it is going to stand with moderate countries and people around the world to form a counterweight.

The world will take note of what Canada decides.

PART II

CHAPTER 12

Cooperation Without Capitulation

ED BROADBENT

We now face an overriding challenge as a nation: the deep integration threat. Such an economic and political surrender to the imperial power of the United States is not inevitable, nor are the moves already made in that direction irreversible. Like the policies that have created two Canadas, one for the rich and one for the rest of us, it is a matter of choice. And the choice that has been proposed to us by the right is the wrong choice. Canadians deserve better than to have their future options framed as inevitabilities.

It is not inevitable that the levers of our economic, environmental, and security structures will be so linked with those of the United States that we cede our capacity to act in our own interests, guided by our own values. The culture of inevitability is one that explicitly denies citizens the right to make a choice. It pretends there are no rational alternatives.

Our challenge in the years ahead must be to make clear to Canadians that there *is* a real alternative to the stripped-down, neoliberal model of citizenship so favoured by the political right in this country, and so deeply entrenched in the United States.

In the aftermath of the 2005 Waco summit of the three NAFTA leaders, Paul Martin, George Bush, and Vicente Fox, we asked in the House of Commons about the deep integration plans so plainly laid out for Canadians by the Canadian Council of Chief Executives and former deputy prime minister John Manley. We were told it wasn't true. But we shouldn't forget that this is the John Manley who has repeatedly advocated the further blurring of sovereignty.

Choosing to succumb to an even tighter American embrace is clearly the wrong choice—not because a close trading relationship with our powerful southern neighbour is bad, per se, but because a continental economy designed mainly to serve the interests of global transnational corporations is bad. It is bad because it opens valuable Canadian resources to corporate exploitation while exposing Canadians to the erosion of social and economic rights, a process that has made the United States the most unequal industrial nation in the world. The Americanization of Canada would lead to a further widening of the gap between our rich and poor, as well as the deterioration of our environment.

It does not suffice, however, simply to register our opposition. The leaders of the right would have us believe that they are the provider of solutions, while the left is portrayed as Dr. No. This is patently false. As a people, we can and do have differences among us on many key issues, from Medicare to child care, from Iraq to the new International Criminal Court and same-sex marriage. We Canadians are proud of our more progressive policies, our more inclusive concept of citizenship. But we cannot afford to be self-deluding. It is true, for example, that we are more egalitarian, and that we have a more socially just concept of citizenship. But, while our governments amassed over $60 billion in surpluses over the past decade, 1.1 million Canadian children still got up in the morning poor, went to school poor, and went to bed poor at night.

We had over $60 billion accumulated in government coffers, and yet many thousands of Canadians right across the country still live in what can only be described as horrible housing conditions.

We also tend to believe, self-righteously, that Canada is greener because our federal government has ratified the Kyoto Protocol [since renounced by the Harper Conservatives] while US President Bush has not. Yet, as the NAFTA Environmental Commission has pointedly reminded us, Canada's record on toxic pollution is demonstrably *worse* than that of the United States. Ours has risen by 5 percent while the United States has reduced its pollution rate by 14 percent.

Keeping a sharp eye on our own reality is not only important and to be done for its own sake, but it can also be useful in pursuing our bilateral relationship with the United States. Integral to that relationship is a recognition that half of the Americans who cast their ballots in the 2004 presidential election voted *against* George W. Bush. Integral, too, is a recognition that sometimes they are more progressive than we are. Demonizing the United States and all its citizens can be self-defeating, since it too often prevents the real policy debates that we require in Canada. Just as we based our Canada Pension Plan thirty years ago on the still superior US model, so, too, can we learn from many American environmental initiatives that surpass ours—from California's emission standards to the EPA's record on toxic site cleanups.

We should be working with progressive American states to clean the air we all share. In many cases, we have to play catch-up—to California, for example. We may rightly deplore the election of Arnold Schwarzenegger as governor, but even under his regime California enforces a regulatory schedule on emissions that mandates steady reductions in automotive pollution. Despite our ongoing efforts in the House of Commons, Canada still does not have a comparable set of mandatory regulations on vehicle emissions.

Even when there is a body like the International Joint Commission that exists to protect our common freshwater resources, Canada—that is to say, our government—often refuses to make use of it to guard against incidents when American policy is demonstrably worse than our own. Such was the case with the Devils Lake project in North Dakota, which threatens Manitoba's Red River ecosystem with new and harmful organisms. Despite immense and continuing pressure from the Manitoba government and the NDP in Parliament, the former Liberal government refused to refer the Devils Lake dispute to the International Joint Commission (IJC)—a refusal that was nothing short of a national disgrace.

Rather than considering policies for further integration with the United States, government should be using the instruments of existing bilateral institutions that are now available to them, if they only had the courage and the political will to do so.

The solution to the failure of the NAFTA dispute settlement mechanism to bring justice to our softwood producers is not to engage in a more draconian integration of our two economies. Rather, it should be to revitalize the notion of an industrial strategy for this country. British Columbia and northern Ontario, for example, would make more economic progress by processing lumber in logging communities than by increasing the export of raw logs, as would inevitably happen under the greater-integration proposals.

In industrial communities in both Canada and the United States, outsourcing is harming workers and the communities in which they live. The textile industry is rapidly being eviscerated in the United States, and has become an endangered species in Canada, as the recent closure of mills in Huntingdon, Quebec, tragically demonstrates.

Production is being shifted not simply to other countries but to countries that totally refuse to comply with international human rights law, including the right to form a union, and which ignore International Labour Organization minimal health and safety standards. This injustice is being aided and abetted by large corporations like Wal-Mart, which gleefully exploit workers both at home and abroad. Rather than pursue an economic policy of deeper integration with the United States, we should be making common cause with progressive Americans—and also with Europeans, Japanese, and Koreans, who are just as vulnerable as we are to the corporations' race-to-the bottom pursuit of cheap labour, low taxes, and inferior environmental protection laws.

Many working Canadians and Americans may not have agreed on whether or not to go to war in Iraq, but they could and should cooperate in building a global trading system in which competitive success does not depend on the denial of basic human rights. Winning competition in fair and decent human circumstances is one thing; winning competition based on the degradation of human beings is quite another.

Those calling for the even deeper integration of our two countries also favour a major change for NORAD. NORAD does provide a security service to both countries in monitoring the airspace we share, but, in terms of security, it should not be expanded into a multi-service defence command. This proposed further reduction of Canadian sovereignty is neither necessary nor desirable. [The Conservative government recently agreed to expand NORAD to cover maritime command.]

There are areas in which we should work closely with the United States—on our oceans, for example, where the two countries'

Coast Guards cooperate today to save lives and stop drug smuggling. And we should have sensible border cooperation with proper border infrastructure because that is what good neighbours need and do.

The Canada that was criticized in Amnesty International's recent report is not the Canada that Canadians want. But if our business and political elites get their way, it is the Canada that we will get, complete with an integrated military structure, more pollution, and trade agreements that ignore the rights of workers and inflict environmental damage on communities.

My proposals are not derived from a jingoistic, nationalist perspective. Rather, they are based on a patriotism that is deeply felt and grounded on the core values of social democracy.

Canada is indeed a different society from the United States. While holding a strong commitment to the autonomy of individuals, we have an equal commitment to cooperation and social equality. It is no accident that Canada has—or that the United States has not—ratified the UN Covenant on Social, Economic and Cultural Rights. Most Canadians, whether they use the term or not (and as every serious social science survey confirms), are social democrats.

To preserve our legacy of more broadly based social justice, we need no further integration with the United States of America. We need the clarity of vision and courage of conviction that sees cooperation to be desirable, but independence for Canada to be essential.

CHAPTER 13

Navigating Canada-US Relations in the Twenty-First Century

LLOYD AXWORTHY

Central to a progressive political agenda is the issue of how we come to grips with sharing North America with the United States—and how we make sure we preserve our space, our culture, and our sovereignty.

I was recalling recently at a family event how my brother Tom and I were recruited back in the 1960s by that legendary Liberal rainmaker, Keith Davey, to come to Ottawa to get involved in the monumental struggle then raging in the Liberal party between Walter Gordon and Mitchell Sharp over the issue of foreign ownership.

I vividly recall lining up at microphones in the Chateau Laurier, beginning at four o'clock in the afternoon and going till one o'clock in the morning, where cabinet ministers got up and argued with young Liberals in a long, knock-down, dragged-out debate. A vote was finally held in the wee hours, which the nationalist Gordon forces lost by seven votes, but it was an opportunity to be engaged, to be connected, to have your say, and it was one of the watersheds in establishing a set of public policies that were going to open up a further level of economic integration.

Of course, later, in the 1988 election, we reached the other watershed in the free trade debate. Since I was the spokesperson for our party on trade matters at that time, I got into the trenches because it was an issue that went deep into your vitals and what you believed in. Again, the outcome was not of my choosing, but at least it was a hard-fought national debate in which millions of Canadians enthusiastically participated. The political system provided that opportunity for both sides of the free trade issue to get actively engaged.

I think we are at a similar watershed now, perhaps an even more pivotal one. You have to measure yourself sometimes by the political periods that you go through, and I see the current political context as crucial for those of us who want to preserve our country's independence. We have a minority government and we have a powerful alliance among elite groups of think tanks and academics and business lobbyists and mandarins in Ottawa who, without much debate or transparency, are trying to force an integrationist, continentalist agenda upon us.

I published a book in 2004, *Navigating a New World*, which necessitated my taking what is laughingly called a book tour. It consisted mainly of going on radio hotline shows at 6:00 a.m. and, somewhere between the hockey scores and the weather, talking about globalization for thirty-three seconds. But it did give me a chance to meet with Canadians from coast to coast, and I could feel this enormous sense of national pride and confidence. It was clear to me that Canadians—especially the younger ones—are no longer tugging the forelock and shuffling the feet when it comes to their relationship with the United States. They're not deferential. They don't buy the continentalist line that we should simply turn the keys over to the Americans. But they are looking for an agenda, for alternatives.

I think what has caused this particular sort of questing by so many Canadians is that the issue of Canadian sovereignty in the post-9/11 era has been connected with the issue of security. The two have been intermixed and argued to the point where the forces of integration are claiming much closer ties with the United States are needed because only the United States has the resources to protect Canadians from terrorists. A lot of fear has been generated, providing a rationale for the thirty-two-step proposal for integration that John Manley signed, and which the business and media pundits hailed as a great hallmark of cross-border cooperation.

In fact, as it ended up, when you begin to dig into the bowels of it, there is a lot going on behind the scenes that nobody knows about. Freedom of information access is not available, not even to Parliament. There is no oversight, no transparency. As a result, decisions are being made without public or even government awareness. Take the Maher Arar case, which came to light thanks only to a concerned group of human rights activists. We learned that his arrest and deportation to Syria by the Americans was not simply a matter of a mistake made by some consul general in New York, but that there was active complicity by Canadian security officials who were acting on their own with the authority given them by Canada's new national security laws.

So we now have this layer of security integration overlaid on top of the long-standing trend toward economic integration. The economic argument has been that we have to keep the trucks rolling; now we have a second line of argument that, because we are threatened by international terrorists, we have to link up with the US anti-terrorist apparatus. This means emulating the US "homeland security" restraints on civil liberties and greatly increasing government powers to bypass due process, invade privacy, arrest and detain people indefinitely without charge, and curb other rights and liberties that Canadians had previously taken for granted.

What we are seeing as a result of this overlay of security issues is that we are now putting in jeopardy our Charter of Rights and Freedoms. The Charter is in danger of being eroded in ways that are hard to see and hard to control. The 2005 *International Policy Review* cites the need to defend ourselves from terrorism as being one of our prime objectives. I don't disagree with that. There is a real threat, and we would be naïve and foolhardy to ignore it. But the question is whether we accept a made-in-Washington definition of what the terrorist threat really is, and, more importantly, whether we accept and adopt the kinds of measures they have taken to respond to it, or devise our own made-in-Canada response.

The debate in Canada has been distorted by the widely held belief that an effective response to the terrorist threat is to greatly increase our defence spending. I don't dispute the need for a more effective defence force, but we have to be careful what we're spending these extra defence billions on, and for what purpose. Surely it's not merely a matter of putting more brigades in the field and leaving it to the generals to decide how and why they are to be deployed. As a result, you pick up the *Globe and Mail* one morning and learn that our new defence chief is establishing a staging base in the Arab Emirates from which to operate our JP-2s. Wait a minute. Who decided that? Why are we all of a sudden getting into a war-fighting mode without any rules of engagement, and without any definition? And why is it all being justified on the basis of buying into Washington's belief that the best—if not only—response for Canada to the terrorist threat should be a military one?

We have to be careful about the terms we use when we talk about defence. Our military stress the need for what they call a rapid reaction capacity, but why is Canada rapidly reacting militarily to Afghanistan and not to Somalia? The answer lies with a whole series of decisions that are being made internally and with hardly any debate.

Canada used to be foremost among the nations that committed troops to UN peacekeeping missions. We now stand at a dismal forty-fifth on the list. Why? Because our military are opposed to continuing in a strong peacekeeping role. They prefer instead to fight alongside the Americans wherever the United States decides to conduct its "war on terror." That is not the kind of "defence" policy space that I think Canada should be occupying, because it derives from a political/military strategy devised in Washington, not in the House of Commons in Ottawa.

Putting it into the broader context of Canada-US relations, I see it as another feature of what could be called à la carte bilateralism. We have carefully negotiated about 270 treaties with the Americans over the last one-hundred years, including NAFTA, but now the United States under its current administration is picking and choosing which of these treaties it will abide by and which it will ignore, depending on what it perceives as being in its narrow national interest.

Take, for example, the Devils Lake dispute, which should have been settled by being referred to the International Joint Commission. But Condoleezza Rice and the US State Department didn't want to risk having the Commission work out a settlement that the Americans might not like. It didn't suit their purpose and might not have served their interests, so they acted arbitrarily to have the Devils Lake diversion go ahead regardless of the adverse environmental and health consequences for Manitoba.

They didn't negotiate, they didn't apologize, they just acted as if the Joint Commission didn't exist. Here we have this great agency that we jointly created to peacefully resolve border disputes through a set of agreed-upon treaties, resolutions, and standards, and we face a US administration that brushes it all aside because it won't accept any restraints on its power to take unilateral action.

This is the same disdain and arrogance that is being displayed in disregarding many other international treaties, in refusing to support an International Criminal Court, in appointing a UN-basher like John Bolton as US ambassador to the United Nations. We Canadians are understandably upset by these and other high-handed actions and policies of the current US administration, but we should always keep in mind that they do not reflect the sentiments of a great many—perhaps even a majority—of American citizens. It would be a mistake to indulge in indiscriminate anti-Americanism. It is absolutely essential to begin engaging actively with our counterparts in the United States on these crucial issues, because they are as dismayed and frustrated as we are about what their government is doing.

The Internet offers a tremendous medium for this kind of international collaboration. I recently became aware of this when I wrote and posted a cheeky "Dear Condy" letter to the US Foreign Secretary. Suddenly I found myself in twelve-hundred blogs and getting an average of fifty to seventy-five responses a day, 90 percent of them from Americans. It struck me forcibly that here was a new and powerful way to connect, link up, ally, and debate with Americans who share our concerns about their political, corporate, and media elites. It opens up a forum for developing a whole new set of propositions for cross-border cooperation—for dealing with water and energy and climate change and diplomacy and security.

Both Americans and Canadians face these and other common problems and need to work together to address them. The best way to start is to develop a serious dialogue with American trade unions, American universities, American NGOs, American environmentalists, American human rights groups. And let's not forget the Mexicans. They should be brought into any continent-wide collaborative grassroots project, too, because they share the same terrain and are plagued by the same problems.

Forging this kind of continent-wide alliance of progressive people and institutions will not be easy, and will be made all the more difficult by the post-9/11 communications and mobility barriers erected as part of the homeland security apparatus. These measures inhibit the sharing of talent and capability in North America and tend to stifle creativity and cooperation. This is why the Internet has become so important as a medium of information and mobilization, although one wonders how long it will escape the intrusive monitoring and surveillance systems that have been set up in the name of security.

In any event, it may be helpful to define more clearly the most important issues that progressive Canadians and institutions need to be grappling with.

First and foremost is Canadian democracy, which is in need of fundamental reform. It is more than a little hypocritical of us to be preaching the virtues of democracy to the rest of the world when our own system is being dangerously eroded. It is eroding in civil liberties and rights, but also fundamentally in the parliamentary system itself, which leaves most of our citizens inadequately represented or not represented at all.

I am not necessarily touting proportional representation, per se, although its basic principles should probably be reflected in some form in whatever changes are made. I was a first-past-the-post politician for twenty-seven years and became adapted to it, learned to succeed electorally in it, and got to know all the angles and all my fellow parliamentarians and support staff. I liked this system, but I was always aware that it was very unrepresentative. The fact that the percentage of women in the House of Commons hasn't risen above 22 percent in the last twenty-five years is enough in itself to show that the system is not truly democratic.

Most of our ethnic and cultural groups are not represented proportionally, either, and our cities get left out of the system, too.

These deficiencies are not simply a matter of mathematics.
They also decide what issues get discussed and are given priority,
because those who occupy the seats in the Commons determine
what is on the parliamentary agenda. And the present mix of
MPs, I think, badly distorts the system.

We really have to get engaged at the national level—as is happening in many of the provinces now—in the serious issue of
democratic reform, the role of the Senate, the role of the monar-
chy, the role of the electoral system itself, and even the role of the
Charter of Rights and Freedoms and the Supreme Court in protecting our civil liberties.

Second on my list of priority issues is climate change, particularly its impact on our North, which is so dramatic and so far
reaching. It potentially creates far more risk and danger than virtually any other threat we face, and here we are ready to save the
world but not ready to save a large and vital part of our own
country.

Yes, we have made a treaty commitment on Kyoto [The Conservative government has renounced this commitment], but we
still haven't made climate change a priority as it affects our
indigenous northern citizens and threatens their whole way of
life. On the contrary, we plan to proceed with development of the
Alberta tar sands, even though it will vastly increase our greenhouse gas emissions and further exacerbate global warming. This
is a flagrant contradiction between what we say and what we do,
and throws doubt on our sincerity in wanting to curb climate
change. Surely we have to find an acceptable answer to this problem, but it seems we will need a much broader alliance of
environmentalists to muster the needed political pressure.

Third on the priority list is labour market, immigration, and
education policies. We may have begun to improve these pro-

grams, but up to now we have failed to use them effectively to attract and mobilize talent, not just in Canada but around the world. I don't mean we necessarily bring such talented people from other countries into Canada, but the skills that are now being deployed in the computer centres of Bangalore to deal with health, technological, and other issues should be part of our alliances as well. We have to conceive of a whole new system of trade and alliances if we are to come to grips with problems that are global in scope.

We are understandably concerned about the outsourcing of jobs. But it is no longer simply a matter of outsourcing; it's a question of how we begin to connect with those areas of business activity that are now springing up regionally around the world, and how to find the best way to relate to them. And I say this speaking from the experience I had in one of my many cabinet posts in human resources and labour and immigration and employment. I know that we are still making policy in these areas on the basis of conditions that prevailed back in the 1960s.

Next on the list is what is arguably our most precious resource—water. Despite the valuable work done by Maude Barlow, Tony Clarke, and other social activists, Canada still does not have a national water policy. And if you don't have a national water policy, how are you going to have a continental water policy? Shockingly, we don't have one. There is no inspiration for it, no political will for it. We urgently need a national water policy that not only defines this resource, but cleans it, preserves it, enhances it, researches it, and develops it not just as another commodity to be sold but as a treasured resource vital to our economy, sovereignty, and way of life.

Finally, there is Canada's international record and image as a peace-loving and peacekeeping nation—an image that has been badly tarnished in recent years as we sharply reduced our participation in UN peacekeeping missions. We have to regain our former much admired status. This is one way we could restore Canada's prestige abroad and energize our own people at home. There are some things that Canada has the ability to do well and to set an example for other countries. That doesn't mean we are flaunting a banner of manifest destiny or that we are any better than other nations. It simply means that we are tapping into our traditions, our history, our experience, our abilities to shape our country's policies at home and abroad.

We Canadians have devoted a lot of time and effort, as have our forebears, in developing an effective public domain in this country, a public domain based upon rules that control the market, institutions that provide for debate, standards that set conducts of behaviour, the preservation of political space for civil organizations to organize and mobilize. We have created a public domain that has served us well. Our challenge now, as Canadians, is to build a global public domain with exactly the same rules, institutions, standards, and practices. That, to me, is really where we provide the leadership. That is where we generate the needed constructive alternatives to the unilateralist and aggressive approach that now prevails in the United States.

If we can do that, we won't have to worry any more about the threat of continental integration. We will have vaulted over it, transcended it, built a global public domain that preserves our distinctive national identity.

CHAPTER 14

Integration and Dis-integration in North America

STEPHEN CLARKSON

In my research, I am trying to understand whether North America exists politically. I am studying the kind of governance that occurs beyond the boundaries of each of the continent's three constituent states: Does it simply amount to three sets of separate bilateral, intergovernmental relationships? Or is North American governance better understood as a continental market operated by transnational corporations? Is it civil society operating across borders? Perhaps what happens in North America is just a regional application of global governance? Is it various combinations of the above?

In terms of the economy, the situation is very complex. Take, for example, steel, which has undergone a tremendous integration ever since the "free trade" agreements proved there wasn't free trade because US firms could still harass Canadian exports using the many tools their congressional representatives had designed to protect them. Canadian steel companies had to put their new investments in the United States and become, in effect, members of the US economy. They have lobbied as Americans in the American Iron and Steel Institute, for instance, to get exemptions for Canada from Washington's protectionist measures.

The Mexican steel industry has done the same, and for a while it looked as though there was a real North American steel sector developing. But now that seems to be split up by the Russians becoming interested in buying Stelco, the Europeans buying Dofasco, and the Brazilians also coming into the market in a big way. So, even in the steel sector, there is not much that is specifically North American governance. Because NAFTA had special rules of origin protecting the powerful US textile/apparel and automotive/auto parts industries, these sectors have established genuine continental governance. However, the penetration of the US auto market from abroad, and the end of the Multi-Fibre Agreement, have broken down these two industries' continental distinctiveness.

And although much of the integration going on in other sectors also seems to be North American, it is really just an aspect of globalization. Banking regulations, for instance, are harmonizing in a sense. Mexico is having to adapt its banking sector regulations. But those come under the global regime, actually run from Basel, Switzerland, by the Bank of International Settlements, in which all the national banking heads participate in working out rules for the world.

Similarly, if you take pharmaceuticals and the problems involved in maintaining some generic drug activity in Canada, that too is driven not by NAFTA but by the WTO and its TRIPS Agreement, which enhances the monopoly intellectual property rights of Big Pharma.

The continental governance issue is especially complex in areas where technology is driving change. In cultural policies, if we are making shifts through the Canadian Radio, Television and

Telecommunications Commission (CRTC), it is not because of NAFTA or the WTO; it is because new technologies are pushing companies to demand more deregulation so they can converge or make other changes.

So it is hard to say that there is a very simple integration process going on. Now, of course, if one shifts to security issues and thinks of the militarization of the Canadian border, there has been a tremendous push, driven by Washington's paranoia about terrorism, to make the peripheral neighbouring countries of Canada and Mexico toughen their standards on anti-terrorism, immigration, and third-country refugees. All those issues have certainly been pushed by the United States and have led to what might be considered a sort of hegemonification of the continent as Washington pressures its contiguous neighbours to conform to American anti-terrorism measures.

It remains unclear, however, whether Canada is therefore proceeding along a deep integration path, and, if so, how rapidly this process is happening. My own feeling is that we have to make a big distinction between the continentalist agenda being pursued by some of our elites and the extent to which they are likely to achieve it. Personally, I doubt the deep integration crowd will succeed. Their continental anti-terrorist policies assume that there is going to be another terrorist strike, leading to another blocking of the border, which is, of course, the great fear of the business community.

Even if there were another terrorist attack, however, it is extremely unlikely the border would be shut down. The officials with the US Department of Homeland Security who deal with Canada know perfectly well that our security system is as good as theirs, and probably better, judging by the failure of the FBI and CIA to prevent the legal immigration into the United States of the nineteen 9/11 hijackers. They certainly didn't cross the alleged "Ontario-Vermont" border, as Hillary Clinton seems to have thought. In any event, my own feeling is that the spectre of another major closing of the border is unreal.

On the broader economic front, I think the possibility of a big "deep integration" deal being made between Canada and the United States is zero. Canada is colossally unimportant in Washington. Not just are we of declining importance globally, but we are politically hopeless as US "allies" in the eyes of George W. Bush and his cabinet. Besides, if any big deal were to be made, it would have to include Mexico.

It strikes me that Washington could not make a deal with Canada that didn't include Mexico because of the powerful presence of Mexicans in the American political system. In addition to the nearly ten million Mexican-Americans who are in the United States legally, there are another four or five million undocumented immigrants whose children, if born in the United States, automatically become US citizens. Together, they comprise a big and influential bloc that would insist that any preferential deal done with Canada should also be extended to Mexico.

We do have to take seriously what the Privy Council Office is apparently pushing through the Policy Research Institute: regulatory harmonization. This move is being described by the Conference Board of Canada and others as simply making some of our "minor" food and drug regulations conform to those of the United States and therefore allowing the US Food and Drug Administration to do the required testing and administering. We would in effect be outsourcing to an agency in another country the testing and approval of painkillers such as some previously approved by the FDA that proved to be patient killers.

It is a logical consequence of the hollowing out of the Canadian state's capacity to do the research and regulation of the food and drugs that Canadians need. The responsibility of protecting our health is to be outsourced to Washington. This is clearly a form of deep integration that we must take seriously and do our utmost to prevent. Once Canadians are made aware of such a dereliction of responsibility for the protection of their health and safety, they will surely massively oppose it.

That leads me to the real issue, which could be called "deep DIS-integration," which I think we need to recognize before we get totally obsessed by doom and gloom. Take social policy, for instance. There is certainly a lot of non-integration going on there. In social policy, think of rights—same-sex marriage and the decriminalization of marijuana possession, for example—where our policies sharply diverge from those in the United States.

On the political side, we have the United States rejecting NAFTA panel decisions favouring Canada in its softwood lumber dispute; blocking the import of Canadian beef; violating the spirit of the Boundary Waters Treaty, which set up the International Joint Commission to manage the quality and quantity of lakes and rivers overlapping the border; and generally acting unilaterally to protect the interests of American industries.

All in all, I think that, politically, there is a real *non*-integration process taking place in North America, or at least a significant slowdown in the impetus toward closer integration. And this is happening for two main reasons. The first is that NAFTA has no institutional reality. There is nothing in North America like the European Union, which is passing regulations all the time that affect its member countries in that continent. Norway, for instance, although it is a rich, small, and otherwise independent country, has to accept regulations passed in Brussels over which it has absolutely no say.

In North America, there is no comparable legislative entity into which Canada is integrated—for better or for worse. But the "for better" means that there is no institutional way to keep changing the regulations, and that is why people like John Manley are on these trilateral commissions, trying to get such comparable EU-style mechanisms, but they are not happening. All the little working groups set up by NAFTA have turned out to be really insignificant.

There is a big institutional reason why deep integration is not actually going ahead very fast and, to the extent that it is going on, if at all, it is largely by stealth, and on very small issues.

The last reason that I think deep integration is not happening is none other than George W. Bush, who makes the American model so unacceptable, who supports American protectionism against successful Canadian exports like beef in the completely Republican-controlled system in Washington. In a way, George Bush is our best ally in maintaining our autonomy.

CHAPTER 15

A Canadian Response to an American War

AVI LEWIS

In our discussions about deep integration with the United States, the wars in Afghanistan and Iraq are mostly treated as add-ons, items in a list of policies that integration is dragging us into. In fact, war is now the primary focus of the economy with which we are integrating. According to a study by PriceWaterhouseCooper, the annual US military budget reached US$417 billion in 2003, almost half of the rest of the world's combined military spending that year. That's a staggering statistic—a massive shift in the economy of the world's only superpower. And that shift is going to be paid for by Americans, by Canadians, by Iraqis, by everyone.

Of course, huge military spending in the United States is nothing new. And neither is the real meaning of war. It is the ultimate expression of the economic agenda that we're fighting. Privatization, radical deregulation, the commodification and control of all public assets—and a beachhead strategy to spread this model to the parts of the world that have not yet embraced it: this is the true meaning of the war in Iraq. As the costs of integrating with a country waging war are becoming clear, now is the time when the war itself is disappearing from view. Correction. Not disappearing. *Being disappeared.*

The *Los Angeles Times* did a study of photographs of the war in America's major newspapers and magazines for a six-month period that encompassed both the second US levelling of Fallujah and the carnage that encompassed the United States and Iraqi elections. Set aside for a moment what was *missing* from the *L.A. Times* study, such as any recognition of the fact that Americans rarely see images that humanize the more than 100,000 Iraqis who have died as a result of the war. But in that bloody six-month period, in which 559 Americans and other Westerners were killed, readers of many major US newspapers and magazines did not see a single picture of a dead soldier. Not a one. Not in the *Atlanta Journal-Constitution,* the *Los Angeles Times,* the *New York Times,* the *St. Louis Post-Dispatch,* the *Washington Post, Time* or *Newsweek.*

It was an entirely transparent plan the Bush administration had—to change the story from that of a brutal and chaotic occupation into the story of a civil war, an ethnic conflict in which Iraqis are killing Iraqis. With the full cooperation of major media in the United States, that strategy is working like a charm. Thousands of people have been killed in Iraq in recent months. But it's no longer even called a war. The daily reports of deaths in Iraq have already settled into a news rhythm to which we are topically anaesthetized.

If we're honest, we'll admit that the horror of war has simply worn off as the pictures have disappeared. That we're unable to generate any substantial outrage despite what we know to be happening right now, every single day, and clearly, for years to come.

The policies that transform our society are political choices, not weather systems out of the reach of mere mortals. And now that we're at risk of watching the generic and sterilized war reports with the equanimity with which we watch weather reports, I think it's worth going deeper into the causes of war as they relate to the fundamental choices we make as societies.

Beyond the rapid transformation of massive US federal surpluses into unprecedented deficits, the war represents a monumental policy choice that is at least partly designed to make other policy options impossible. In the war appropriation approved in 2005 by the US Congress, the price tag for Iraq alone is US$220 billion. Of course, that's the tip of the iceberg in real terms, but let's take a look at what that figure represents. For that much spending, the United States could have paid for health insurance for 103 million children, hired three million new teachers, or built one-and-a-half million new units of housing.

Globally, that money could have almost single-handedly met the UN's Millenium Development Goal of cutting world hunger in half by 2015, or filled the Global AIDS Fund for at least fifteen years. These political choices, like the ones governments have been making in Canada for a generation, reveal an underlying world view that must be named and fought for what it is.

So I would argue that the Bush administration's war, inspired by its central ideological text, the Project for a New American Century, and its doctrine of pre-emptive warfare, represents nothing less than the elevation of radical individualism to the status of a national ideology. At its core, the guiding belief is that what's good for America is good for the world. That justice, freedom, and democracy for all will be best served by an aggressive pursuit of what the United States considers to be in its own interest.

This deeply Darwinian philosophy is echoed in the White House's catchphrase for its domestic agenda, the "Ownership Society." I've become obsessed with it. Because I think it's a useful lens through which to zoom in on the cellular structure of this ideology, the DNA of American capitalism. The Ownership Society was first used by the Bush team to sell the privatization of social security by recasting what has been seen historically as a truly public project—the wider society taking care of people after they retire—as an individual, private responsibility. But it has since been embraced by the Bush administration as a term that represents its entire domestic agenda.

As White House advisor Peter Wehner explained the phrase in a memo to conservative supporters, "we have it within our grasp to move away from dependency on government and toward giving greater power and responsibility to individuals." What's so revealing about the language of the Ownership Society is the way that it elevates individualism—which has always been a strong streak in American society—to the status of a nation-defining quality.

Everything previously considered in the collective realm redefined in terms of private ownership, private gain, and private responsibility. A society in which the collective interest is best served by individuals aggressively pursuing self-interest. In other words, the Project for a New American Century, the blueprint for American Empire, scaled down for application at home.

This fundamental struggle of two world views, one more collective, one more individualist, is how many of us characterize the difference between Canadian and American values. For the record, I don't like those reductionist and oversimplified constructions. I don't believe we've earned it, historically, in Canada, and I believe there's a difference between the American people and the US regime. But I do believe that it's still possible to appeal, in Canada, to a common interest, the public good, a notion of taking care of one another that transcends the human impulse to self-interest. And those are the terms in which we ought to engage with the war economy and the security state, and their active transformation of Canadian society.

If John Manley, Tom d'Aquino, and their US counterparts are

going to bundle security issues with economic integration, then we ought to respond to war and security with the same energy that we muster to fight their economic agenda. The secretary-general of Amnesty International has called the US detention centre in Guantanamo Bay the "Gulag of our times," and the United States "a leading purveyor and practitioner of torture." To quote Amnesty further: "When the most powerful country in the world thumbs its nose at the rule of law and human rights, it grants a license to others to commit abuse with impunity and audacity."

In the case of a country like Canada, already deeply integrated with the United States, it doesn't just grant a licence, it actively implicates us in these crimes. First we learned at the Arar inquiry that CSIS encouraged the consular officials who visited Maher Arar in that Syrian prison to gather intelligence on him, rather than focus on getting him out. Then came the smoking gun memo. CSIS actively lobbied to keep Arar in prison in Syria because they knew they didn't have enough evidence to jail him under Canadian law. So not only is Canada cooperating with the American outsourcing of torture—that alone is illegal and unacceptable, and we've been slammed by the UN Committee Against Torture for it—but worse, our intelligence service clearly views the process of deporting people to torture the way the United States does as a great intelligence-gathering tool and, more importantly, as an efficient and acceptable means of implanting fear, and therefore obedience, in specific ethnic communities. This is integration at its most insidious, the integration of world view.

Now, the good news, of course, is that the majority of Canadians are offended by the war, against the occupation, and dead set opposed to extraordinary rendition and giving up our sovereignty to the US economic and security agenda. The problem, as always, is how to make this latent resistance active. To change our government's behaviour. To move from defensive campaigns—fighting against developments that come to light after they're already enshrined in government practice—to positive policy alternatives that we can put forward, campaign on, and win.

But I would go further. Instead of concentrating mainly on how the United States is transforming our domestic policy, I think it's time we devoted some collective brain power to figuring out how we can start transforming theirs. I have a concrete, if modest, proposal of one place to start. But first, let's take a quick look at the major recent victories for Canadian sovereignty, and see what we can learn from them. I want to propose a policy that I think would represent a major victory for Canadian sovereignty, and it has to be qualitatively different from the kind we've had in the last few years.

It's generally accepted that the two biggest examples of Canada standing up to the United States recently were Chrétien's stand on the Iraq war and Martin's position on ballistic missile defence. But let's be honest about what they represent as victories. Both are testaments to the classic model for achieving change to which organizations like the Canadian Centre for Policy Alternatives are rightly committed. You do the research, get the facts and arguments right, and fuel the debate. You don't spend your life lobbying behind closed doors to achieve micro-tweaks in the language of legislation; you go right to the public and make the case against the war, against missile defence. Then, in coalition with progressive forces across society, who take your research and turn it into energetic campaigns, you swing the supertanker of public opinion around so that the pragmatic power-addicted leaders see their political capital enhanced by doing the right thing.

I mean, do we really believe that Paul Martin and Jean Chrétien located their inner Trudeau and decided to give Uncle Sam the finger? (Actually, if memory serves, it was not the United States, but Canadians exercising their right to dissent, who received that gesture of respect from Trudeau.) But of course not. Martin and Chrétien didn't locate their inner Trudeau; they located their in-house pollster and did what the majority of Canadians clearly wanted them to.

But here's the problem with this model of change. It lends itself to symbolic gestures that we cling to as evidence of our sovereignty, but we slip away when we examine the record later. Chrétien's stand against the invasion of Iraq, we learned later, was part of a savvy bait-and-switch, which saw Canadian troops providing backup to US operations in Afghanistan and the Persian Gulf, and hundreds of millions of dollars of foreign aid money redirected to the so-called reconstruction of Afghanistan and Iraq.

As a report co-sponsored by the Canadian Council of Chief Executives approvingly notes, "when Canadian troops hunt terrorists and support democracy in Afghanistan, or when Canadian ships lead patrols in the Persian Gulf, they engage in the 'forward defense' of North America by attacking the bases of support for international terrorism around the world." So our status as little brother, tag-along pre-emptive warrior is intact, despite or actually *because* of Chretien's decisions.

And then the story broke that Ottawa is negotiating with the United Arab Emirates to make our so-called secret Camp Mirage, which everyone knows is just outside Dubai, a permanent base to support the Canadian presence in Afghanistan. Permanent bases in the region kind of undercuts our principled stand on the war, doesn't it? But as a piece of propaganda, it was marvellous. And I believe that the symbolic effect around the world was real.

And then there's Paul Martin on missile defence. Let me quote one extraordinary account of the reaction to the prime minister's decision, from Lawrence Martin in the *Globe and Mail*:

> The media, to the tune of about 90 percent,
> ripped the Martin government to pieces over its

decision to reject Washington's missile-defense plan. The people went the other way; they favoured the decision ... by a 20 percent margin, which, in political terms, is a landslide. Today's press, most strikingly on the question of US relations (missile defence, Iraq, defence spending, taxation, etc.), has become concertedly conservative, moving to the right of the people. The conservative media tend to favour a closer embrace of the United States and its values. Canadians themselves show little inclination to go that route. It is a storyline—the press versus the people—that runs right to the heart of the debate over the future of the country.

He goes on to say that, in the right-wing media, missile defence

was examined not so much on the basis of what Canadians think, but on what the Bush administration would think. It was as if—after 138 years of existence—we were still strapped down to a client-state mentality wherein the driving imperative was approval from a higher authority.

It was with almost cosmic relief, two months later, that I stumbled on a tiny, digest-style story that put the whole missile defence incident in perspective.

Dateline Whitehorse: The Governments of the Yukon and Alaska have agreed to co-finance a study to show the benefits of a long-discussed rail link between Alaska and Canada. A consultant's report commissioned by the Yukon government announces enthusiastically that the railroad would support missile-defence silos now being built in Fort Greeley, Alaska, and would allow

Washington to develop an Alaskan port to station up to three missile defence ships in the northern Pacific, outside Korean territorial waters.

We have a long-standing pattern here. Canadian leaders, playing the nationalist card, make the right noises or even take the right stands when it comes to the decisive issues of sovereignty from the United States. But then, over the years, the information trickles out that we cooperated anyway. That our government had a tacit agreement that certain symbolic spasms of independence were an unpleasant political necessity, but that compliance would always be there for the little technical matters.

Like US nuclear weapons on our soil. Canadian troops mopping up after invasions in the Middle East. A US-sponsored coup in Haiti. Canadian citizens being deported to torture, or held on security certificates, without charges, without hearing the evidence against them, in solitary confinement, without seeing their families. For years. We need to fight these violations of human rights and this Canadian complicity in a global American war. We need to reclaim, not harmonize, our immigration and refugee policy. We have to put integration, with its insidious bundling of security and economic issues, back on the front burner, like it was in the free trade fights of the late eighties and early nineties. We have to abolish security certificates, ensure that we will never again deport anyone to torture, reverse Canada's supporting military role for US adventures in Haiti, Iraq, Afghanistan, and whatever comes next. We need to fight on all the economic fronts and audaciously advance progressive policy alternatives at every opportunity.

But we also need a real sovereignty victory to re-assert our distinctive values. One we can measure. One that is symbolic in its scope, but utterly concrete in its achievement. And this sovereignty victory must achieve a number of objectives. It needs to address the American war, not just in Iraq but wherever the doctrine of pre-emptive warfare will focus its beam next. It needs to affirm a different set of values from the underpinnings of a privatized military economy: radical individualism and the Ownership Society. It needs to support and preserve those achievements of our deeper faith in the public sphere, those very policies that are eroding so ominously in this era of carefully cultivated insecurity, and sneaky integration.

And finally, it ought to link progressive people across the border, to tap into the tremendous collective power of American liberals. That is the millions in the United States who feel that they are trapped in a nightmare of war in the name of democracy; the same people who believe that there is a utopian land of a pot-powered same-sex community to the north. (We can let them hold on to that fantasy for a while—it's potent political fuel, after all ...)

So here it is: We have in our midst a group of Americans who have come here because they refuse to serve in an illegal war. They are facing harsh sentences if returned to the United States. One conscientious objector named Pablo Paredes was recently sentenced to three months hard labour for refusing to fight in Iraq. Jeremy Hinzman, Brandon Hughey, and others seeking refugee status in Canada face the possibility of years in prison if they are returned to the United States. They are the draft dodgers of today—people who want to live in a country where war is not celebrated, where they can raise their children in public child care with public health care, where you can say "social justice" and not be sniggered at, where you can consume media that is infuriating and right-wing but not yet Orwellian. They want to live in the Canada they have found and the Canada they want to help build.

So we need to reaffirm, as a matter of public policy, the most progressive thing, in my view, that Pierre Trudeau ever said: *that Canada should be a refuge from militarism.* We need a special immigration program to welcome US war resisters to this country. We've done it many times before: for people fleeing the former Soviet Union, for "boat people" in the 1970s. Canada's courts have consistently ruled that those fleeing a regime engaging in an illegal war should be granted asylum if they are coming to Canada because they oppose the war. That's how we dealt with the Iraqis who refused to participate in Saddam's war on Kuwait, and with Serbs who deserted from the war in Kosovo.

Set in the context of deep integration, and the myriad, intractable issues of trade, security, privatization, and sovereignty, this may seem like a proposal that is too modest by half. So let me take a moment to articulate why I think it is effective, powerful, progressive, futuristic—and winnable.

1.   A special immigration program to welcome US war resisters is not yet prevented by any trade or security deal, and, better still, it would drive the White House and David Frum absolutely crazy.

2.   It directly addresses the war, and the economic logic which it embodies and enforces, by posing Canada as a clear global alternative to American Empire and the Ownership Society. We may cause some hernias in the beltway, but around the world we'd be heroes.

3.   It directly recalls the last time the Canadian government embraced a dramatically different social vision with a massive social result: fifty-thousand progressive Americans who came in the Vietnam period, half of whom stayed and helped build Canada's system of public health, broadcasting, justice, and social services, not to mention lefty think tanks.

4.   The US military is desperate, and talk of a draft in America cannot be dismissed. There are more

than five thousand soldiers who are officially
acknowledged to be AWOL in the United States—
the real number could be many times that.

The US Marines are missing their recruiting targets. The US Army's top recruiter said last fall he
would be starting with the smallest pool of
recruits in at least a decade, and the Rand Corporation described this prediction as "near
disastrous." Frantic recruiters are threatening
young people with prison time for not keeping
appointments, giving others laxatives to help meet
weight requirements, and instructing others on
how to cover up past drug use for medical tests.
Counter-recruiter groups have started throwing
recruiters out of high schools across the United
States. And an unprecedented one-day stand-
down was called recently so the Army could give
its recruiters emergency ethics training. Okay, they
might need more than a day. So, if there is another
US invasion, or major terrorist attack, the likeli-
hood of a draft is real. If we were already fighting
for, or had already won, an official policy of
accepting war resisters, the floodgates would open.
And we would be ready.

5. Let's talk openly about those floodgates. Despite
    an ugly backlash in the early 1970s—remember
    the danger of appealing to nationalism and
    "Canadian values"—Vietnam-era draft dodgers
    made an historic contribution to the very things
    about Canada that progressive Americans now
    look at with naked envy. We could really use an
    infusion of immigrants who would fight for public
    health care, national child care, a more inclusive

immigration and refugee system, a public broadcaster that stays public, and against deeper
integration with the very system they are fleeing.

With another 35,000 to 50,000 people in this country repulsed
by war and the fundamentalist takeover of their government, we
might actually save those things worth saving about Canada. And
talk about making alliances with progressive movements in the
States. Why don't we go further and start a grassroots campaign
to recruit Americans who are disgusted by what their country has
become. *Move to Canada!* It could be the most successful move-
ment-building slogan this country has ever heard.

This is an ideal moment to push the idea of a special immigration program to the forefront. Although this policy alternative
would be excoriated in all the daily papers in Canada, it would be
embraced, I believe, by most Canadians. This is something worth
spending political capital on. This is a policy that says: "We're not
anti-American, we're anti-war!" We're against the racism of war,
and the racial profiling of all its victims. We're against the clas-
sism of war. We're against the war economy—its distorted
priorities, its scandalous corporate welfare, its attack on civil liberties.

And we're against the economy of war: war as the extreme
trade agreement, the harshest structural adjustment program, the
unmasked face of neoliberalism. And we believe that our country
should be a refuge. We welcome people who feel the same way to
come and join us in building something better.

CHAPTER 16

Selling Off Our Country

MEL HURTIG

In the late 1960s and throughout the first half of the 1970s, Canadians became increasingly concerned about the already high and rapidly increasing level of foreign ownership in Canada, which had reached over one-third of all non-financial industry corporate assets and over 37.4 percent of all revenues.

One result of this concern was the formation of the Committee for an Independent Canada (CIC), the Watkins Report, the Gray Report, and a steady stream of public opinion polls that reflected growing Canadian unease about foreign ownership—so much so that, after being presented with a 176,000-name petition by the CIC, Pierre Trudeau and his government brought in the *Foreign Investment Review Act* in 1975. Within a decade, foreign control dropped all the way down to 21.4 percent—still very high compared to other industrialized countries, but at least it was decreasing instead of continuing to increase at an alarming rate.

After Brian Mulroney abolished the Foreign Investment

Review Agency and replaced it with the rubber-stamp Investment Canada, foreign direct investment and foreign control began to increase once again. By 2000, the foreign control of non-financial industries was at about the same level as in the mid-1960s. The latest official Statistics Canada figures at this writing are for 2003, when foreign control was back up to 29.3 percent, the highest level in thirty years.

In 2006, there is little doubt that we have already passed the levels that caused such great concern in the 1970s, and are rapidly proceeding well beyond all previous record levels.

In this respect, it's interesting to note that, in compiling its figures, Statistics Canada does not consider companies such as Air Canada, the CNR, Petro-Canada, or Canada's largest oil and gas producer, Encana, in its foreign ownership calculations, even though all four and dozens of other important "Canadian" corporations are already majority foreign owned, mostly by Americans. Many other countries consider that as little as 10 percent foreign ownership can and often will represent effective foreign control. (And hasn't it been wonderful to see the CNR holding its annual meeting in the United States for the first time in its history?)

Today, about 35 percent of Canada's largest corporations are thought to be foreign owned, although this number is undoubtedly too low since in the annual business magazine listings the information about ownership is often shown as NA (not available) or many firms are only classified as "widely held." For those right-wing continentalists and their comprador colleagues who make their perpetual, widely publicized pleas for more foreign direct investment (for example, Chamber of Commerce, Conference Board, Canadian Council of Chief Executives, C.D. Howe and Fraser Institutes, our leading newspapers), we should have nothing but contempt. As we shall see, what they are asking for is plain and simple: more foreign ownership and control of our resources, our industry, our high-tech companies, and other businesses. How so?

Let's look at the startling figures for foreign direct investment since Brian Mulroney declared Canada open for business and dumped the Foreign Investment Review Agency. To the end of December 2005, there were 11,501 companies in Canada taken over by non-resident-controlled corporations. The total dollar amount monitored by Investment Canada was an enormous $620.7 billion. Of this amount, 97.1 percent was for takeovers, and only a pathetic 2.9 percent was for the hoped-for new business investment!

Since Investment Canada began keeping track (June 30, 1985), some 64 percent of these foreign direct investments have been attributed to American firms. Far behind in second place is the United Kingdom at just over 9 percent. So, essentially, when we talk about foreign ownership and control in Canada, it's predominantly American. And, contrary to all the nonsense in our newspapers about Canadian direct investment in the United States exceeding US direct investment in Canada, the American ownership of Canada was over $63.5 billion higher, and of course represented a much greater percentage of assets and GDP.

As might be expected, a very large percentage of Canadian direct investment abroad was by our good old patriotic Canadian banks—42 percent, to be exact. For some very good reasons, most Americans think that they have the right to buy up as much of the ownership and control of Canada as they wish. For some truly bizarre reasons, many of our leading politicians and journalists see no problem with all of this. In fact, many of our political leaders and our most prominent editorial writers and columnists encourage more US investment at almost every opportunity when the topic comes up, seemingly ignorant of the fact that what they are asking for is even more foreign ownership and foreign control of our country.

The following industries in Canada are now majority or heavily foreign owned: manufacturing, the petroleum industry, chemicals and chemical products, mineral fuels, non-metallic mineral products, food processing and packaging, electric products, tobacco products, machinery, transportation equipment, computers, major advertising firms, meat packing, aircraft, etc., etc., and etc. Altogether, some thirty-six different sectors of the Canadian economy are heavily or majority foreign owned and/or controlled. And now the Harper government is under increasing pressure to allow the foreign takeovers of Canadian utilities, airlines, book stores and book publishers, telecommunication companies, and others.

In comparison, in the United States, there's not one major industry that is majority foreign owned or controlled. Seven smaller industry groupings have majority foreign ownership, but overall only 4.7 percent of US private industry employment is in foreign-owned firms. Another way of comparing foreign direct investment in Canada and the United States is as a percentage of GDP. In Canada in the 1990s it averaged 22 percent. In the United States it was only 8 percent.

Well over half of all manufacturing in Canada is foreign owned. In comparison, among the other twenty-nine OECD countries, all of the following have below 4 percent foreign ownership: Japan, Germany, the United States, Poland, Norway, Italy, the Netherlands, Finland, the United Kingdom, France, Sweden, and the Czech Republic. *No other major industrialized country has a level of foreign ownership of its manufacturing even a third as high as Canada's.*

As I pointed out in my book *The Vanishing Country*,

> Tom d'Aquino and his fellow patriots at the Business Council on National Issues (now the Canadian Council of Chief Executives) have been complaining for

years that Canada isn't getting enough foreign investment. Let's turn to official Statistics Canada figures and
look at recent foreign direct investment which in the
1990s amounted to $126 billion for the entire decade.
In 2000, it exploded to a new annual record greater
than in any G-7 country, and a record 509 Canadian
firms were taken over. The value of these takeovers was
a startling $81.8 billion. The previous record, set the
year before, was $18.1 billion.

By 2000, foreign direct investment in Canada was over two-
and-a half times as much as it was in 1990, and over
four-and-a-half times as much as it was in 1980.

So much for all the misleading complaints from our continentalist corporate sellouts that Canada hasn't been getting enough
foreign direct investment.

It's always interesting to ask these people just how much of the
country they're prepared to sell off. None of them will ever give
you an answer. Try writing Stephen Harper a letter asking him
this question and see what you get.

If you have a strong stomach, go to the Investment Canada
website (investcan.ic.gc.ca) and have a look at any one month of
takeovers of businesses in Canada. Month after month, year after
year, in every region of the country, the long list of takeovers is
appalling: petroleum and mining companies, forestry and energy
distribution companies, clothing and design companies, computer and software companies, wholesale and retail operations, hotels
and entire resorts, tar sands companies, a multitude of important
service industry companies, our largest and most successful steel
producer, insurance and finance firms, real estate and construction companies, home heating and power companies, asset
management firms, restaurants, breweries, bakeries, research
firms—and the list, month after month, goes on and on and on.

It's remarkable, but too sad to be laughable, to hear the constant whining about such things as poor productivity, lack of Canadian patents and innovation, poor levels of high-tech exports when almost every day another Canadian high-tech company is taken over by foreign corporations. As others have pointed out, 125 such companies in the Ottawa area alone were taken over in the decade ending in 2003.

In the late 1990s, there were over forty large Canadian petroleum companies. Since then, US companies have purchased over twenty. Now there are only six left.

In April, 2005, then liberal minister of industry, David Emerson, wrote to concerned citizens that he strongly believed that the well-being of Canada's petroleum and manufacturing industries "is very much in the national interest," and that "a key element in supporting these industries is to allow and indeed promote foreign investment." The hapless Emerson seemed quite unaware that both the petroleum and manufacturing industries were already majority foreign owned. One must wonder just at what level Mr. Emerson and his political and corporate colleagues would be satisfied that enough is enough. Would it be 60 percent? 70 percent? 80 percent? Or should it be 100 percent foreign ownership and control? Too bad that some MP or some press gallery member hasn't long ago asked such a question of our political leaders.

Emerson also indicated that Canadians need not be concerned about the investment review process, which he described as "rigorous," with "systematic and well-established systems." What total bunk! *Since FIRA was dumped by Brian Mulroney, not one single takeover of over 11,500 has been denied.*

Bear in mind that the current goal of Investment Canada is to facilitate and solicit even *more* foreign direct investment, not to limit or control it. This was the Mulroney government goal when it abolished the Foreign Investment Revenue Agency, and both the Chrétien and Martin governments enthusiastically continued this policy and continued selling off the ownership and control of our country. If anything, the Harper government will almost certainly open the door even wider to new record levels of takeovers of more of our businesses, resources, and land.

While the Mulroney, Chrétien, and Martin governments actively encouraged more foreign direct investment, the Harper government will likely make all three look like rabid nationalists in comparison. At the same time, consistently the Canadian people have shown that they want otherwise. Year after year, poll after poll, Canadians say we already have too much foreign ownership and control and we don't need more.

Under Stephen Harper's new government, is there anything that will not be for sale? American corporations are eyeing our airlines, our telecommunications firms, our mining companies, our book publishers, and what is left of the petroleum and manufacturing industries. What can we expect in the future? *Globe and Mail* business columnist Andrew Willis is to the point: "expect takeovers to continue at a red-hot pace."

Virtually universal conventional wisdom among our corporate elite, our blinkered media, and our federal and provincial politicians leads us to believe that the development of Canada and our standard of living has been largely due to the influx of foreign capital. Not so. In fact, most of the massive takeover of corporations in Canada has been financed by Canada's good old reliable Canadian banks and our other financial institutions, including the Caisse and our very own pension funds. For example, the Recreational Products Division of Bombardier's takeover was financed by two Canadian banks (BMO and RBC) and a Quebec caisse. The CIBC was the leading lender in the takeover of Shoppers Drug Mart. The CIBC and the Bank of Nova Scotia helped finance the Yellow Pages sale.

As I have pointed out many times in the past, no one in Ottawa knows just how much of the sale of our country has been financed with our own money—not the Department of Finance, not the Bank of Canada, not Statistics Canada, not the Prime Minister's Office or the Privy Council Office: no one! Why is that? Simple. None of them are interested. They don't care. One thing is for sure. It could happen in no other developed country. Meanwhile, incredibly, thanks mostly to our banks and other Canadian financial institutions, the outflow of foreign direct investment from Canada in the period 1995–2004 was greater than such outflows for Germany, the United States, Italy, Finland, Sweden, and, all-combined, Portugal, Belgium, Luxembourg, Norway, Austria, New Zealand, Australia, and Ireland.

As every year goes by, it becomes increasingly clear how poorly Canada's negotiators emerged from both the FTA and the NAFTA talks. Here we will mention only the egregious mandatory energy-sharing clauses, our inability to control our own petroleum prices, the notorious Chapter 11, the absurd straight-jacketing of industrial strategy options, and the mandatory treatment of American corporations as if they were 100 percent Canadian. I cannot imagine any other country giving away so many vitally important policy options. (Mexico laughed at the Americans when the United States proposed NAFTA petroleum clauses similar to the ones Canadians so stupidly accepted.)

Under the terms of both the FTA and NAFTA, Canada gave away many of the tools used by nations around the world to keep a reasonable check on excessive and/or detrimental foreign ownership and control, and even abandoned many of the options to ensure takeovers had to clearly bring benefits to this country.

All of this raises two very interesting and important questions, one easy to answer, the other very difficult to answer. The first and easy question is why do other developed countries reject such high levels of foreign ownership and foreign control?

There are many important reasons, too many to do justice to

in this chapter, but, to begin, here's just one: Foreign firms import much of their goods and services from their parent company, almost always at high non-arms-length prices. Here are G-7 figures for imports of goods and services as a percentage of GDP that I have published before:

Canada	41 percent
Germany	28 percent
United Kingdom	27 percent
France	24 percent
Italy	24 percent
United States	13 percent
Japan	9 percent

These figures represent a huge loss of jobs, profits, and overall economic activity caused by excessive imports resulting from excessive foreign ownership and control. Overall, foreign firms operating in Canada import three times as many parts and components and services as similarly sized Canadian companies. In a truly remarkable comparison, an OECD study showed that the ratio of foreign parts and components in manufacturing in the US was 13 percent, in Japan 7 percent, *and in Canada it was over 50 percent.*

In the United States, when China National Offshore Oil Corporation tried to take over the American oil firm Unocal Corp., the ninth largest US oil company, Washington stepped in to take steps to block the Chinese bid. In France, when Pepsi attempted a takeover of the famous Danone SA food company, French prime minister Dominique de Villepin warned Pepsi not to proceed further. And there are many, many other examples of governments stepping in to curb foreign takeovers in every part of the world every year.

Transfer pricing is another important reason other countries limit foreign ownership. Foreign subsidiaries are charged high or even outrageous prices for goods and services which *must* be purchased from their parent companies. Firms such as Safeway, Ford, Coca-Cola, and the large pharmaceutical companies, to mention a few, transfer their profits out of Canada before they are taxable here. Hence, every Canadian reading these words gets the privilege of paying more tax.

Another reason excessive foreign ownership is discouraged is that the dominance of foreign corporations in an industrial sector inevitably brings pressure on government policy in both domestic and foreign policy development. The job of foreign subsidiaries is to make as much profit as possible for their foreign parent. There is no such thing as a Canadian national interest in any such considerations. ExxonMobil, as one example, tells Imperial Oil what to do about maximizing or minimizing their public positions on petroleum reserves, and the result no doubt benefits ExxonMobil, but it may well not be in Canada's national interest.

Other downsides include the fact that key decisions on the opening and closing of plants, the level of wages and dividends, the marginalization of Canadian directors, the inability of subsidiaries to compete with their parent in export markets unless permission is granted, and the adoption of US standards, values, and policies are made by the foreign parent.

There's no room here to do proper justice to all the other foreign ownership negatives, but much can be summed up in my favorite quote on the subject of takeovers, which comes from none other than Brian Mulroney: "I've yet to see a takeover that has created a single job, except of course for lawyers and accountants." Try looking at the number of jobs per million dollars in sales and compare Canadian firms and US subsidiaries. The numbers are shocking and most revealing. In 2000, foreign firms in Canada made 53 percent of all manufacturing shipments in this country, but employed under 32 percent of manufacturing workers.

The second question is much more difficult and truly borders on the bizarre. After the takeover of the Hudson's Bay Company, the marvellous Fairmont Hotel icons, and Dofasco, the *Economist* put it this way: "In many other countries, the sale of national heirlooms would spark fierce opposition. Not in Canada." Peter C. Newman says: "In all other developed countries, the economic elite defend their country's sovereignty because not only is it in their own interest to do so, but they are proud of their country and wish it to be more than a place where their children and grandchildren can best look forward to being serfs."

David Crane, columnist for the *Toronto Star,* pinpoints one element of the problem: "The upsurge in foreign ownership and control in the Canadian economy would not be taking place if our financial markets were focused on building Canadian companies, rather than selling them."

It would take at least several chapters like this to properly try to explain the sell-off of our country. Yes, some or even much of it is related pure and simple to greed, but that alone cannot explain the extraordinary and virtually unique-in-the-world absence of patriotism and loyalty to one's homeland among so many of our corporate establishment. Surely, though, the fact that so much of our media is either American or controlled by our own far-right conservative continentalists is a factor in our country's silent sleepwalking to colonial status.

CHAPTER 17

A Progressive American Perspective

THEA LEE

While I was at the Economic Policy Institute in Washington in the early 1990s, it was a thrill for me to discover that the EPI had a sister institution in Canada, the Canada Centre for Policy Alternatives, that was doing very similar intellectual work. I have fond memories of the early tri-national meetings we had around NAFTA—which was my first experience with deep integration from the progressive perspective—memories of meeting and working with labour, environmental, and social activists from Mexico and Canada and the United States.

We are still having the exact same debate we had fifteen years ago: asking ourselves how, if we were in charge, would we want to carry out the economic and social integration of our countries in a way that really puts a priority on the things we care about, on workers' rights, human rights, environmental protection, democracy, and so on.

We learned a lot of important lessons back then that are still of enormous value, especially as this transnational world order is expanding to the western hemisphere with the Free Trade Area of the Americas talks, and indeed around the world through the World Trade Organization, the IMF, and the World Bank.

We learned much from these joint endeavours—two lessons in particular. The first was that we don't always entirely agree with each other, even though we all come from progressive backgrounds, but that such disagreements are invariably about means rather than ends, and thus relatively easy to work around. I think one of the important things we have to learn about our transnational work is to be respectful of each other's domestic political context and constituencies, and that it is still possible to find common ground and put together a joint political agenda. But we have to do so carefully and not in a way that assumes activists in other countries come from exactly the same place we do, because we all don't.

The second lesson is that, despite these differences, it is absolutely crucial for us to be able to understand each other's issues and views, to be able to craft a common agenda where it is possible, and to coordinate the pressure on our own governments in order to maximize the leverage that we can collectively bring to bear. Even after doing this work for more than fifteen years, I feel that we constantly have to remind ourselves that the crucial divisions between us are not in fact national divisions but class divisions.

It is easier to think about our social and economic issues in terms of winners and losers. We know who the winners are: they're the multinational corporate elite, and they're laughing all the way to the bank. And we know who the losers are: they're my folks and your folks, the most vulnerable, the workers, the small farmers, the average citizens—the people who don't have a voice in these integration debates, but desperately need one.

The Canadian Centre for Policy Alternatives has exposed the rise in corporate profits and the stagnation of wages in Canada, and, of course, that is exactly what we are experiencing in the United States, and it is exactly what is happening in Mexico as well. It is really crystal clear that the whole point of these integration agreements is not about trade liberalization but about bargaining power, about strengthening the influence of multinational corporations while weakening national governments, weakening labour unions, weakening environmental activists. And it works.

We have had twelve years of NAFTA and five more years with the Canada-US Free Trade Agreement to see that this has been a very effective agenda from the corporate perspective but not from anyone else's. It is really important for all of us to constantly remind ourselves that our enemies are not geographically located across national borders but are operating on a global scale.

Many of the Canadians I meet feel a necessity to defend themselves from the charge of being anti-American. I can sympathize with Canadians who are anti the American government, and I appreciate their being so careful to make the distinction between our government and the American people. Many millions of us are your friends, not your enemies. Unfortunately, as you know, we failed you, and we failed ourselves, in the last election. We allowed George W. Bush to usurp yet another four years of power in which to ruin both our lives and yours.

But, to get back to the prospects for this proposed deepening of US-Canada economic integration, I have to say, first of all, that this project is "nowheresville" in the United States, in terms of the political agenda. Nobody in Washington is talking about deeper economic integration with Canada. It is nowhere on our politicians' priority list. We are talking about a lot of other things, mostly having to do with the opposite of integration. Our politicians are running for the exits, trying to distance themselves from NAFTA.

On our side of the border, we have stressed the failure of NAFTA—and the FTA before it—to help American workers. They certainly haven't created the promised jobs or improved living standards. They have been a flop in alleviating poverty in Mexico or in lifting that country out of its Third World status. And the Central Americans have heard of NAFTA's flop from the Mexicans, and they are very skeptical that the recently ratified Central American Free Trade Agreement is the golden answer to all their problems.

Of course, the other context for the United States is that we are running huge trade deficits. We are sucking in imports from the rest of the world, running up trillions of dollars in external debt, and borrowing to pay the bills, with our debts rising twice as fast as our incomes.

Wages—real wages—are falling in the United States at a time when productive growth is excellent and economic growth very rapid, and yet somehow workers are not getting their fair share of that growth. In this context, the idea that we are going to actually deepen and expand NAFTA is almost laughable. On the other hand, we shouldn't underestimate the deep integrationists' ability to operate by stealth. Unless we are vigilant, they could take a series of insidious small steps towards deeper integration that happen under the radar screen and could ultimately be more dangerous than a big bang or a single legislative bill that you can rally around and fight.

In terms of strategy, when we consider how we are going to work together to block this integration-by-stealth agenda, there are many differences between the way Canadian and American activists approach this challenge. You Canadians obviously have more to protect and more to fear than we do. I think the emphasis Canadians are putting on sovereignty and democratic control is exactly right in the Canadian context. You have superior social programs, especially your health care, you have a vibrant and distinctive culture, and you have large and valuable resources—all of which you need to protect from the envious and avaricious grasp of your "Uncle" next door.

We activists in the United States are really energized and encouraged by your successes in Canada. When your political activism gets results and you are able to make progress, it creates hope and a sense of possibility for us in the States that is very important.

In the United States today, as you know, we progressives are totally out of power. We face a hostile congress and president, and now a very conservative judiciary system as well, which is deeply depressing, and which may be laying the groundwork for decades of conservative politics. And we see the dominance of the corporate agenda everywhere. Every morning, picking up the newspaper, it's a terrifying prospect. Whether it's food safety or the environment or trade policy, the corporations are holding all the cards and setting the priorities for our politicians. The other irony about the deep integration agenda is that there is so much else that we desperately need to do together in North America. We need a common social agenda. There are so many issues that we ought to be addressing, given the fact that our economies are so tightly intertwined and given that we have so much in common.

In Mexico, even Carla Hills, the former US trade representative, has conceded that maybe the distributional impact of NAFTA in that country wasn't great. That is about as far as she will go. Then you think to yourself: well, maybe, if we had mustered a major workers' rights campaign, it might have helped empower Mexican workers and enabled them to gain a fair share of the economic growth from NAFTA. As it stands, real wages in Mexico are lower today than they were twelve years ago before NAFTA, throwing many more Mexican families into poverty.

The workers' rights agenda is not one that we are going to

reopen because it would necessitate renegotiating NAFTA, something we don't trust any of the three governments in North America to do in a way that would benefit workers. We have, however, been involved in several worker-to-worker campaigns that have been interesting and from which we have learned a lot. Even under the North American Agreement on Labour Cooperation, the very weak and ineffective NAFTA labour side agreement that wasn't really worth much, at least some of the worker-to-worker connections that were made were constructive, even if the outcome of any of the NAFTA labour side agreement cases were not.

But projects such as a tri-national Wal-Mart campaign could be really interesting. We could share the frustrations as well as the experiences we are all having around Wal-Mart, both in terms of the supplier side and the kind of downward pressure on prices and wages that Wal-Mart applies worldwide to the supply chain, and then of course at the retail level. We are all following very closely what's happening with the Canadian attempts to organize in Wal-Mart, and trying to use the Canadian experience and the Canadian examples to strengthen our efforts in the United States. Our goal is to expand the community efforts and build a strong community alliance against Wal-Mart, which I think is coming along pretty well in the United States, and it is something on which we hope to work more closely with Canadian organizers and activists.

The NAFTA Chapter 11 issue also resonates very well in the United States, as it does in Canada, and for all of us to use the concrete outcomes of Chapter 11—the truly outrageous challenges to public health and environmental and labour protections that have come out of that notorious section of NAFTA—is vitally important. It is important for us also to spread the word about these shocking Chapter 11 examples transnationally so that people in Central and South America can be alerted to them and spurred to increase their opposition to the hemispheric expansion of NAFTA.

Finally, I think the immigration issue is a perplexing and difficult one. I see in the tri-national big business report on deepening integration that they want to expand the temporary migrant worker programs. Our view on this issue is that the focus really needs to be on protecting the most vulnerable—the migrant workers—and protecting their rights, their labour rights.

In the United States, we have seen from experience that workers' undocumented status is often used against them in organizing campaigns where chambermaids or construction workers try to either form a union or even stand up for their rights or ask for their illegally withheld wages. If they are branded as troublemakers, they can be blacklisted or sent back to their home countries. Employers shamelessly use the undocumented or temporary status of workers as a way of weakening labour's bargaining power.

That is one of the reasons we have focused not so much on these temporary guest worker programs, which seem to us blatantly tailor-made for unscrupulous employers, but rather to devise ways of protecting the illegal immigrants already in the country and eventually winning for them the rights of citizenship. That is sort of a progressive immigration agenda. I think it is clearly going have to be part of our progressive North American dialogue.

It has been a pleasure to work with our Canadian counterparts on the left over the last sixteen years, trying desperately to chart out what a progressive alternative integration agenda would look like, while also doing our best to oppose the regressive kind of deep integration being pushed by the CEOs of the big corporations and their neoliberal political partners.

NOTES

Chapter 1: The North American Deep Integration Agenda: A Critical Overview

1   John McDougall, "The Long Run Determinants of Deep/Political Canada-US Integration," in *Thinking North America, The Art of the State* II, ed. Thomas Courchene, 1–29, (Montreal: Institute for Research on Public Policy, 2004).

2   Stephen Clarkson, *Uncle Sam and Us: Globalization, Neoconservatism and the Canadian State* (Toronto: University of Toronto Press, 2002).

3   Frank Graves, "Identity, Globalization and North American Integration: Canada at the Crossroads" (paper presented to the Canadian Club, 16 January 2001). See also Michael Adams (2003), *Fire and Ice*, Penguin; Robert Wolfe and Matthew Mendelson, "Embedded Liberalism and the Global Era," *International Journal*, spring 2004, 261–80.

4   Matthew Mendelson, Robert Wolfe, and Andrew Parkin, "Globalization, Trade Policy and the Permissive Consensus in Canada, " Canadian Public Policy, vol. 28, no. 3 (2002): 351–71.

5   See for example, Wendy Dobson, *Shaping the Future of the North American Economic Space*, C.D. Howe Institute, 2002; and Allan Gotlieb, Romanticism and Realism in Canada's Foreign Policy, C.D. Howe Institute Benefactors Lecture, November 2004.

6   Bruce Campbell, "North American Monetary Union: A Critical Assessment" (briefing note for University of Victoria, Centre for Global Studies conference, Canada and the New American Empire, 26–28 November 2004), http://www.globalcentres.org/can-us/economic_campbell.pdfMarc Lee, "Indecent Proposal: The Case Against a Canada-US Customs Union," Canadian Centre for Policy Alternatives, August 2004.

7   .Marc Lee, "Indecent Proposal: The Case Against a Canada-US Customs Union," Canadian Centre for Policy Alternatives, August 2004.

8   Mario Seccareccia, "North American Monetary Integration: Should Canada Join the Dollarization Bandwagon?" Canadian Centre for Policy Alternatives, November 2002.

9   Council on Foreign Relations, "Building a North American Community: Report of the Independent Task Force on the Future of North America," co-sponsored with the Canadian Council of Chief Executives and the Consejo Mexicano de Asuntos Internacionales, May 2005.

10   Canada is a more deliberately constructed federation than most—with vast geography, a small population strung out along the US border, and decentralized governing structures. Built on three pillars—English, French and the (long-subordinated) Aboriginal peoples, and on subsequent ethnic layers—the federation has had to contend with two sets of (often interrelated) forces that threaten its integrity—the pull of the United States and the pull of regional divisions. The sinews of Canadian nationhood have, of necessity, been primarily in the realm of government and in the activities shaped by government.

11   Ram C. Acharya, Prakash Sharma, and Someshwar Rao, Canada's Trade and Foreign Direct Investment Patterns with the United States, paper presented to North American Linkages Conference, Calgary.

12   P. Dungan and S. Murphy, "The Changing Industry and Skill Mix of Canada's International Trade," Perspectives on North American Free Trade, paper no. 4, Industry Canada, 1999.

13   See Stanford in this volume.

14   E. Saez and M. Veall, The Evolution of High Incomes in Canada, 1920–2000, National Bureau of Economic Research, working paper, June 2003.

15   Elizabeth May and Sarah Dover, "Breaking the Free Trade Addiction: An Intervention on Environmental Grounds," in *Canada, Free Trade and Deep Integration in North America*, eds. Ricardo Grinspun and Yasmine Shamsie (Montreal: McGill-Queen's University Press,

2006 forthcoming).

16   Gordon Ritchie, *Wrestling with the Elephant: The Inside Story of Canada-US Trade Wars* (Toronto: Macfarlane, Walter and Ross, 1997).

17   Derek Burney, *Getting It Done: A Memoir* (Montreal: McGill-Queen's University Press, 2005).

18   See Gibson and Thompson in this volume.

19   Bruce Campbell, "Managing Canada-US Relations: An Alternative to Deep Integration" in *Canada, Free Trade and Deep Integration in North America*, eds. Ricardo Grinspun and Yasmine Shamsie (Montreal: McGill-Queen's University Press, 2006 forthcoming).

20   Stephane Roussel, "Canada-US Security and Defense Relations: A Continentalist-Institutionalist Perpective" (briefing note for University of Victoria, Centre for Global Studies conference, Canada and the New American Empire, 26–28 November 2004), http://www.globalcentres.org/can-us/security_roussel.pdf.

21   See Jeff Faux, *The Global Class War* (Hoboken: John Wiley and Sons, 2006), for an American perspective on a progressive North American integration agenda. Faux makes a number of proposals including continental citizens economic bill of rights, a continental citizens' congress, and cohesion funds for less developed regions, namely Mexico.

22   In making this argument, I have drawn heavily on a presentation made by Scott Sinclair and Pierre Laliberté at a CLC symposium in October 2005—the basis for a forthcoming CCPA monograph.

23   John W. Holmes, *Life with Uncle: The Canadian-American Relationship* (Toronto: University of Toronto Press, 1981).

Chapter 2: The Security Agenda Driving Deep Integration

24   Maureen Webb is the author of a forthcoming book about the emergence, since 9/11, of a global infrastructure for mass registration and surveillance and its implications for democratic societies and movements. Entitled *Ilusions of Security: Global Surveillance and Democracy in the Post 9/11 World*, it will be published in fall 2006 by City Lights (San Francisco) and will be available through www.citylights.com or www.Amazon.com.

25   Produced by the Project for a New American Century.

26   Ryan Singel, "CAPPS II Stands Alone, Feds Say," *Wired News*, January 2004.

27   "… an information-hungry US government [is] increasingly buying personal data on Americans and foreigners alike from commercial vendors including ChoicePoint and LexisNexis." Jim Krane (Associated Press), "US Buys Latin American's Personal Data," *Seattle Times*, 14 April 2003.

28   American Civil Liberties Union, The Surveillance-Industrial Complex: How the American Government Is Conscripting Businesses and Individuals in the Construction of a Surveillance Society, August 2004, 10–11. In 2001, 195 US universities and colleges voluntarily turned over personal information about their students to government agencies. Also in 2001, 64 percent of US travel and transportation companies voluntarily turned over information about their customers and employees. In 2002 the American Professional Association of Diving Instructors voluntarily gave the FBI a disk with the personal information of about two million people on it. US airlines have voluntarily given the Pentagon, FBI and TSA millions of passenger records.

29   Sections 215 and 505.

30   Jim Krane (Associated Press), "Information Bank Reaches into Latin America: US Buys Access to Personal Data," *Daily News* (Los Angeles), 20 April 2003. The US government, for example, has bought the driving records of six million Mexico City residents and Mexico's entire voter registry from the data aggregator, ChoicePoint Inc.

31   Under Section 365 of the *USA Patriot Act* banks, credit unions and "any person engaged in a trade or business" must now report transactions involving cash amounts of US$10,000

or more. Under Section 505 of the *USA Patriot Act*, the FBI can issue a "National Security Letter" to access the records of "financial institutions" without judicial authorization and subject the institution to a gag order. In the *Intelligence Authorization Act for Fiscal Year 2004*, the definition of "financial institution" was significantly expanded to include stock-brokers, car dealerships, casinos, credit card companies, insurance agencies, jewellers, airlines, the US Post Office, and any other business "whose cash transactions have a high degree of usefulness in criminal, tax, or regulatory matters." David Martin, "With a Whis-per, Not a Bang: Bush Signs Parts of Patriot Act II into Law—Stealthily," *San Antonio Current*, 24 December 2003. Section 326 of the *USA Patriot Act* requires financial institu-tions to check customers against government watch lists, and Executive Order No. 13224 issued September 24, 2001, requires businesses involved in the buying and selling of cer-tain property to do the same. Regulations stemming from Section 314 of the *USA Patriot Act* require financial institutions to search through their records for any transaction made by individuals suspected of money laundering by any arm of the US government with a law enforcement function. The US Treasury Department is currently developing a plan pursuant to a provision of the *Intelligence Reform and Terrorism Prevention Act* of 2004 that would give the government access to the logs of hundreds of millions of international wire transfers in and out of American banks. Eric Lichtlau, "US Seeks Access to Bank Records to Deter Terrorism," *New York Times*, 10 April 2005.

32   The Mutual Legal Assistance Agreement signed by the EU and US in June 2003 gives "US law enforcement authorities access to bank accounts throughout the EU in the context of investigations into serious crimes, including terrorism, organized crime and financial crime." European Union Fact Sheet, "Extradition and Mutual Legal Assistance," http://europa.eu.int/comm/external_relations/us/sum06_03/extra.pdf.

33   See the Council of Europe's *Convention on Cyerbercrime*, ETS 185; Seymour Hersh, "Lis-tening In", *The New Yorker*, May 29, 2006; and Nick Hagar, *Secret Power: New Zealand's role in the International Spy Network* (Nelson, New Zealand: Craig Potton Publishing, 1996). See also European Parliament, *Report on the existence of a global system for the interception of private and commercial communications (ECHELON interception system) 2001/2098 (INI)*, Final A5-0264/2001 PAR 1, July 11, 2001: http://www.europarl.eu.int/tempcon/eche-lon/pdf/rapport_echelon_en.pdf.

34   US-Europol Cooperation Agreements signed 2001 and 2002 allow US law enforcement authorities and Europol to share strategic information (threat tips, crime patterns and risk assessments) as well as "personal information relating to individuals." See Kristin Archick, "US–EU Cooperation Against Terrorism," Congressional Research Service RS22030, 12 July 2005.

35   US-VISIT, for example, links together over twenty US federal databases. Eric Lichtblau and John Markoff, "US Nearing Deal on Way to Track Foreign Visitors," *New York Times*, 24 May 2004. See also, Stephen W. Yale-Loehr and Matthew X. Vernon, "An Overview of US Immigration Watchlists and Inspection Procedures, Including US-Canadian Information Sharing," (submission to the Commission of Inquiry into the Actions of Canadian Offi-cials in Relation to Maher Arar, 31 May 2005).

36   Lichtblau, and Markoff, "US Nearing Deal." (see this chap., no. 35).

37   Sara Kehaulani Goo, "US to Push Airlines for Passenger Records," *Washington Post*, 12 Jan-uary 2004.

38   The CAPPS II program was killed by Congress over privacy concerns, and the Transporta-tion Security Administration gave Congress assurances that it would not use private sector databases in the successor program, Secure Flight. However, it was subsequently revealed that the TSA had done so. "The federal agency in charge of aviation security revealed that it bought and is storing commercial data about some passengers—even though officials said they wouldn't do it and Congress told them not to." Leslie Miller, "Government Col-

NOTES 261

lected Data on Airline Passengers," Common Dreams News Center, 21 June 2005.

3

January 2006.

58   Ibid.

Chapter 5: Canada's Oil and Gas: Security, Sustainability, and Prosperity

59   US National Energy Policy Development Group, *National Energy Policy: Report of the National Energy Policy Development Group*, Washington, DC: US Government Printing Office, May 2001, 5–3. Available online at http://www.whitehouse.gov/energy (accessed 10 January 2006).

60   Wendy Dobson, "Shaping the Future of the North American Economic Space: A Framework for Action," CD Howe Institute Commentary N.162, April 2002, 14.

61   US National Energy Policy Development Group, *National Energy Policy*, 1–7 (see this chap., no. 59).

62   Based on data from Canadian Association of Petroleum Producers, "Canadian Statistics for the Past Eight Years," available at http://www.capp.ca/raw.asp?x=1&dt=NTV&e=PDF&dn =34087 (accessed 18 January 2006).

63   The chapter focuses heavily on Alberta because the bulk of the nation's natural gas and oil reserves are located there, and because the limitations of this chapter make it impossible to cover the issues related to all producing regions. The broader issues related to the status of reserves and provincial policies need to be elaborated further and should be part of any national debate on energy security.

64   US National Energy Policy Development Group. *National Energy Policy* (see this chap., n.59).

65   Dobson, "Shaping the Future," 14 (see this chap., n.60).

66   T. Turner and D. Gibson, *Back to Hewers of Wood and Drawers of Water: Energy, Trade and the Demise of Petrochemicals in Alberta* (Edmonton: Parkland Institute, University of Alberta, 2005), 25. Also available at http://www.ualberta.ca/~parkland/research/studies/PetroChemWeb.pdf (accessed 29 November 2005).

67   The text of NAFTA is available at http://www.dfait-maeci.gc.ca/nafta-alena/chap06-en.asp?#Article605.

68   Article 6.05 states that "a Party may adopt or maintain a restriction … with respect to the export of … energy … only if … the restriction does not reduce the proportion of the total export shipments of the specific energy … made available to that other Party relative to the total supply of that good of the Party" [emphasis added]. *Total supply* is defined to include domestic production and imports.

69   Maude Barlow, *The Free Trade Area of the Americas: The Threat to Social Programs, Environmental Sustainability, and Social Justice*, The International Forum on Globalization (IFG), February 2001. Cited in Martinez 2004:9.

70   Alberta, *Enquiry into Reserves and Consumption of Natural Gas in the Province of Alberta*, Natural Gas Commission, 1949.

71   J. Richards and L. Pratt, *Prairie Capitalism* (Toronto: McClelland and Stewart, 1979), 64.

72   Proved reserves are the quantity of gas that can be produced and brought to market under current conditions.

73   Paul G. Bradley and G. Campbell Watkins, *Canada and the US: A Seamless Energy Border?* (Ottawa: CD Howe Institute, 2003), 6–7. http://www.cdhowe.org/pdf/commentary_178.pdf (accessed 30 November 2005).

74   Bradley and Watkins, *Canada and the US*, 7 (see this chap., n.73).

75   Turner and Gibson, *Back to Hewers of Wood*, 19 (see this chap., n.66).

76   Personal communication, B. Bingham, Technical Leader, North American Gas Markets, National Energy Board of Canada, 30 November 2005.

77   Statistics Canada, CANSIM table 128-0002.

78   US Department of Energy, Country Analysis Brief, Canada, http://www.eia.doe.gov/emeu/cabs/canada.html (accessed 28 November 2005).

79   http://www.sice.oas.org/trade/nafta.asp.

80   Statistics Canada, CANSIM table 128-0002.

81   Ibid.

82   This calculation is made based on statistics taken from the Canadian Association of Petroleum Producers table, Alberta Statistics for the Past Eight Years, website address: http://www.capp.ca/raw.asp?x=1&dt=NTV&e=PDF&dn=34090. Calculated from Statistics Canada, 1991 to 2000, table 6 and table 7. See also Anonymous, "Report Predicts Falloff in Western Gas Production," *National Post*, 2 April 2004, FP6.

83   For more information on the impacts of the tar sands see Fuelling Fortress America: A Report on the Athabasca Tar Sands and US Demands for Continental Security, a CCPA, Polaris and Parkland Institute, March 2006. Also see *Oil Sands Fever: The Environmental Implications of Canada's Oil Sands Rush* (Pembina Institute for Appropriate Development: Drayton Valley, November 2005).

84   As the name suggests, CBM is the methane present in coal formations.

85   *The Globe and Mail*, "Canada's Greenhouse-gas Emissions Increase," 28 November 2005. http://www.theglobeandmail.com/servlet/story/RTGAM.20051128.wxemissions28/EmailB-NStory/National/ (accessed 28 November 2005).

86   Government of Canada, Project Green: Moving Forward on Climate Change: A Plan for Honouring our Kyoto Commitment, Annex 3: Canada's Kyoto Commitment, 1. http://www.climatechange.gc.ca/kyoto_commitments/ann3.asp (accessed 28 November 2005).

87   Other avenues for collecting rent include taxes, lease sales and dividends from public ownership.

88   A carefully structured incentive for private resource corporations to reduce costs, whether structured as a tax break or a grant, can increase rents available to the public.

89   Parkland Institute, *Giving Away the Alberta Advantage: Are Albertans Receiving Maximum Revenue from Our Oil and Gas?* (Edmonton: Parkland Institute, 1999), 4. Executive Summary available at http://www.ualberta.ca/~parkland/research/studies/execsum/ESABAdv.html (accessed November 29, 2005). A.Taylor, C. Severson-Baker, M. Winfield, D. Woynillowicz, M. Griffiths, *When the Government Is the Landlord* (Drayton Valley: Pembina Institute, 2004), http://www.pembina.org/publications_item.asp?id=171 (accessed 29 November 2005).

90   Taylor et al. *When the Government is the Landlord*, 29 (see this chap., n. 89).

91   US National Energy Policy Development Group, *National Energy Policy*, 8–9 (see this chap., n.59).

92   Quoted in Canadian Council of Chief Executives, "Building a 21st Century Canada-United States Partnership in North America, April 2004," http://www.ceocouncil.ca/en/view/?document_id=365&area_id=7 (accessed 18 January 2006).

93   Canadian Council of Chief Executives, "Building a 21st Century" (see this chap., n.92).

94   Dobson, "Shaping the Future," 14 (see this chap., n.60).

95   Canadian Council of Chief Executives, "Building a 21st Century" (see this chap., n.35).

96   Dobson, "Shaping the Future," 13 (see this chap., n.2).

97   Independent Task Force on the Future of North America, Chairmen's Statement, available at http://www.ceocouncil.ca/en/view/?area_id=1&document_id=396 (accessed 10 January 2006).

98   Ibid.

99   US National Energy Policy Development Group, *National Energy Policy*, 8–10 (see this chap., n.59).

100 "The biggest challenge to be addressed in forging an energy strategy for Canada and for the continent lies in reducing regulatory obstacles." Canadian Council of Chief Executives, "Building a 21st Century" (see this chap., n.92).

101 Parkland Institute, *Toward an Energy Security Strategy for Canada* (Parkland Institute: Edmonton, December 2005), http://www.ualberta.ca/~parkland/ media releases/PRDec1_2005Energy.htm.

102 Articles 1905 and 2005. Article 1905 allows a signatory country to open the agreement if another is violating the provisions of the agreement (i.e., softwood lumber). Article 2005 provides that any party may withdraw from the agreement by providing six months' notice in writing to the other parties.

103 parkland@ualberta.ca.

Chapter 7: Turning on the Tap? Water Exports to the United States

104 The information in this section is taken from Maude Barlow and Tony Clarke, Blue Gold: *The Battle Against the Corporate Takeover of the World's Water* (Toronto: Stoddart, 2002), chapters 1 and 2.

105 It should be noted that these figures do not include the vast potential sources of glacial water found in the Arctic, Alaska, Greenland, Siberia, and the Antarctic, which would add countries like Norway, Austria, and the United States [Alaska] to this list.

106 *Time* magazine, 6 December 2004.

107 Frederic Lasserre, "Les Projets de Transferts Massifs d'Eau en Amerique du Nord," *Vertigo*, hors-serie no 1.

108 Richard Bocking, *Canada's Water: For Sale?* (Toronto: James Lewis & Samuel, 1972).

109 See, for example, Barlow and Clarke, *Blue Gold*, chapter 6 (see this chap., n.104); and Lasserre, "Les Projets de Transferts Massifs d'Eau en Amerique du Nord," 4–5 (see this chap., n.107).

110 Mark Reisner, *Cadillac Desert: The American West and Its Disappearing Water* (New York: Penguin Books, 1986), 506. Cited in Aruni de Silva, "The Sale of Canadian Water to the United States," *Environment Probe*, 1997.

111 Quotations in this paragraph are taken from the Department of Foreign Affairs and International Trade, An Act to Amend the International Boundary Waters Treaty Act: Questions and Answers, February 2001.

112 Quotations in this paragraph are taken from "A Legal Opinion Concerning Water Export Controls and Canadian Obligations Under NAFTA and the WTO," prepared by Steven Shrybman, West Coast Environmental Law Association, 15 September 1999.

113 See NAFTA articles 302, 309.2 and 314.

114 It is worth noting that President Fox of Mexico has taken steps to have water declared a matter of national security in Mexico.

115 Maude Barlow, *Too Close for Comfort: Canada's Future Within Fortress America* (Toronto: McClelland & Stewart, 2005), 223–224.

Chapter 8: Deregulation and Continental Regulatory Harmonization

116 External Advisory Committee on Smart Regulation, Smart Regulation: A Regulatory Strategy for Canada, Report to the Government of Canada, Ottawa, September 2004.

117 Data from Paul Reed, "Estimating Government Regulatory Expenditures from the Public Accounts. Presentation to Privy Council Office," Office of the Chief Social Scientist, Statistics Canada, 15 April 2005.

118 External Advisory Committee on Smart Regulation, Smart Regulation, 22 (see this

chap., n.116).

119 Michael Hart, Risks and Rewards: New Frontiers in International Regulatory Cooperation (paper prepared for the External Advisory Committee on Smart Regulation, 2004).

120 Council on Foreign Relations, Building a North American Community: Report of the Independent Task Force on the Future of North America (co-sponsored with the Canadian Council of Chief Executives and the Consejo Mexicano de Asuntos Internacionales, May 2005).

121 Fidele Ndayisenga and Andre Downs, *Ecomomic Impacts of Regulatory Convergence between Canada and the United States* (Ottawa: Policy Research Initiative, August 2004).

122 Doug Blair, *Measuring the Potential Gains of Canada-US Regulatory Cooperation in Five Selected Product Markets: A Cash Flow Approach* (Ottawa: Policy Research Initiative, September 2004).

123 For a detailed analysis of the PRI studies, see M. Lee and B. Campbell, Foxes and Henhouses: A Critical Analysis of the Federal Smart Regulation and Continental Regulatory Harmonization Initiatives, CCPA, April 2006.

124 Policy Research Institute, *Canada-US Regulatory Cooperation: Charting a Path Forward,* Interim Report (Ottawa: Privy Council Office, December 2004).

125 Dr. David J. Graham, Testimony before the United States Senate Finance Committee, 18 November 2005. (Reproduced in the *CCPA Monitor,* May 2005).

126 Phil B. Fontanarosa, Drummond Rennie, and Catherine D. DeAngelis, "Postmarketing Surveillance—Lack of Vigilance, Lack of Trust," *Journal of the American Medical Association* 292 (1 December 2004): 2647–2650.

127 Public Broadcasting System (PBS), "Dangerous Prescription," *Frontline,* 18 November 2003.

128 External Advisory Committee on Smart Regulation, Smart Regulation, 80 (see this chap., n.116).

129 US Office of Management and Budget, *Informing Regulatory Decisions: 2003 Report to Congress on the Costs and Benefits of Federal Regulations and Unfunded Mandates on State, Local and Tribal Entities* (Washington: Executive Office of the President of the United States, September 2003).

130 David Michaels, "Doubt is their Product, " *Scientific American* (June 2005): 101.

131 Differences in regulations are also common at the provincial level, reflecting the same principles of responding to the differential needs of citizens. The Agreement on Internal Trade has been developed as a means of harmonizing provincial regulations. See Marc Lee, "In Search of a Problem: The Future Agreement on Internal Trade and Canadian Federalism," Canadian Centre for Policy Alternatives, October 2000.

Chapter 10: Modelling North American Integration: Pushing the Envelope on Reality

132 Portions of this chapter appeared in Jim Stanford, "Economic Models and Economic Reality: North American Free Trade and the Predictions of Economists," *International Journal of Political Economy* 33 (3): 28–49.

133 Andrew Sharpe, "Why Are Americans More Productive Than Canadians?" CSLS Research Report 2003–04, Ottawa: Centre for the Study of Living Standards, 2003; Steven Globerman and Daniel Shapiro, "Assessing Recent Patterns of Foreign Direct Investment in Canada and the United States," in Richard G. Harris, ed., *North American Linkages: Opportunities and Challenges for Canada* (Calgary: University of Calgary Press, 2003).

134 Robert E. Scott, "The High Price of 'Free' Trade" (briefing paper #147, Washington, Economic Policy Institute, 2003).

135 Gerardo Esquivel and Jose Antonio Rodriguez-Lopez, "Technology, Trade, and Wage Inequality in Mexico Before and After NAFTA," *Journal of Development Economics* 72 (2003): 543–565; Miguel D. Ramirez, "Mexico Under NAFTA: A Critical Assessment,"

Quarterly Review of Economics and Finance 43 (2003): 863–892.

136 Aaron Tornell, Frank Westerman, and Lorenza Marinez, "NAFTA and Mexico's Less-than-Stellar Performance" (NBER working paper #10289, Cambridge, Mass., National Bureau for Economic Research, 2004); Donald J. Daly, "Canadian Research on the Production Effects of Free Trade: A Summary and Implications for Mexico," *North American Journal of Economics and Finance* 9 (1998): 147–167. In the case of Mexico, for example, Tornell, Westerman, and Marinez blame the failure to modernize capital markets for Mexico's sluggish growth, while Daly fingers the substantial expansion of small business in Canada during the 1990s for the post-FTA stagnation of productivity levels there.

137 Rules of origin specify that a product must embody minimum levels of North American content before it can qualify for NAFTA's special tariff-free privileges. They are held by conventional economists to constitute a "cost" because of their administrative burden (requiring companies to keep track of the value added in various locations) and because they may stimulate "inefficient" relocation of certain supply-chain activities toward NAFTA from other, more "competitive" jurisdictions.

138 An *elasticity* is the measure of how responsive one variable is to changes in another, related variable—for example, how much would demand for a product change in response to changes in its price.

139 Ray C. Fair, *Specification, Estimation, and Analysis of Macroeconometric Models* (Cambridge: Harvard University Press, 1984), 18.

140 Lance Taylor, *Income Distribution, Inflation and Growth: Lectures on Structuralist Macroeconomic Theory* (Cambridge, MA: MIT Press, 1991).

141 See the UK Department of Trade and Industry, "Estimations of Global Welfare Gains from Trade Liberalization," in *Trade and the Global Economy: The Role of International Trade in Productivity, Economic Reform, and Growth* (Norwich: HM Treasury, 2004); Frank Ackerman, "The Shrinking Gains from Trade: A Critical Assessment of Doha Round Projections," (working paper # 05-01, Global Development and Environment Institute, Tufts University, 2005); and Lance Taylor and Rudiger von Arnim, "Computable General Equilibrium Models of Trade Liberalization: The Doha Debate," (mimeo, New School University, New York, 2006) for surveys of CGE models of other trade policy issues—the latter two more critical in perspective.

142 Taylor, *Income Distribution, Inflation and Growth*

143 Peter S. Armington, *A Theory of Demand for Products Distinguished by Place of Production* (Washington, DC: International Monetary Fund, 1968).

144 Robert K. McCleery, "An Intertemporal, Linked, Macroeconomic CGE Model of the United States and Mexico, Focusing on Demographic Change and Factor Flows," in *Economy-Wide Modeling of the Economic Implications of a FTA with Mexico and a NAFTA with Canada and Mexico* (Washington, DC: US International Trade Commission, 1992); Leslie Young and Jose Romero, "A Dynamic Dual Model of the Free Trade Agreement," in *Economy-Wide Modeling of the Economic Implications of a FTA with Mexico and a NAFTA with Canada and Mexico.*

145 Carlos Bachrach and Lorris Mizrahi, "The Economic Impact of a Free Trade Agreement Between the United States and Mexico: A CGE Analysis," in *Economy-Wide Modeling of the Economic Implications of a FTA with Mexico and a NAFTA with Canada and Mexico;* Drusilla K. Brown, Alan V. Deardorff, and Robert M. Stern, "Impacts on NAFTA Members of Multilateral and Regional Trading Arrangements and Initiatives and Harmonization of NAFTA's External Tariffs," (discussion paper #471, School of Public Policy, University of Michigan, 2001); David Cox and Richard G. Harris, "North American Free Trade and its Implications for Canada: Results From a CGE Model of North American Trade," *World Economy* 15, no. 1 (1992); Bob Hamilton and John Whalley, "Geographically Discriminatory Trade Arrangements," *Review of Economics and Statistics* 67, no. 3 (August 1985):

446–455; Raul Hinojosa-Ojeda and Sherman Robinson, "Alternative Scenarios of US-Mexico Integration: A Computable General Equilibrium Approach," (mimeo, Department of Agricultural and Resource Economics, University of California at Berkeley, 1991); Santiago Levy and Sweder van Wijnbergen, "Transition Problems in Economic Reform: Agriculture in the Mexico-US Free Trade Agreement," in *Economy-Wide Modeling of the Economic Implications of a FTA with Mexico and a NAFTA with Canada and Mexico*; McCleery, "An Intertemporal, Linked, Macroeconomic CGE Model"; David W. Roland-Holst, Kenneth A. Reinert and Clinton R. Shiells, "North American Trade Liberalization and the Role of Non-Tariff Barriers," in *Economy-Wide Modeling of the Economic Implications of a FTA with Mexico and a NAFTA with Canada and Mexico*; Horacio E. Sobarzo, "A General Equilibrium Analysis of the Gains from Trade for the Mexican Economy of a North American Free Trade Agreement," in *Economy-Wide Modeling of the Economic Implications of a FTA with Mexico and a NAFTA with Canada and Mexico*; William E. Spriggs, "Potential Effects of Direct Foreign Investments Shifts Due to the Proposed US-Mexico Free Trade Agreement," (briefing paper, Washington, Economic Policy Institute, 1991); Jim Stanford, *Estimating the Effects of North American Free Trade: A Three-Country General Equilibrium Model with "Real-World" Assumptions* (Ottawa: Canadian Centre for Policy Alternatives, 1993); US International Trade Commission, 2003; Randall Wigle, "General Equilibrium Evaluation of Canada-US Trade Liberalization in a Global Context," *Canadian Journal of Economics* 21, no. 3 (1988): 539–564; Young and Romero, "A Dynamic Dual Model of the Free Trade Agreement".

146 Hamilton and Whalley, "Geographically Discriminatory Trade Arrangements," 446–455. As discussed further below, some models allow for economies of scale (in which firms' production becomes more efficient as they become larger), while others do not (constant returns to scale, in which productivity does not depend on size).

147 Cox and Harris, "North American Free Trade and Its Implications for Canada," 31–44 (see this chap., n.145); Richard G. Harris, "Symposium—The Canada-US FTA, Economic Impact and Transition Effects," *Journal of Policy Modeling* 13, no. 3 (1991): 421–434.

148 Drusilla K. Brown, Alan V. Deardorff, and Robert M. Stern, "The North American Free Trade Agreement: Analytical Issues and a Computational Assessment," *World Economy* 15, no. 1 (1992): 15–29; Roland-Holst, Reinert, and Shiells, "North American Trade Liberalization" (see this chap., n.145); Sobarzo, "A General Equilibrium Analysis" (see this chap., n.145); Cox and Harris, "North American Free Trade and Its Implications for Canada," 31–44 (see this chap., n.145).

149 Wigle, "General Equilibrium Evaluation," 539–564 (see this chap., n.145); Levy and van Wijnbergen, "Transition Problems in Economic Reform" (see this chap., n.145); Roland-Holst, Reinert, and Shiells, "North American Trade Liberalization" (see this chap., n.145); Young and Romero, "A Dynamic Dual Model of the Free Trade Agreement" (see this chap., n.145).

150 Cox and Harris, "North American Free Trade and Its Implications for Canada, 31–44 (see this chap., n.145); Sobarzo, "A General Equilibrium Analysis" (see this chap., n.145).

151 Bachrach and Mizrahi, "The Economic Impact of a Free Trade Agreement" (see this chap., n.145); Brown, Deardorff and Stern, "Impacts on NAFTA Members" (see this chap., n.145).

152 McCleery, "An Intertemporal, Linked, Macroeconomic CGE Model" (see this chap., n.144); Stanford, *Estimating the Effects of North American Free Trade* (see this chap., n.15); Spriggs, "Potential Effects of Direct Foreign Investments Shifts" (see this chap., n.145).

153 Hinojosa-Ojeda and Robinson. "Alternative Scenarios of US-Mexico Integration" (see this chap., n.15).

154 Saskia Sassen, *The Mobility of Labour and Capital: A Study in International Investment and Labour Flow* (Cambridge: Cambridge University Press, 1988).

155 Stanford, *Estimating the Effects of North American Free Trade* (see this chap., n.145).

156 Roland-Holst, Reinert, and Shiells, "North American Trade Liberalization" (see this chap., n.145).

157 Noel Gaston and Daniel Trefler, "The Labour Market Consequences of the Canada-US Free Trade Agreement," *Canadian Journal of Economics* 30, no. 1 (1997): 18–41; Daniel Schwanen, "Trading Up: The Impact of Increased Continental Integration on Trade, Investment and Jobs in Canada," (commentary #89, Toronto, C.D. Howe Institute, 1997).

158 The simple export share of GDP actually overstates the importance of Canadian exports, because of a significant increase in the "import share" of those exports—that is, an increase in the imported content that is reflected in the gross value of exports. P Cross, "Cyclical Implications of the Rising Import Content in Exports," *Canadian Economic Observer*, Catalogue 11-010-XPB, Statistics Canada, December 2002, 3.1–3.9 finds that over half of the growth of the export share since the FTA is attributable to this rise in the import share of exports. This suggests a growing and complex intensity of two-way trade in intermediate products, but not so much a growth in the importance of final export demand to Canadian macroeconomic aggregates.

159 Schwanen, "Trading Up" (see this chap., n.157); Daniel Trefler, "The Long and Short of the Canada-US Free Trade Agreement," *Perspectives on North American Free Trade* Series #6. Ottawa: Industry Canada, 1999; Head, Keith and John Ries. 2003. "Free Trade and Canadian Economic Performance: Which Theories Does the Evidence Support?" in Richard G. Harris, ed., *North American Linkages: Opportunities and Challenges for Canada* (Calgary: University of Calgary Press).

160 Centre for the Study of Living Standards, *Aggregate Income and Productivity Trends: Canada vs. United States, 1961–2003* (Ottawa: Centre for the Study of Living Standards, 2003).

161 A fourth, unpublished model of deep integration was developed several years ago by Appiah. It utilizes a pre-FTA database, however, calibrating the model's base case solution to a pre–free trade equilibrium, and hence is likely to conflate some of the predicted "gains" from a customs union with already realized "gains" from continental tariff elimination. (Alex Appiah, "An Applied General Equilibrium Model of North American Integration with Rules of Origin," PhD thesis, Simon Fraser University, 1999).

162 Brown, Deardorff, and Stern, "Impacts on NAFTA Members" (see this chap., n.145); Madanmohan Ghosh and Someshwar Rao, "A Canada-US Customs Union: Potential Economic Impacts in NAFTA Countries," *Journal of Policy Modeling* 27, no. 10 (2005): 805–827; Evangelia Papadaki, Marcel Merette, Yu Lan, and Jorge Hernandez, "Toward a Canada-USA 'Deeper' Integration: A Computable General Equilibrium Investigation," (mimeo, International Trade Canada, 2006).

163 Brown, Deardorff, and Stern, "Impacts on NAFTA Members" (see this chap., n.145).

164 Danielle Goldfarb, The Road to a Canada-US Customs Union (report #184, Toronto: C.D. Howe, 2003).

165 Ghosh and Rao, "A Canada-US Customs Union," 805–827 (see this chap., n.162).

166 An interesting feature of neoclassical CGE models is that any growth in imports must be offset by an equal growth in exports, thanks to the income-expenditure equilibrium conditions that are implied. Thus even a unilateral tariff reduction sparks welfare-enhancing two-way trade flows. The fact that real-world governments almost never reduce tariffs unilaterally, despite this finding, suggests that policy makers do not really believe the results of the CGE models they invoke when it is politically convenient to do so.

167 The authors themselves report that only about fifty federal officials are employed to supervise rule of origin submissions from all importers to Canada.

168 Canada still applies some tariffs within NAFTA, or non-tariff barriers that have a tariff equivalent, on certain products—mostly agricultural products and food and beverages.

And tariffs may be collected on other intra-NAFTA imports, which do not qualify under the rules of origin.

169 This assumption merely reflects the existing reality of extensive two-way intra-industry trade in autos, especially between Canada and the US; the Armington model "interprets" this reality not as the structural result of history and policy (for example, the Canada-US Auto Pact, which integrated the two countries' auto industries beginning in 1965), but as a greater willingness on the part of consumers to try other countries' products.

170 For comparison purposes, consider that direct labour in the assembly stage of automotive production constitutes just over 5 percent of total gross production costs; reducing the assumed rules-of-origin cost of Canadian automotive exports to the US by 2.5 percent (the value of the US MFN tariff on passenger vehicles) would thus be of equivalent value to a 50 percent cut in labour costs by Canadian autoworkers.

171 Papadaki, Merette, Lan, and Hernandez, "Toward a Canada-USA 'Deeper' Integration" (see this chap., n.162).

172 The authors refer to the findings of so-called gravity models of trade to estimate what they expect would be observed trade levels in the absence of these unobserved trade frictions.

173 Since these trade frictions are "unobservable," the question is begged as to how policy makers would know how to eliminate them, let alone how they would know when they had finished the job.

174 The fact that trade "barriers" are assumed to be greatest in both countries in private services industries (such as wholesale trade, transportation, and personal services) reflects the model's conflation of purported trade "barriers" with a distinct concept in economics: namely, the fact that certain commodities are inherently more "tradeable" than others, due to differences in their physical properties, transportability, and inherent consumer practices. A lack of tradeability is interpreted, in this model, as proof of the existence of some kind of trade barrier.

175 Ghosh and Rao, "A Canada-US Customs Union," 805–827 (see this chap., n.32).

Chapter 11: Another Path for Canada

176 This chapter is adapted from *Too Close for Comfort: Canada's Future with Fortress North America* (Toronto: McClelland & Stewart, 2005).

177 World Bank report, Poverty in Mexico: An Assessment of Conditions, Trends and Government Strategies, 2004.

178 China Daily, 19 June 2005. "An Alternative Defence Policy", 61

CONTRIBUTORS

Lloyd Axworthy is president and vice-chancellor of the University of Winnipeg. He was Canada's foreign minister from 1995 to 2000. For his leadership on the landmark global treaty banning anti-personnel landmines, he was nominated for the Nobel Peace Prize. Lloyd Axworthy has been the recipient of numerous prestigious awards and honours, including the Order of Canada. His most recent book is Navigating a New World: Canada's Global Future, Knopf Canada, 2003.

Maude Barlow is the national chairperson of the Council of Canadians. She is the recipient of numerous awards and honourary doctorates. Most recently she received (with Tony Clarke) the 2005 Right Livelihood Award given by the Swedish parliament and widely referred to as the Alternative Nobel. Maude Barlow is the author or co-author of fifteen books. Her most recent book is Too Close for Comfort: Canada's Future Within Fortress North America, McClelland and Stewart, 2005.

Ed Broadbent was leader of the New Democratic Party of Canada from 1975 to 1989. Mr. Broadbent was the first president of the International Centre for Human Rights and Democratic Development (renamed Rights and Democracy). He has been a visiting fellow at Oxford, Carleton, McGill, and Queen's universities. He edited Democratic Equality: What Went Wrong, University of Toronto Press, 2001. Mr. Broadbent is a member of the Privy Council and a Companion of the Order of Canada.

Michael Byers holds a Canada Research chair (Tier 1) in global politics and international law at the University of British Columbia, where he teaches and also serves as academic director of the Liu Institute for Global Issues. He is the author, most recently, of War Law: Understanding International Law and Armed Conflict, Atlantic Books and Douglas & McIntyre, 2005.

Bruce Campbell is executive director of the Canadian Centre for Policy Alternatives. He has written widely on public policy issues, including on Canada-US relations. He is author or co-author of three books including (with Maude Barlow) Straight Through the Heart: How the Liberals Abandoned the Just Society, HarperCollins, 1995, and Pulling Apart: The Deterioration of Employment and Income in North America Under Free Trade, CCPA, 1999.

Tony Clarke is the founding director of the Polaris Institute, former chair of the Action Canada Network, and director of social affairs at the Canadian Conference of Catholic Bishops. His books include Silent Coup: Confronting the Big Business Takeover of Canada, CCPA/Lorimer, 1997; and Blue Gold: The Battle Against Corporate Theft of the World's Water (with Maude Barlow), which is published in forty countries. He was 2005 co-recipient (with Maude Barlow) of the Swedish Right Livelihood Award. He is a member of the CCPA Board.

Stephen Clarkson is professor of political science at University of Toronto. He is the author of many books, including Uncle Sam and Us: Globalization, Neoconservatism, and the Canadian State, University of Toronto and Woodrow Wilson Presses, 2002. His Trudeau and Our Times, Vol. 1, McClelland and Stewart, 1990, (with Christina McCall) won the Governor General's Literary Award. He is a research associate with the CCPA.

Marjorie Griffin Cohen is professor of political science and chair of women's studies at Simon Fraser University. She has written extensively on international trade agreements, electricity deregulation, women, and labour. Her books include Free Trade and the Future of Women's Work, and Women's Work, Markets and Economic Development. Professor Cohen has served on several boards, including BC Hydro. She is a research associate with the CCPA.

Ed Finn is founding editor of the CCPA Monitor. Formerly, as a journalist, he worked at the Western Star (Corner Brook, NL), the Montreal Gazette and the Toronto Star, for which he wrote a weekly column on labour relations. He served for twenty-seven years as a communicator for several labour organizations, including the Canadian Labour Congress and the Canadian Union of Public Employees. He received an honourary doctorate from Memorial University in 1996.

Diana Gibson is research director with the Alberta-based Parkland Institute. She has an extensive background in public policy on topics ranging from health care and education to energy and international trade agreements. She is co-author of The Bottom Line: The Truth Behind Private Health Insurance in Canada, Parkland/NeWest Press, 2006; and Back to Hewers of Wood and Drawers of Water: Energy Trade and the Demise of Petrochemicals in Alberta, Parkland, 2005.

Mel Hurtig is founder and past-chair of the Council of Canadians and former chairman of the Committee for an Independent Canada. He is an Officer of the Order of Canada and has honourary degrees from six universities. His best-selling books include The Vanishing Country, The Betrayal of Canada, Pay the Rent or Feed the Kids, and a memoir, At Twilight in the Country.

Andrew Jackson is chief economist with the Canadian Labour Congress, and a research associate with the Canadian Centre for Policy Alternatives. He has written numerous articles on economic and social policy issues for popular and academic publications. His books include, most recently, Work and Labour in Canada: Critical Issues, published by Canadian Scholars Press, 2005. Andrew Jackson is research professor at Carleton University's Institute of Political Economy.

Marc Lee is a senior economist with the BC office of the Canadian Centre for Policy Alternatives. He has authored many CCPA

272   LIVING WITH UNCLE

publications, including Tax Cuts and the Fiscal Imbalance, Indecent Proposal: The Case Against a Canada-US Customs Union, and In Search of a Problem: The Future of the Agreement on Internal Trade and Canadian Federalism.

Thea Lee is policy director with the AFL-CIO. Previously, she worked as an international trade economist at the Economic Policy Institute in Washington, DC. She appears frequently before US Congressional committees and on American media. Thea Lee is the author of numerous publications on international economic issues, including NAFTA, and is co-author of A Field Guide to the Global Economy, published by WW Norton, 2005.

Avi Lewis is a Gemini award-winning broadcaster and documentary filmmaker. As the host and producer of CounterSpin on CBC Newsworld, he presided over more than five-hundred nationally televised debates. His first feature-length film, The Take, CBC/NFB, 2004, a story of hope and resistance in the global economy, has screened to acclaim in theatres worldwide.

Kent Roach is professor of law at the University of Toronto, with cross-appointments in criminology and political science, and a Fellow of the Royal Society of Canada. His many books include September 11: Consequences for Canada, University of Toronto Press, 2001. Since 1998, Professor Roach has been editor-in-chief of Criminal Law Quarterly.

Jim Stanford is chief economist with the Canadian Auto Workers union. His research and analysis on a wide range of economic topics has been published in numerous academic and popular publications. He is the author of Paper Boom, CCPA/Lorimer, 1999. Jim Stanford writes regular column for the Globe and Mail. He is a research associate with the CCPA.

David Thompson is an independent public policy researcher and organizational development consultant. His recent research interests include environmental policy, corporate accountability, energy, tobacco control, and public finance. He practised environmental law and holds postgraduate degrees in law and economics. He is co-author of Curing the Addiction to Profits: A Supply Side Approach to Phasing out Tobacco, CCPA Books, 2005.

Maureen Webb is a human rights and labour lawyer with the Canadian Association of University Teachers. She is the author of Illusions of Security: Global Surveillance and Democracy in the Post 9-11 World, forthcoming, fall 2006 by City Lights (San Francisco). She is co-chair of the International Civil Liberties Monitoring Group, a founder of the International Campaign Against Mass Surveillance (www.i-cams.org), and coordinator for security and human rights issues for Lawyers' Rights Watch Canada.

INDEX

MEMBER OF SCABRINI GROUP

Québec, Canada
2006